Resolving
public conflict

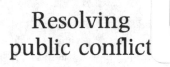

Political Analyses

This major new series, a flagship for Manchester University Press, will include some of the best new writing across the range of political science subdisciplines. All of them will present exciting new research or provocative syntheses in an accessible style, and will be available in paperback.

Series editors: Bill Jones, Michael Clarke and Michael Moran

Brendan Evans and Andrew Taylor
From Salisbury to Major: continuity and change in Conservative politics

Michael Foley and John E. Owens
Congress and the Presidency: institutional politics in a separated system

E. Franklin Dukes
Resolving public conflict: transforming community and governance

Stuart Croft
Strategies of arms control: a history and typology

Roland Axtmann
Liberal democracy into the twenty-first century: globalization, integration and the nation state

Resolving
public conflict

*Transforming community
and governance*

E. Franklin Dukes

Manchester University Press

Manchester and New York

distributed exclusively in the USA by St. Martin's Press

Published by Manchester University Press
Oxford Road, Manchester M13 9NR, UK
and Room 400, 175 Fifth Avenue, New York, NY 10010, USA

Distributed exclusively in the USA
by St Martin's Press, Inc., 175 Fifth Avenue, New York, NY 10010, USA

British Library Cataloguing-in-Publication Data
A catalogue record for this book is available from the British Library

Library of Congress Cataloging-in-Publication Data
Dukes, E. Franklin.
    Resolving public conflict : transforming community and governance
/ E. Franklin Dukes.
        p.   cm. — (Political analyses)
    Includes bibliograhical references
    ISBN 0–7190–4512–6 — ISBN 0–7190–4513–4 (pbk.)
    1. Conflict management.   2. Mediation.   3. Dispute resolution
(Law)   I. Title.   II. Series.
    HM136.D783   1996
    303.6—dc20   95–26495
                                                                             CIP

ISBN 0 7190 4512 6 *hardback*
      0 7190 4513 4 *paperback*

First published 1996

00 99 98 97 96   10 9 8 7 6 5 4 3 2 1

Typeset in Great Britain
by Northern Phototypesetting Co, Ltd, Bolton
Printed in Great Britain
by Redwood Books, Trowbridge

Contents

To my family: my parents, Franklin and Marie-Anne Dukes, for instilling in me the values I have attempted to enact here; my children, Jesse and Noni, who have given my life a meaning I have tried to share here; and, especially, to Linda, whose example this work aspires to honor.

Series editors' foreword

The Politics Today series has been running successfully since the late 1970s, aimed mainly at an undergraduate audience. After over a decade in which a dozen or more titles have been produced, some of which have run to multiple copies, MUP thought it time to launch a new politics series, aimed at a different audience and a different need.

The Political Analyses series is prompted by the relative dearth of research-based political science series which persists despite the fecund source of publication ideas provided by current political developments.

At home we observe, for example: the rapid evolution of Labour politics as the party seeks to find a reliable electoral base; the continuing development of the post-Thatcher Conservative Party; the growth of pressure group activity and lobbying in modern British politics; and the irresistible moves towards constitutional reform of an arguably outdated state.

Abroad, there are even more themes upon which to draw, for example: the ending of the Thatcher-Reagan axis; the parallel collapse of communism in Europe and Russia; and the gradual retreat of socialism from the former heartlands in Western Europe.

This series will seek to explore some of these new ideas to a depth beyond the scope of the Politics Today series – whilst maintaining a similar direct and accessible style – and to serve an audience of academics, practitioners and the well-informed reader as well as undergraduates. The series has three editors: Bill Jones and Michael Moran, who will concentrate on domestic topics, and Michael Clarke, who will attend to international issues.

Preface

Vision

Much of public life is about conflict and its resolution.

The ability to reconcile competing public interests is necessary in order to formulate good public policy. But a sustainable democratic society requires much more than good public policy. It requires neighborhoods and communities where people care about, as well as care for, one another. And it requires processes of governance which both demand and reward such qualities as honesty and integrity, respect and tolerance, fairness and compassion, and individual and corporate responsibility.

This book is the story of a movement which is working to satisfy these needs: to foster community, to create a responsive governance, and to develop peaceful and productive ways of solving problems and resolving public conflict. It is the story of the public conflict resolution field, a broad range of mediated and facilitated processes and forums which engage individuals and representatives of public interests in dialogue and negotiation. It is the story of public conflict resolution's history and its practices, yes, but most of all its promise.

What is perhaps most intriguing about public conflict resolution is this: there already exists a field, including a broad set of practices and practitioners, which is working in some of the most sensitive areas of the public domain, trigger points where minimal shifts can have maximum effect. And the practice is still at a developing stage, facing a future in which it will encounter many choices, and which will offer many possibilities. The potential of public conflict resolution to address the many difficult challenges posed by contemporary democratic society is as yet largely untapped.

Many thoughtful analysts of the human condition have offered persuasive critiques of contemporary democratic society. And perhaps even more important than what they have said about what we are, they have served as beacons of hope by providing visions of what we may yet become.

But discovering a realistic guide for moving from that critique to actualize those visions is another matter entirely. There is a story about the owl and the grasshopper which is relevant. The grasshopper, a prudent insect, is concerned about surviving through the cold winter. The wise owl, pondering this question, finally comes up with a solution that works: the grasshopper is told, 'Turn yourself into a cricket, and hibernate through the winter.' When the grasshopper, quite naturally, complains about being unable to do so, the owl gripes, 'I told you what you need to do; it's up to you to figure out how to do so.'

Public conflict resolution may be one way to figure out 'how to do so'.

Audience

This book is intended to be a practical work. It is not a 'how-to' primer on mediating public disputes, but it presents a way of thinking about mediation and facilitation, about community and governance, and about the requirements of democratic society, which may have a real impact upon the public conflict resolution field. By identifying the variety of existing goals and functions of public conflict resolution; by providing a critical analysis of the field; and by offering credible direction, I hope that what is presented here will inform and alter the future of public conflict resolution, through practitioners, through public officials, and through those who participate in the forums and processes of the field.

This work is intended as a bridge between many worlds. It is intended for democratic and other social theorists, in and out of academia; for planners, administrators, and elected officials; for students, formal and informal, of conflict resolution and public policy; and finally, it is directed at the public conflict resolution community of practitioners, researchers, funders, and participants.

The focus is necessarily on practice in the United States, which has led the development of public conflict resolution as a field. However, while the context of practice may certainly be different in other nations where public conflict resolution is developing, concerns about its purposes and practices are similar, and it is hoped that readers outside the United States will find the discussion and arguments relevant.

Overview

The first chapter introduces the key themes of the book. These include the inability of traditional institutions of governance to address problems of contemporary democratic society and the potential offered by the practices of public conflict resolution. Public conflict resolution risks becoming dominated by an emerging ideology of 'management' which offers an unduly limited vision of its potential. Public conflict resolution ought instead to challenge fundamental problems of community and governance.

The first section of the book, entitled 'The genesis of public conflict resolution', offers an overview of the development of the field. The first chapter of this section presents an assessment of the social, cultural, and political changes in the United States in recent decades which pointed to the limitations of traditional legislative, judicial, and administrative institutions. An important distinction is made between those circumstances and concerns which prompted the development of public conflict resolution practices, and the problems which might best deserve the attention of the field.

This assessment is followed in Chapter Three by an outline of the history and development of public conflict resolution. This history considers the antecedents of conciliation within the American experience as well as the actions of practitioners, philosophers, funders, and convenors responsible for the development of the field.

The second section of the book, 'A portrait of current practice', provides an overview of current practice. Chapters Four and Five describe the variety of mediated and facilitated processes which make up the arena of public conflict resolution, including ad hoc mediation, policy dialogues, negotiated rulemaking, and community visioning, with brief examples of each.

The sixth chapter describes the individuals and institutions practicing in the public conflict resolution field. The chapter ends with a brief sampler of public conflict resolution developments in other democratic nations.

Chapter Seven offers a review of how the purposes and goals of public conflict resolution are assessed. The focus here is primarily on mediation.

This section concludes with Chapter Eight, which presents a closer look at the construction of the ideology of management, an ideology flourishing throughout the public arena. Within public conflict resolution, the main components of this ideology are:

1 the problem public conflict resolution is designed to address – the so-called 'crisis of governance' – and the intended consumers of the product: authorities in the executive, legislative, and judicial branches of government;
2 the public conflict resolution practice, including most importantly an explanation of disputes, conflict, and dispute resolution, a singular view of the third party role, and distinctive goals and objectives; and,
3 a vision of human nature, society, and the role government plays in fulfilling this vision consistent with this problem, audience, and practice.

The third and final section, 'Developing a transformative practice', focuses on the future of public conflict resolution. The ninth chapter critiques the assumptions underlying the 'crisis of governance,' suggesting other problems of contemporary democratic society more deserving of attention. Three problems in particular are highlighted here: disintegration of community and the meaning found in community life, alienation from the institutions and practices of governance, and the inability to solve public problems and resolve public conflicts.

The tenth chapter returns to the problems of community, governance, and conflict, tracing these problems to the legacy of modernity. It outlines the philosophical, social, and political foundations of a transformative public conflict resolution practice which would address these problems. This foundation begins by challenging the vision of human nature, society, and governance offered by the ideology of management. It embraces a rethinking of modernity, including an understanding of humans and human nature which rebuts 'possessive individualism', a vision of a society which honors this human being, and a conception of democratic governance which supports such individuals and this society.

Chapter Eleven enunciates the practical implications of this foundation. It does so by suggesting the ways by which society might satisfy its members' needs for affiliation and community and the methods by which citizens might become more fully engaged in governance. The chapter concludes with a call for the development of public conflict resolution processes which foster relatedness among citizens.

The final chapter offers an agenda for a transformative public conflict resolution practice consistent with these philosophical and practical foundations. This last chapter concludes with a series of recommendations about developing a transformative field of public conflict resolution, centered around six themes:

1 a conception of disputes and dispute resolution which emphasizes an appeal to relatedness;
2 a third party role of independence and responsibility;
3 a broad range of problems addressed in casework;
4 goals and standards for success and failure which incorporate, but go beyond, agreements;
5 a research agenda which stresses dissemination of information to intended audiences; and,
6 responsibility for development of the field.

E. Franklin Dukes
Virginia
1996

Acknowledgments

I firmly believe that one's views develop best in interaction with others. This is true whether one is working through differences over a public policy issue or assessing the import of the public conflict resolution field, as I do here. I do not particularly like lecturing or writing, not so much because I don't like expounding my thoughts and ideas but because of the absence of immediate feedback and opportunity for consideration. The best ideas are like fine knives: they may cut well, but they are best brought out periodically and sharpened, tested on hard surfaces, and put away for a while before repeating the process. The analysis and arguments offered here are intended not as final pronouncements but as a continuation of an ongoing conversation, a conversation involving many hundreds of practitioners, researchers, public officials, and citizens.

I have had the privilege of engaging in this conversation through conflict resolution practice since 1984, the first five years primarily as a volunteer advocate for community mediation and a graduate student at the innovative conflict program at George Mason University, and since 1989 professionally in the public conflict resolution arena. I owe thanks to many, many individuals and organizations who began and advanced that conversation and who invited me to participate in it.

Many thanks go to John Burton, who offered an uncertain student his first opportunities in this field, and much more; to the late Jim Laue, whose combination of reflection and practice offered a model for my own work, and whose support set me on the path for that work; to Rich Rubenstein, Dennis Sandole, Chris Mitchell, Maire Dugan, Mary Clark, Wallace Warfield, and the other faculty at the Institute for Conflict Analysis and Resolution, whose continued encouragement I have valued more than they realize; to Bill Potapchuk, who gave generously of his time and valued expertise in reading and discussing much of what is presented here; to Mary Lynn Boland, who always has the important answers (or knows where to find them); and to Bill Breslin, whose cogent analysis is much valued.

Although I do not share their faith, the example of Mennonite and Quaker communities of peacemakers is continually inspirational. Particular thanks go to Barry Hart, who offered me my first mediation training and who remains a good friend and colleague.

Parts of this book previously appeared in Dukes, E. F. (1993), 'Public Conflict Resolution: A Transformative Approach', *Negotiation Journal*, 9, 1, 45–57 and acknowledgement is made to the editors and publishers for their permission to use this material.

Too many busy practitioners to list without fail demonstrated the generosity which characterizes so much of the conflict resolution field when discussing the issues addressed in this work. Rich Collins and Bruce Dotson of the Institute of Environmental Negotiation at the University of Virginia have provided me the best perspective of all, and made me the beneficiary of hours of informative discussion and debate about the merits of practice.

I would like especially to acknowledge the many friends of George Mason University's Institute for Conflict Analysis and Resolution, including the Advisory Board. Without their financial support, this work may not have been possible; it certainly would have been much more difficult.

Abbreviations

AAA	American Arbitration Association
ABA	American Bar Association
ACUS	Administrative Conference of the United States
ADR	alternative dispute resolution
APHIS	Animal and Plant Health Inspection Service
BAPE	Bureau d'audiences publiques sur l'environment
CEDR	Centre for Dispute Resolution
COE	Army Corps of Engineers
CRS	Community Relations Service
DPA	Domestic Policy Association
EPA	Environmental Protection Agency
FACA	Federal Advisory Committee Act
FMCS	Federal Mediation and Conciliation Service
FRDR	Fund for Research in Dispute Resolution
GDNP	Gross Domestic National Product
GNP	Gross National Product
IAP3	International Association of Public Participation Practitioners
NCPCR	National Conference on Peacemaking and Conflict Resolution
NEPA	National Environmental Policy Act
NFMA	National Forest Management Act
NGO	non-governmental organization
NIDR	National Institute for Dispute Resolution
NIF	National Issues Forum
NIS	Negotiated Investment Strategy
SCRC	Study Circles Resource Center
SPIDR	Society of Professionals in Dispute Resolution

1

Introduction: The role of public conflict resolution

- The Chesapeake Bay, a magnificent body of water and ecosystem providing sustenance for fish, shellfish, waterfowl, and the individuals and communities who make both a living and a life from them, is slowly dying.
- Voter intimidation, violence, and partisan conflict threaten the first all-race election as South Africa attempts to lay to rest the awful legacy of apartheid.
- Residents of a small-town neighborhood in Virginia organize to oppose the expansion of a heavy equipment business in their midst.
- Chattanooga, Tennessee watches itself succumb to the fate of other urban areas whose declining industry continues to poison its air and water at the same time as it inexorably reduces employment.[1]

These situations, differing in location, actors, and issues, nonetheless share two significant features. They are, first, characteristic demonstrations of the difficulties of traditional institutions and practices – judicial, legislative, and administrative – to come to terms with the complexities of contemporary public issues. But they are, second, and most importantly, exceptions to the fates which commonly befall such cases. For in each of these circumstances the use of facilitated, inclusive, consensual processes – those which fall under the rubric *public conflict resolution*[2] – was able to change the course of these problems.

During the past two decades, many elected public officials, administrators of public agencies, citizen advocates, corporate managers, and other participants in contemporary public conflicts have begun a revolution in governance. Efforts to overpower opposition, to manipulate administrative procedures, to legislate solutions, or to shift political (and moral) disputes to judicial battlegrounds, are not always feasible, and are even less often effective, ways to achieve public good. Increasingly, the practical need to gain agreement among divergent interests who have a stake in public decisions, who share limited power, and who have very different goals, has led to new kinds of decision-making forums.

And beyond the practical need for agreement is the moral need to move beyond the type of fighting which characterizes so much public conflict. This moral need has led to the search not only for common ground, but for *higher* ground: a ground for engagement in public issues on terms such as fairness, integrity, openness, compassion, and responsibility. It is the search for forums and processes where individuals and organizations can be forceful advocates without being adversarial, where public officials can make effective decisions without being dictatorial, and where communities can come together rather than split apart when faced with tough problems and divisive conflicts.

For some issues, where basic consensus about the direction of policy exists, such change has meant no more than new ways of ensuring effective public participation. But for many occasions, the adjustments in decision-making have been radical: in effect, the proverbial lions sitting down with the lambs.

The scope of this work is extensive. Issues range from problems of small localities such as school redistricting, to regional issues such as Native American fishing rights, to national and even trans-national concerns such as the siting of a multi-billion dollar airport. The processes used in addressing these issues vary from highly stylized mediations supervised by the judiciary or legislature to informal neighborhood discussions hosted in individual homes. And the practitioners involved in designing and facilitating these procedures may be independent professionals, volunteers trained through local community-based institutions, or public officials.

The growth of public conflict resolution has been nothing short of phenomenal. From scattered efforts in the 1960s and 1970s to apply the procedures of labor-management mediation to such public problems as racial and environmental conflict have emerged a set of practices, an established profession, a body of literature, and entry into virtually every level and every arena of public life. Its impact is felt in decisions made every day and at every level inside and outside of government. And questions about its purpose and direction need to be raised.

The problems of contemporary democratic society

Contemporary democratic society struggles with an array of seemingly intractable problems. Whether in the former Soviet Bloc countries of Eastern Europe, or onetime dictatorships of Latin America, or industrial leaders such as the United States, Great Britain, or Germany, the litany of these problems is both long and dismal. As one observer wryly noted not so long ago, 'There is, as usual, much that is wrong with the world' (Dryzek, 1990: 3).

There is indeed always much wrong with the world. But there seems to be something extraordinarily unsettling about our current plight. What is unique about this era may be represented by three unprecedented concerns about these problems. First, there seems to be a sense that, not only are there many problems, but things seem only to be getting worse. Literate observers – and there seem to be fewer of them than before – can read of continually escalating problems such as the growth of a permanently disenfranchised underclass; a decaying infrastructure, including roads, bridges, and transport; health-care systems breaking down; and a future in which acts of disorder and rebellion are expected to increase as problems go unattended and palliatives prove inadequate.

The entire planet is threatened with destruction. Nuclear weapons continue to proliferate. Should we manage to avert nuclear destruction, it may only be to witness a slower doom through poisoning of the biosphere or some other unforeseen environmental catastrophe.

Much of the population suffers from untreated disease and malnutrition. There are unprecedented deficits and enormous foreign debt. There is little confidence in public education. The costs of environmental degradation, abused drugs, the continuing spread of AIDS, and inadequate and insufficient housing are visible to all.

There is a measurable decline in the standard of living. Farmers are losing their lands; unprecedented numbers of banks and savings and loans are failing. Not surprisingly, accompanying these problems are rising murder, suicide and divorce rates.

These problems are manifested in the growth of a permanent disenfranchised underclass amidst unprecedented prosperity and cultures of violence even within the most vulnerable populations. And solace is sought in the escapism of rampant materialism, gang membership, and drug and alcohol abuse.[3]

The second distinctive concern of contemporary democratic society is that there seems to be little hope that effective remedies to these problems can be found. There is certainly little promise offered by the political and social theorists whose traditions contemporary society have inherited (Giddens, 1989). On the left, orthodox Marxism has been unable to free itself from the shadows of totalitaranism. The promise of social planning to eliminate social problems is no longer an item of faith; indeed, such planning is now often seen as one cause of these problems. On the right, concentration on individual freedom and market rationality has discounted the need for social responsibility and civic engagement. And the antagonism between advocates for these different perspectives has intensified to such a level that the bitterness, cynicism, and even hatred among those engaged in 'culture wars' (Hunter, 1991; 1994) has destroyed long-standing standards of civility.

The third distinctive contemporary concern is that even if solutions to these problems might be found, there is little expectation that governing institutions are capable of enacting them. Witness the withdrawal of central governments from active problem solving; the fear of changes brought by the radically increasing diversity in the population; and the disconnection of citizens from their communities and society, expressed in a virtual boycott of the democratic processes by a wary electorate.[4]

The public conflict resolution response

Given the enormous scope of these problems – this intensification of public conflict and public problems, this lost confidence, this deterioration of civic life – what can public conflict resolution possibly have to offer of any significance at all? After all, only a tiny number of public disputes are ever mediated. Of those, the little research there is indicates mixed success.

And if the mediation of public disputes were all the public conflict resolution field had to offer, then its role would indeed be extremely limited. But a focus on the mediation of public disputes miscalculates the nature of the problems confronting contemporary society, and overlooks the potential and even the current actuality of public conflict resolution.

The 'ideology of management'

There is a myth which permeates much of politics in democratic society, a myth which has become ingrained as a foundation of public culture. This myth is that of the fundamental division between liberals and conservatives, a partition constantly reinforced in blaring terms on radio talk shows and elsewhere. This division, when offered in neutral terms, is between those who favor a significant role for government and those who do not. In terms which have actual currency, the language is less decorous: big spending versus greed, godless versus bigot, welfare versus wealthy, bleeding heart versus heartless.

These differences are sometimes real. But they mask a much stronger and disturbing consensus which transcends party affiliation and party differences. This consensus, what I term an 'ideology of management', embraces a way of viewing the world, society, and human nature and behavior. The primary political problem, according to those holding this ideology, has been popularly termed the 'crisis of governance'. The main theme of this problem, dramatized by the attention of government officials, the media, and academia, is the inability of authorities to govern: legislative, judicial, and administrative gridlock (Cloud, 1989). Among the explanations for this failure are:

- the proliferation of powerful single-interest groups and a resultant par-

alyzing diffusion of power;
- overregulation by the growing bureaucracy of an inefficient state administrative apparatus;
- a glut of costly and untimely litigation;
- an apathetic citizenry; and,
- the resultant general moral, economic, and political decline of democratic nations relative both to their own past and, in the case of the United States, to current rivals such as Germany and Japan.

The worldview implicit in the 'crisis of governance' includes a society whose aggregation of Hobbesian individuals is brought together into temporary associations in order to best pursue their own self-interest, a pursuit that is celebrated as the basis of economic and social well-being. In this view, it is through the process of private competition that the public good will best be realized. Freedom is the absence of constraints; equality the opportunity for all to utilize the resources given by one's station in life.

Public life, to all but 'policy junkies,' is seen as the dominion either of cynical, manipulative, ruthless politicians or devious, Gucci-clad, special-interest lobbyists. To enter the area of public issues is to be adversarial, a paradigm of conflict settlement extended from the judiciary to legislative processes, to administrative procedures, and to the arena of public opinion. The only visible alternative to adversarialism and its inevitable accompaniment of rancor and antagonism is dis-engagement, an option reluctantly accepted by most citizens.

The influence of this ideology of management is found in planning, in public administration, in electoral politics, and in every other area of public life. And, not surprisingly, public conflict resolution has not escaped its grasp.

How does this ideology manifest itself in the practice of public conflict resolution? Within the management practice the most important goals are those of efficiency and productivity. Attention is devoted to what Bacow and Wheeler (1984) term the 'microanalysis' of disputes – such process issues as who should be at the table, what incentives there are for negotiation, how to bind the parties to their agreements, and so forth.

The mantle of the labor mediator weighs heavily in this practice, with its accompanying trappings of neutrality, power bargaining, and compromise. The intended purpose of engagement with opponents is to find the optimal accommodation of differing interests. These interests mainly concern protection or allocation of resources, and they remain constant during negotiations.

The range of issues considered suitable for public intervention is limited in the management framework. Attention is focused on problems and disputes within the domain of the responsible governing body or bodies. Thus, a sharp dividing line separates certain public concerns, which are considered government responsibility and hence amenable to intervention, and other concerns (e.g. community identity, quality of life) which, since they are not brought under government control, are either considered private matters or not considered at all.

The emphasis on management in public conflict resolution is not so much a product of deliberate efforts to define the field's role as it is a creation of structural factors. For instance, the very sensible attention devoted within the conflict resolution literature to process and cases has the unfortunate corollary of excluding the larger questions about the meaning of practice. And practitioners' efforts to make their services attractive to their paying customers – which increasingly means government agencies – are framed in terms of the use these authorities may make of them, in the language of management (Forester, 1992). Furthermore, there is a distinct absence of any convincing countervailing argument which is sensitive to the realities of practice.

The ideology of management offers a decidedly unsatisfactory future for the public conflict resolution field. Most importantly, the 'crisis of governance' is an inadequate representation of the problems of contemporary democratic society, and hence inappropriate as the basis for efforts directed at those problems, including public conflict resolution.

What is conflict resolution for?
What, indeed, is conflict resolution for? Is it simply one more instrument in the toolbox of judicial efficiency? Is it a (derailed) movement for social justice and change? This is certainly one of the most persistent, urgent, and daunting questions facing the conflict resolution field of practitioners, researchers, funders, and supporters. And yet, it is a question that only a few interested parties have been willing to confront publicly.[5]

In part, this reticence is caused by the attention demanded by the practical tasks facing those who have imagined, designed, and implemented new varieties of dispute and conflict resolution processes. Besides the actual 'doing' of those processes, the conflict resolution community must also confront the obvious inadequacies of democratic society's established institutions of dispute settlement – problems such as expense, delay, unproductive decisions, and consumer dissatisfaction. This reticence may also be a product of the dilemma faced by those who do come to the conflict resolution field with a desire for systemic change, who find themselves dealing with institutions as they are, and who risk being ignored or labeled 'soft' or 'unrealistic' if they speak too loudly of their values.[6]

The public conflict resolution component of the larger conflict resolution field is hardly an exception to this neglect; indeed, it demonstrates perhaps the least attention to the goals and values of conflict resolution of any area within that family. The literature of public conflict resolution is dominated by questions of process and descriptions of successful ventures. This is the case despite the quality of its practitioners, many of whom are quite sophisticated politically, who recognize the larger implications of their work, and who often speak in impassioned terms of their values and goals.

I suggest that this reticence, this failure to grapple publicly with the question of the role of public conflict resolution, may soon extract a high price on the field. This price is foreshadowed by an unfounded sense of complacency about the impact of its practices, and by an emerging consensus consistent with the ideology of management which may, if it continues to develop, forge an unnecessarily proscribed role for public conflict resolution.

The goal of transformation

I suggest that there is a more significant role for public conflict resolution than that offered by the ideology of management. This role recognizes that the conflict resolution work already being done in the public arena, including not only mediation of public disputes but a much wider range of activities centered around facilitated dialogue and public participation, has considerable potential for challenging the sense of decline, hopelessness, and distrust permeating civic culture. Public conflict resolution is not limited to the settlement of disputes; rather, it is a vehicle for transforming citizenry, communities, and the private and public institutions of contemporary democratic society.

Public conflict resolution is not just the application of mediation to a small number of public disputes, however useful such work may be. Public conflict resolution practices encompass a host of processes of which mediation is only one small part. Some of these processes are new. Others have been in use for some time, but have been altered by a reconception of the use of such conflict resolution elements as an independent third party, consensus-based decision-making, inclusiveness, and openness.

And public conflict resolution thinking encompasses more than a theory of resolving disputes. Such thinking is contributing to an evolution in the understanding of what conflict means, when conflict is valuable, where it is destructive, and how it can be transformed. It is leading to a reevaluation of who we are as human beings in relationship with one another. It is becoming part of the reconception of how democratic institutions and communities may be sustained.

And finally, the field of public conflict resolution practitioners encompasses more than a group of professional facilitators and mediators. There are many individuals and organizations who are doing the work described here who would not consider themselves part of any field, much less a movement. They are elected officials, civil servants, teachers, attorneys, and citizens from every walk of life. One does not have to belong to a profes-

7

sional organization, or use the title 'mediator' or 'facilitator', to be doing this work.

The body of this new work argues for a larger role for the field than that envisioned in the ideology of management. What may be termed the 'transformative'[7] ideal of public conflict resolution, while currently overshadowed by the management vision and practice, does have supporters within the conflict resolution field, allies in related fields such as planning and law, and a rich historical and theoretical foundation. Although it has yet to be fully articulated as an integrated body of theory and practice within the conflict resolution field, there is some thought and practice within the field which highlights this transformative potential.[8]

A transformative ideal of public conflict resolution suggests a direction for the public conflict resolution field quite different from that of the management ideology. This difference begins with the kinds of problems it is intended to address. Transformative public conflict resolution is rooted, not in the 'crisis of governance', but in a critical assessment of society that recognizes the fundamental problems which are the legacy of modernity.[9] These problems may be divided into three broad categories:

1 disintegration of community, and the relationships and meaning found in community life;
2 alienation from the institutions and practices of governance;
3 inability to solve public problems and resolve public conflict.

A transformative public conflict resolution envisions a direct challenge to these three sets of problems, a challenge which, if accepted, means a substantially broader and more ambitious role for public conflict resolution than that offered by the ideology of management. This practice would be aligned with a larger ongoing and vital movement within democratic society to reconstitute, where appropriate, and otherwise create, nurture, and sustain a life-affirming and democratic public domain.

The antecedents of this movement are found in such varied places as Enlightenment philosophy, Jeffersonian democracy, and American pragmatism, including the conflict resolution field's own recently-claimed prophet, Mary Parker Follett (1918; 1930). It has been newly invigorated by the theories and practices of strong participatory democracy, communitarianism, feminism, civil rights, environmentalism, the peace movement, and the larger field of conflict resolution.[10]

This movement is neither of the right nor of the left. It rejects that aspect of postmodern critical thought and practice which is infused with a sense of victimization and which offers no realistic program of change. It finds within the traditions of liberal democracy an enduring core of values and practices whose affirmation offers a powerful force for productive change. Yet, neither is it afraid to critique the excesses and failures of this democratic tradition, nor to reach outside of this tradition for new visions and new practices.

There is a need to develop a foundation for a practice of public conflict resolution consistent with this transformative movement to challenge the problems of the public domain. As a keystone for that foundation, I advocate three broad goals for the public conflict resolution field, consistent with the three categories of problems identified earlier. These goals are:

1 inspiring, nurturing, and sustaining a vital communal life: *an engaged community*;
2 invigorating the institutions and practices of governance: *a responsive governance*;
3 enhancing society's ability to solve problems and resolve conflicts: *a capacity for problem solving and conflict resolution.*[11]

It is to these ends – and to the search for higher ground – that this work is devoted.

Notes

1 These and other situations are briefly profiled in Chapters Four and Five.
2 See the Appendix for clarification of vocabulary, including the term 'public conflict resolution'.
3 Elaboration of these problems may be seen in most newspapers or news magazines. But for this particular litany see specifically The National Civic League's Citizen Democracy Project (1990), Burton (1989), Ziegler (1985), Rohatyn (1990), and Kellner (1989).
4 See The National Civic League's Citizen Democracy Project (1990), *Citizens and Politics* (1991), and Dionne (1991).
5 The greater part of such discussion is concerned with the community mediation movement. Three traditions in particular dominate the discourse: scholars working close to the law and society or critical legal studies tradition (e.g. Abel, 1982; Harrington, 1985), advocates for community mediation (e.g. Bush, 1984; 1988; 1989; Bush and Folger, 1994), and religious social activists (e.g. Price, 1989; Chupp, 1991).
6 See, e.g., Davis (1986).
7 The choice of the term 'transformation' for this vision is somewhat problematical. I wish to differentiate between the type of personal change and individual moral development endorsed as the essential goal of mediation by Bush and Folger (1994) and the changes in relations, in community life, and in governance I advocate. While a transformative public conflict resolution does not preclude such personal growth, and indeed is open to its development, it is not the goal of such practice to transform individuals. Furthermore, as my colleague Chris Mitchell has observed, the term does not admit to the merit of preserving that which is valued. But there is also a tradition of usage which is consistent with my purposes. Following Friedmann (1987), transformative

9

theory focuses on structural problems such as racism, patriarchy, class domination, resource degradation, impoverishment, exploitation, and alienation. It provides a critique which anticipates the future course of these problems, it creates a vision for a preferred outcome, and it indicates strategies for overcoming resistance to achieving desired outcomes.

8   See Laue and Cormick (1973; 1978) and Susskind (1981) for early manifestations of this potential. See especially Handler (1988), Forester (1992), Caspary (1991), Chesler (1992), and Bush and Folger (1994) for the public conflict resolution arena, and Schwerin (1995) for a well-articulated vision of the transformative potential of community mediation. In the United States, perhaps the most adventurous institutional vehicle within this arena has been the National Institute for Dispute Resolution (NIDR) Innovation Fund.

9   An introduction to the critique of modernity might begin with Clark (1989), Friedmann (1989), Habermas (1984), and Lenz and Shell (1986).

10   See, e.g., Lea (1982), Barber (1984), Boyte and Evans (1986), Weedon (1987), Gould (1988), Lappé (1989), Etzioni (1993), and Lappé and DuBois (1994).

11   Thanks to Albie Davis for her suggestions for these roles.

Part I

The genesis of public conflict resolution

2

The origins of public
conflict resolution

The extraordinary development of public conflict resolution is a singular response to a particular confluence of social, cultural, and political circumstances. While some of these circumstances are characteristic of other democratic societies, their overall complexion is peculiar to the United States, and it is the United States which has led the development of public conflict resolution. This is true despite the considerable embrace and advances offered to public conflict resolution in other nations such as South Africa, Germany, and Australia. Understanding these circumstances will be particularly helpful in appreciating the appeal of the ideology of management.

Five developments of the latter part of the twentieth century spawned the search for new forums for addressing public problems and public conflicts.[1] These developments, while not entirely unique to the United States, are nonetheless distinctive. They are:

1 the emergence, growth, and dominance of the administrative apparatus of state governance;
2 a diffusion of power away from central authority, a diffusion spawned by growth in numbers, size, and involvement of citizens and competing interest groups in issues of public concern;
3 changes in the legal landscape in critical areas of public policy, particularly civil rights and environmental legislation accompanied by an increasingly activist judiciary;
4 the growth of persistent public problems with new and perplexing qualities, including scientific and technical complexity and uncertainty, multiple causality and resistance to unilateral solutions, and transcendence of existing political jurisdictions;
5 recognition of the inability of existing institutions and practices to meet these new demands.

These five developments do not stand alone; they evolved in conjunction with one another and are necessarily interrelated. Nonetheless, for analytical purposes it is appropriate to consider them in turn.

The growth of the liberal state: The rise of the administrative role

One of the central features of contemporary life in the United States, as in other democratic societies, is the dominant role a bureaucracy of administrative agencies plays in public and private lives. If the nineteenth-century liberal state was dominated by the courts and political parties (Hawley, 1988), then in the twentieth century their roles have to a great degree been appropriated by this bureaucracy.[2]

These roles are not limited to policy implementation, as originally intended; this bureaucracy is deeply involved in policymaking as well. And the agencies are not alone. The complex created by this bureaucracy includes each agency's cluster of client/advocacy groups, research/consultant capacity, and corporate estates, a complex particularly evident at the federal level thanks to its concentration in Washington, but replicated to varying degrees at state and local levels as well. This complex developed in part out of the upheaval of economic and social changes accompanying the pressures of industrial and population growth. But there would have been no such development without the creation of an optimistic class of administrators and planners who altered the conception of the capacity of government to perform such tasks (Hawley, 1988).

Friedmann (1988) traces the genesis of this latter change to the eighteenth-century philosopher Jeremy Bentham, who shifted the basis for ethical judgment, and hence evaluation and choice, away from rules and intention to the results of action. This shift, in conjunction with the Enlightenment's expectations of the power of reason and science, spawned a revolutionary concept: that society's problems could be solved through the application of scientific methods of research, application, and evaluation. By the 1930s, this concept, and its enactment through the new profession of planning, promised a vision for the future. The representative democracy which these specialists would serve – and transform – would work something like this. A general preference for how public problems should be handled would be expressed by the people through the electoral process. The elected representatives would assign the search for solutions to the appropriate experts. These experts would perform a rigorous analysis of the problems and determine the best solutions. The task of carrying out the solutions would be assigned to other management experts. Efficiency and effectiveness were to be triumphant, and both the public and their representatives would be satisfied.

Even allowing that this scenario is oversimplified, the reality as played out during the next several decades was far from the ideal. On the technical side, according to Friedmann, the philosophers of planning were never a monolithic group; there were always competing visions of the planning and administrative roles. In addition, rigorous analysis did not ensure objectivity; technical advice about the nature of social problems can only rarely, if ever, be freed from socially significant judgments of value. And some problems seem particularly resistant to planned solutions.

The continuing failure of this proposed system of governance to live up to its ideals did not destroy it, however; in fact, according to Friedmann, just the opposite occurred. The blame for these failures was pinned upon immature methodology rather than an inadequate theoretical foundation, and a search for better methods intensified. A number of new fields developed as methodology became increasingly sophisticated. These included not only the key disciplines, public administration and public planning, but sub-specialties such as policy analysis and systems analysis.

Within government, these disciplines spawned specialists who became the staff and employees of elected representatives and administrative agencies and organizations. Outside of government, growing numbers of private consultants, including academics, created new uses and demands for their services.

Two needs evolved out of this enormous bureaucratic growth. On the one hand, as these agencies discovered that they did not operate in a political vacuum, they realized that they needed to develop support for their policies, to legitimate them with their constituencies (Langton, 1978a). Public officials have two constituencies to satisfy: the political constituency, which grants authority to the 'regime', and the economic one, which provides it with legitimacy (Critchlow, 1988). Thus, government is no 'neutral executor' of forces arising in society (Hawley, 1988). Rather, the contemporary liberal state is characterized by the conflict between public welfare and private economic interests, a conflict which is mediated by officials who have a strong interest in cultivating their own bases of support (Critchlow, 1988).

On the other hand, this discretionary power meant that there was a second need: to limit abuse of discretionary power, to 'regulate the regulators'. Administrative procedures were put in place to limit contact between regulators and the regulated community. However, these efforts to enhance the propriety and legitimacy of the administrative decision-making processes also made such processes cumbersome, time consuming, and easily susceptible to judicial challenge (Susskind and Cruikshank, 1987). Changes such as sunshine laws, blockage of communication with regulatees during review of regulations, and increased eligibility of parties to challenge rules, all decreased rather than increased the effectiveness of government. As Susskind and Cruikshank (1987) observe, the bureaucratization of administrative agencies, the shackling of discretion through the obeisance to procedural rules, led to indecision, delay, and stalemate.

The diffusion of power: New players in the policy arena

The possibility that there might be substantial differences between the interests of those holding power and portions of the general public affected by policy decisions had not been adequately considered by the most influential advocates of planning. Thus, the potential response of the affected public to the solutions imposed upon them by experts was largely ignored by the philosophers of planning and administration.

The costs of this neglect became apparent during the 1960s. Ever-increasing portions of the public traditionally shut out of policy decision-making, developed political consciousness and began insisting upon access to power. These new interests were led by the civil rights movement; they included student and antiwar, black power/community control, women's, gay/lesbian, environmental, and neighborhood organization/protection (Fisher and Kling, 1989). Their weapons of organization, protest and litigation enabled many of them to delay, block, and sometimes change both the decision-making processes and the outcomes of those processes.

The decline of the activism of the 1960s has been greatly exaggerated. Activism has been muted only in the recognition it receives; in fact, today there are far more advocacy groups representing local, national, and global interests than ever before. Low voter turnout hides the actual growth of a strong core of citizenry – those who keep up with current events, who participate in political campaigns, and who contribute to candidates and causes (Walker, 1988; Lappé and DuBois, 1994). And these citizens are represented by more organizations and professional advocates than ever before (Walker, 1988).

There really were two citizen participation movements which arose in the late 1960s and 1970s (Langton, 1978b). The first of these, the citizen action movement, involved the appearance and growth of grass-roots organizations, public-interest groups, consumer groups, and voluntary service organizations. The civil rights crusade was particularly influential, as it not only raised the expectations of minority and poor persons but gained tangible results in the war on poverty, with its emphasis on 'maximum feasible participation'.

This citizen action movement was linked to a second citizen participation movement, government-initiated public participation. The development of official requirements and guidelines was spurred by the advance of the public-interest movement, emphasizing governmental accountability to the public as well as openness of, and access to, government (Langton, 1978b). Beginning with the Administrative Procedures Act of 1946, almost all major federal programs were required to provide for some type of citizen participation. The expansion of the federal government's reach, along with the growth of an educated middle class and the support of new institutions, caused a 'vast' increase in participation in political activity by citizens (Langton, 1978b). Much of that increase was oppositional. Policies and programs such as federal planning assistance, urban renewal, model cities, and the War on Poverty developed a clientele which both used and generated opposition to those programs (Kaplan, 1988).

Part of this increase in political participation can also be attributed to changes in communications media. A greater proportion of the population became aware of public problems than ever before. An expanding news media of cable and broadcast television and public and private radio meant that most of the citizenry had nearly instantaneous access to significant public events. Oppositional groups developed an enormous capacity for mobilization with instant access to their populace through direct-mail, copiers, computers, and fax ('Electronic democracy', 1991).

Of course, these activists do not all represent forces for challenges to existing power. Some of these groups lie squarely within the political mainstream. Furthermore, citizen advocacy groups emerging from social movements often collapse, and associations based upon occupational interests have always wielded more power than citizen groups (Langton, 1978a).[3] Nonetheless, the cumulative effect of this dispersion of power was a permanent change in the way the business of public decision-making is done. Administrative and elected officials were not only besieged by these new interests, they became forced to be more responsive to their demands (Bosso, 1988).

While there remains a good deal of disagreement about who really rules America (Bendix, 1991) – how, and by whom, power is acquired, maintained, and exercised – there can be little doubt that the past few decades have seen major new players fight their way into the policymaking arena. Control of policy decisions by a single political leader, or one party apparatus, or a single set of interests, is no longer possible; power has been permanently dispersed.[4]

Changes in the legal landscape

Legislative and legal influence

The increasing strength and activity of these new players in the policy arena would have had little meaning without some measure of systemic acceptance of their interests. The twin factors of unprecedented legislative endorsement of their rights and the acceptance of an activist role by the judiciary legitimized and institutionalized the power won by these new interests. While these changes were particularly evident within the environmental arena, it was the case in other areas of social concern as well. As a consequence, these new parties were able to use the judicial system to force a more level playing field, despite the greater resources of more established interests.

Part of this new playing field has been the ability of these new groups to work at the most intimate levels of policymaking in local, state, and federal arenas. Not only did they get involved in the development of new policy; they gained an increasing ability to block implementation of legislative, administrative, or corporate actions through threatened or actual litigation. Civil rights legislation (e.g. the Civil Rights Act of 1964) created entitlements people demanded as well as the legal basis for obtaining them. With the muscle available in such legislation as the National Environmental Policy Act (NEPA), as well as the Clean Air, Clean Water, Toxic Substances Control, Resources Conservation and Recovery, and Superfund Acts, environmental activists were able not only to win particular cases but to broaden and strengthen the entire environmental movement (Sachs, 1982; Bacow and Wheeler, 1984). And other public interest groups made similar gains.

An activist role for the judiciary

In addition to the new legislation, the courts in the 1960s and 1970s began to take a more active role in policymaking and implementation. What is termed the 'adaptationist' view of the role of the judiciary highlights the transformation of the relationship between courts and institutions such as legislatures and executive agencies. In this view, it is the failures of these other institutions which have left a vacuum that the courts have been filling.

Besides a willingness to intervene themselves, courts liberalized rules of standing. The result was a substantial increase in litigation (Cutler, in Wondolleck, 1988).[5] With active courts willing to examine agency decisions, the administrative, legislative, and implementation processes took much longer to perform their tasks (Susskind and Cruikshank, 1987).

Other developments in the legal arena complemented these changes. These included the federal legal aid programs, the development of class-action lawsuits, the new concern for public-interest law, and the use of litigation as a vehicle for opening to scrutiny and regulation previously closed institutions such as prisons, schools, and hospitals (Auerbach, 1983).

Wondolleck (1988) has documented the sources of increased conflict on public lands, particularly those involving the US Forest Service. Both environmental and commodity groups have been able successfully to challenge agency decisions. The National Forest Management Act (NFMA) of 1976, (16 U.S.C. 1600[note]), mandated the Forest Service to produce and periodically revise management plans for each of the 155 national forests. Assessments must be made each five years, plans every ten to fifteen years, with fifty-year scope, must satisfy the National Environmental Policy Act of

1970, and include at least ten points of public participation.

According to Wondolleck, officials expected 200–300 appeals for the 155 plans. But by April 1987 they had received 600 appeals on just the first 75 plans. Timber harvesting and management, oil and gas leasing and permitting, and planning in general; these issues have provided both fertile ground for disputing and the judicial system as a vehicle for traversing that ground. She describes a Forest Service which finds itself conducting a good part of its business of land management in the courts, which now regularly review administrative decisions.

New qualities of problems and conflicts: Complexity and interdependence

Does the contemporary era really have more problems than ever before? It may not be wise to argue the case for such an increase, as surely every generation's attention turns more to its own problems than to those of the past. But it is true that a substantial change in the qualities of problems occurred during the past few decades.

To describe the type of problems which seemed completely resistant to planned efforts of change, Rittel and Webber (1973) invented the dichotomy of 'tame' versus 'wicked' problems. Wicked problems include nearly all public policy issues where there is no definitive formulation and no finite set of potential solutions. Every wicked problem is symptomatic of another problem, and can be explained, and approached, in numerous ways.

An examination of contemporary problems appears to offer four components of these problems which might merit the qualification, 'wicked'. These are:

1 interrelatedness: problems integrally linked to one another;
2 scientific and technical complexity and uncertainty;
3 resistance to monocausal explanations and unilateral action; and, most significantly in terms of the search for solutions,
4 transcendence of existing political jurisdictions.

Not too long ago, the National Civic League (1989) identified an array of persistent social problems. Each appears to qualify for the designation, 'wicked'. The list includes environmental issues such as appropriate land use, air pollution and excessive solid and industrial waste, as well as social welfare concerns about homelessness, inadequate housing, rising racism, child care, and abandonment of children.

None of these can be addressed independently of other, related problems. None can be 'solved' in one locality without implications for other areas. For none of these problems could one say with any degree of certainty that a particular remedy would both succeed and avoid raising additional problems. And there is no single public body or agency one could identify which has not only the responsibility but also the authority to deal with any of these problems.

There is an increasing recognition that these problems are not confined to existing political jurisdictions. An examination by Pierce (1991) of the jurisdictional issue suggests that most of the truly critical issues, such as air quality, mass transit, land use, and economic development, are in significant measure regional concerns.[6] If this is the case then it makes sense to address them on a regional basis. But existing institutions of governance are bounded by locational strictures. Furthermore, these institutions are usually organized by service (e.g. transportation or housing) or media (air, water, toxics), rather than by problem. Thus, within each level of government, agencies share jurisdiction with other agencies. Also, state and local governments often bear the responsibility for implementing federal programs (Gray, 1989). Thus, the boundaries of responsibility among federal, state, and local authorities have become increasingly blurred as they share responsibility for a host of policies, including taxes, environmental protection, and commerce (Gray, 1989), as well as health care, education, and business regulation.

As a consequence, this multitude of jurisdictional authorities, each with different policies and interests, has made coordination of approaches for dealing with these issues difficult (Bradley, undated). To take just one example: there are approximately 2,600 units of government within the Chesapeake Bay watershed, an area whose ecological interdependence is widely recognized, and yet many of these units retain authority over land use decisions (Pierce, 1991).

Lee (1982) summarizes the problem succinctly:

> Complexity is the greatest challenge to implementing social and environmental policies. Attempts to deliver social services, in a setting where state and local governments share responsibility with national agencies and the Congress, can become entangled in a welter of incompatibilities: jurisdictional problems, competing professional criteria, ethnic and regional sensitivities, and divergent economic interests (p. 1).

Recognition of failure

Of course, none of these circumstances – the growth of the state, the diffusion of power, changes in the legal landscape, and new qualities of problems – would have the impact they do had existing institutions been adequate to the task of adapting to new needs. But they were not. And recognition of the failures of mechanisms traditionally used to deal with public disputes – science, the courts, administration, the legislature – has, more than anything else, drawn attention to the potential of public conflict resolution.

The criticisms of these traditional mechanisms generally fall within one or more of four categories:

1 excessive cost and delay;
2 limited access and participation;
3 undesired wider effects; and,
4 unsuitability of the forum for the question being addressed.

Lengthy battles over public issues consume resources that could be better directed towards the problem under consideration ('Paths to justice', 1983). Formal decision-making forums often appear shrouded in mystery to an outsider. They require special intermediaries (e.g. attorneys, lobbyists). Inequities between parties occur as the quality of service depends upon knowledge of the system and the resources a party can bring, including not only the ability to pay costs, but the capacity to endure delay and uncertainty ('Paths to justice', 1983). Parties with few resources sometimes cannot even gain access to the courts (Madigan *et al.*, 1990).

An adversarial process subjected to judicial processing may shape disputes so as to obscure the real issues. Litigation may introduce process issues holding no interest for the principals (Gray, 1989). The settlement imposed upon the parties, or negotiated within the 'shadow of the law' (Harrington, 1985), may not remedy the real sources of the dispute ('Paths to justice', 1983). And the adversarial nature of many of these processes disrupts relationships, and resultant decisions may lead to further adversarial encounters rather than problem solving ('Paths to justice', 1983).

The judiciary is burdened with new duties: interpreting environmental policy statutes, reviewing complex environmental impact statements and highly technical pollution-control legislation, correcting deficient welfare systems, and supervising schools, mental hospitals, and prisons (Ford Foundation, 1978). But the judiciary has neither the time nor the competency to settle complex technical issues and to monitor enforcement of decrees. A judge (and, in some cases, jurors) may lack expertise – or interest – in the subject matter.

The administrative procedures offered by the regulatory agencies often have similar problems. In fact, their formality makes them 'quasi-adjudicative' in nature (Ford Foundation, 1978). Procedural concerns often outweigh substance, constraining the use of potentially valuable information, overlooking possible compromises and innovative solutions, and resulting in awards with little relation to the actual substantive issues (Madigan *et al.*, 1990). Decisions may be delayed beyond the point where intervention might have mattered. And the administrative process can be biased, as parties bring different levels of financial resources and familiarity with the lobbying process to the table (Susskind and Cruikshank, 1987).

21

Conclusion

Wondolleck's (1988) reflection about environmental concerns provides an apt conclusion for these arguments:

> Society has a penchant for leaning on scientists and experts for making the tough social choices that inevitably must be made, precisely because these decisions are difficult, controversial, and many outcomes are possible ... As seen, technical analysis fails at this task. Congressional intervention and judicial rulings have similarly failed. Other means must be found (p. 152).

And just what might these other means be? In the past, mediating institutions such as church, political parties, community, and fraternal organizations played an important role (Berger and Neuhaus, 1977). But their influence declined during the past several decades as well (Langton, 1978a). More authoritative decision-making seems merely to generate increased opposition (Susskind and Cruikshank, 1987).

The answer to this question has depended upon the explanations for the problems. For many parties, the answer has been in the processes of public conflict resolution.

Notes

1   A number of public conflict resolution theorists have offered somewhat different circumstances. Dotson *et al.* (1989) identify five factors they contend are responsible for increased planning controversy and, hence, the search for new vehicles of dealing with such controversy. These are:
1   more active interest groups;
2   greater legal scrutiny of public actions;
3   increased scarcity of government resources;
4   higher public awareness of planning impacts; and,
5   more complex planning problems (p. A6).

Susskind and Cruikshank (1987) specify five 'major flaws' in representative democracy which 'foster and prolong distributional disputes'. These flaws are the conditions under which dispute resolution procedures have become necessary. They are:
1   the 'tyranny of the majority';
2   short-term political solutions for long-term problems;
3   weaknesses of voting as a decision-making process;
4   technical complexity; and,
5   'winner-takes-all' thinking (pp. 38–9).

Gray (1989) suggests six components of turbulent conditions recently faced by organizations (including business and non-profit organizatons as well as government) that shift institutional relations globally as well as locally. Because of these conditions, the consequences of unilateral actions by any single entity are unpredictable. They thus create 'increasing interdependence', an interde-

pendence which offers many incentives for them to collaborate. These conditions are:
1 economic and technological change;
2 declining productivity growth and increasing competitive pressures;
3 global interdependence [the economic, political, and social linkage of local,
national and international communities];
4 blurring of boundaries between business, government, and labor;
5 shrinking federal revenues for social programs;
6 dissatisfaction with the judicial process for solving problems (p. 29).

2 As one indicator of the rapidity of this change, by the mid-1970s there were
some 80 such federal agencies, as opposed to only 20 in 1960 (Ford Foundation, 1978).

3 These industrial, professional, and trade associations began at the turn of the
last century, a product of the industrial economy (Walker, 1988). The business groups were formed less as a response to organized labor than to undesirable government intervention (Langton, 1978a). Similarly, the growth of
the public sector also spawned 'numerous' professional associations for
providers of public services (Langton, 1978a).

4 The results of these changes are not lost on the public conflict resolution field.
See Laue (1988) and Carpenter (1989).

5 Legal 'standing' refers to the conditions under which a party or parties may
seek redress. In *Duke Power Co. v. Carolina Environmental Study Group, Inc.*, 438
US 59, 72 (1978), the United States Supreme Court ruled that the Constitu-
tion requires a 'distinct and palpable injury' to a plaintiff with a 'fairly trace-
able' causal connection between the claimed injury and the challenged
conduct (Waite, 1991).

A prime example of the increased standing granted environmental organizations was the ruling of *Sierra Club v. Morton*, 405 US 727, 734 (1972). In
this case, the Supreme Court ruled as follows:

> harm to the aesthetics and the ecology of an area can constitute sufficient
> injury, to a person who uses the area, to provide standing under the FAPA
> [the Federal Administrative Procedure Act] ... The fact that particular
> environmental interests are shared by the many rather than the few does
> not make them less deserving of protection (Waite, 1991: 3).

In an interesting twist to the issue of standing, in 1991–92 the Institute for
Environmental Negotiation of the University of Virginia convened a roundtable
consisting of attorneys, legislators, environmentalists, and representatives from
businesses, to negotiate procedures for determing judicial standing in Virginia.
One indication of the importance granted to the issue was the opposition
offered even to consideration of the issue. The enabling legislation authorizing
the roundtable passed only upon a tiebreaking vote of the Lieutenant Governor, even though no state funds were to be allocated for expenses. The group
was unable to reach consensus.

6 Pierce also suggests that the patterns of growth of cities and towns are such
that municipal boundaries have little relevance for work, sports, concerts,
restaurants, and parks. 'Urban villages', where 60 percent of the nation's

offices are located, are replacing residential suburbs, which in 1970 had only 25 percent. He quotes the LA 2000 committee, which warns of 'a Balkanized landscape of political fortresses, each guarding its own resources in the midst of divisiveness, overcrowded freeways, antiquated sewers, ineffective schools, inadequate human services and a polluted environment' (Pierce, 1991: 3).

3

History and development

The early American experience: Justice without law

An observer talking to most advocates and practitioners of conflict resolution in any field might form the impression that the use of mediation and facilitation is an entirely modern phenomenon. Some of these advocates might credit other cultures (often non-Western) with appreciation for informal means of reconciliation, and many are discovering and endorsing the consensus-based decision-making wisdom of Native American and other aboriginal populations. Yet these cultural offerings, however valuable they might be, are generally and correctly viewed as supplements to, rather than antecedents of, the mainstream (Nader, undated). Most undoubtedly would argue that the extraordinary growth of the field is entirely a product of the contemporary conditions discussed earlier, including dissatisfaction with legal and administrative procedures, political gridlock, and the search for solutions to such problems as increasing levels of violence and environmental degradation.

These advocates are only partially correct. It is true that the 1970s and 1980s saw an extraordinary growth in the development of conflict resolution procedures in the United States and in their application to family, school, neighborhood, commercial, administrative, legal, and public policy settings. In fact, however, the conflict resolution field did not emerge, Venus-like, sprung miraculously full-grown. On the contrary, there is a considerable foundation of thought and practice embedded in the American experience with dispute resolution, an experience rooted in a deep strain of anti-formalism running throughout the nation's history.

Historically, citizenry have relied less on law than on community and religious institutions to settle conflict and to promote community social values (Shonholtz, 1987). America's Judeo-Christian heritage brought an emphasis on individual and social responsibilty for maintaining social harmony; for example, in certain communities a lawsuit was considered a violation of social norms as well as a failure of individual moral responsibility (Shon-holtz, 1987). Indeed, some religious communities today continue to renounce the dispute resolution mechanisms of the state.[1]

Auerbach (1983) has conducted a highly informative and entertaining assessment of these roots of what he terms 'informalism' in the United States. He observes that throughout American history mechanisms for set-tling disputes have been considerably more varied than is reflected by what the current legal perspective would indicate. He finds a rich history of citi-zenry who consistently sought 'justice beyond law', a justice maintained without courts or lawyers. During colonial times, the legal system was only one small part of an 'intricate mosaic' of dispute resolution mechanisms. The kinds of communities that rejected the formalization of legalized dispute settlement were defined by geography, ideology, religion, ethnicity, and, perhaps surprisingly, commercial interest. These communities included reli-gious groups such as New England congregations, Quakers, Amish, Men-nonites, and Mormons; ethnic groups such as the Chinese in San Francisco, the Dutch in New Amsterdam, the Jews of Lower East Side of Manhattan, and Scandinavians in Minnesota; and businessmen of various persuasions. Yet despite the differences in the types of communities, the processes they used were at heart the same, because of their appeal to the foundations of communal life: mutual access, responsibility, and trust.

It is a curious irony that some of what are currently termed 'alternatives' and 'innovations' were firmly in place by the time first European pioneers had barely established a toehold in the New World. For instance, Auerbach notes that a Boston town meeting in 1635 ordered against litigation with-out a prior effort at arbitration (a practice that certain jurisdictions and many commercial enterprises are currently advocating as well). Virginia fol-lowed Boston in its bias against attorneys; indeed, they disbarred those who were paid and fined them when they appeared in court! Auerbach argues that this reaction cannot be explained simply as an anti-lawyer sentiment. Rather, it was a product of a strong communitarian value which saw dependency upon the law as a threat to community existence.

Inevitably, the economic and social changes of the eighteenth century weakened the strong communitarian bonds which attended the earlier set-tlers. The transformation of agrarian communities into commercial centers, the continuing differentiation between secular and religious life, the contests for land which pitted fathers against sons and brother against brother, all pulled apart the communal framework. Economic and social stratification, declining participation in religious life, and continuing immigration led to increasing dependency on appeals for legal adjudication as a vehicle for set-tling disputes. By the late 1700s, when the Enlightenment's project of indi-vidual rights of liberty and property was enshrined, the law's triumph was finally ensured.

But the triumph was not total. Even until the Civil War, the practice of non-judicial dispute settlement bespoke an 'ideology' of community justice. Utopian communities proliferated in New England and the mid-west. But eventually this quest for justice collapsed into a search for 'judicial effi-ciency', a shift of such significance that its effects are felt in the practice of dispute resolution today.

A watershed event for informalism, according to Auerbach, was Justice Pound's famed address ('Social Justice and Legal Justice') to a convention of attorneys in 1912. He indicted the justice system for its congested courts, excessive delay, high costs, and obsolete law. And he asserted that the dis-parity between rich and poor in access to the law 'mocked the promise of equal justice and gravely menaced social stability' (in Auerbach, 1983: 95). In response to the concerns Pound's speech articulated, the next decade saw a flurry of activities, in many ways previewing the current alternatives movement. Reformers designed new institutions and procedures to provide more humane remedies and increase both the responsiveness and efficiency of the justice system. Enduring reforms such as small-claims, domestic-rela-tions and juvenile courts, public defenders and legal aid societies, and indus-trial accident commissions began then.

Auerbach suggests that the contemporary movement towards concilia-tion actually began in Cleveland, in 1913, with the advent of a court-run alternative to adjudication. The movement slowly spread, along with its rhetoric of harmony and amity, and along with the continuing concerns of second-class justice and imposition of alternatives on unwilling beneficia-ries. Yet the movement remained mostly dormant until the most recent revival began in the 1960s.

Contemporary sources

The larger conflict resolution field

It is with this background, and in the socio-political context described ear-lier, that proponents began the revival of informalism in the 1960s, with renewed interest in mediation, conciliation, arbitration, and a host of other innovative dispute resolution procedures (Burton and Dukes, 1990). Handler (1988) suggests that two sources of the 'alternative dispute resolution' (ADR) movement correspond in large part to the competing views of management and transformation: the establishment interests, on the one hand, and social activists on the other. These latter are what Price (1989a) calls the 'Halls of Justice,' that is, the legal establishment (and, sometimes, counter-establish-ment). To this pair she adds a third, the 'Social Gospel,' those individuals who come to the field inspired by Judeo-Christian teachings.

Laue (1990) suggests a number of other sources of the conflict resolution field. A prominent intellectual source is Marxist sociology and philosophy, in which conflict is viewed as the driving dynamic of society. Other sources include political science and small group dynamics. Yet another is peace research, which includes not only studies of warfare and international relations, but studies of human aggresson and conflict. In the intercultural and international arena he cites the pioneering efforts of Burton (1987) and Kelman (1990) and their development of 'problem-solving workshops' as a major influence on the field.

Just as community mediation reforms have come from judicial reformers, religious leaders, and community organizers (Harrington and Merry, 1988), public conflict resolution practice draws its procedures and inspiration from a variety of sources. It is too simplistic to view the development of the field as a linear path. It is important to realize that the public conflict resolution arena has developed very much within the context of a larger field of conflict resolution. This larger field, which embraces the many components within interpersonal, family, organization, community, and international areas of practice, precedes as well as encompasses the arena of public conflict resolution. Not only has there been a cross-fertilization of ideas within and between different areas of practice; many of the leading institutions, foundations, and practitioners of public conflict resolution are active in other areas as well.

Despite the disclaimer against questionable claims offered at the beginning of this chapter, the experience of other cultures has indeed had some influence upon contemporary dispute resolution practices.[2] However, the influence of the practices of other cultures is easily exaggerated.[3] Indeed, Nader (undated) contends that the lines of influence run in the other direction, as Christian missionaries in Africa and the Pacific have left their mark on indigenous law.

In some cases development of processes in separate fields, such as family or public policy mediation, has been along parallel but separate paths; in others, practices in one field have reinforced those in another; while in some cases, concepts or practices in one area have been borrowed wholesale by another. The combination of opportunity, cross-fertilization, visionary leadership by forceful and influential individuals, and growing dissatisfaction with the status quo, are all ingredients in the mix of contemporary practice, theory, and ideals.

Three sources of public conflict resolution

Industrial relations

The early efforts to resolve public disputes drew their inspiration from several sources, including particularly industrial relations, social psychology and small group dynamics, and social activism. It is the industrial relations arena which initially offered the greatest influence. The institutionalization of procedures for settling disputes between labor and management, which evolved from the turbulent history of intractable class conflict, provided not only a framework for understanding the sources of public conflict and the dynamics of public disputes but also a model of third-party intervention for those seeking a remedy for racial and ethnic conflict and environmental disputes.

Several early advocates for mediation of public disputes (e.g. Chalmers and Cormick, 1971; Laue and Cormick, 1973) noted the similarities between the tactics of labor organizing and those of community (racial, in particular) activism, including picketing, boycotts, sit-ins, and strikes. They also observed many parallels between labor-management negotiations and those involving parties to community disputes. It is not surprising, given these similarities, that mediation, a process used with a good deal of success in the labor-management arena, would be suggested for these public disputes. Nor is it surprising that these efforts to mediate public disputes would draw heavily from the procedures used in labor-management mediation (Laue and Cormick, 1973; Bellman, *et al.*, 1982).

As mediation moved from labor-management disputes to community disputes in the late 1960s and early 1970s, and to environmental and other public policy disputes in the 1970s and 1980s, the labor relations model continued to serve as a benchmark. For example, Cormick and Patton (1980) define environmental mediation as much by its differences from labor-management mediation as by its own characteristics, and refer to their 'continuing attempt to apply third party dispute resolution techniques to non-labor social conflicts in the United States' (p. 76). Lee (1982), in an article entitled 'Defining success in environmental dispute resolution', offers several criteria of 'orderly' dispute resolution transferrable from the labor relations experience to the environmental arena. These include the mutual recognition of parties, legal and administrative procedures, and the continuing relationship among parties. Lentz (1986) even argues that a 'revisionist' mediator who abandons labor model standards so alters the role of the mediator that the resultant practice ought not be called mediation at all.

Small group dynamics

Another influence on the development of public conflict resolution was the work of psychologists, psychiatrists, and intergroup sensitivity and encounter facilitators.[4] This approach was being tested in the international arena (Doob, 1970). Laue and Cormick (1973) suggest the importance of these processes in early attempts at conflict resolution in racial disputes. Their critique of such an approach – that it ignores structural power disparities in favor of personal change – was duplicated by critics of the sensitivity training approach in international disputes as well.[5] Despite these criticisms, which did much to slow the use of these procedures, their methodology has continued to attract a following.[6]

Social activism

A surprisingly large number of practitioners identify social activism as the beginnings of their conflict resolution work (Dukes, 1992). Areas of former activity include civil rights, community organization, and environmental activism. It is perhaps not unexpected, then, that community organizer Saul Alinsky (1972) is offered as a source of inspiration for many practitioners' work.[7]

The first phase: Pioneers and exploration

Brunet (1987) speaks of 'first' and 'second' waves of thinking about ADR. The first he terms an 'evangelical' movement; the second has been a more measured, and even skeptical, current. The development of the field of public conflict resolution might be viewed in similar terms. During the first phase, dating from the late 1960s and continuing even perhaps until the early 1980s, a relatively small number of individuals pioneered efforts to apply techniques of mediation and conciliation to public disputes. This was a phase of innovation, of experiment, of advocacy. It was also a phase of much uncertainty. There were significant concerns about the viability of such efforts, and about their advisability; about the role of the third party and whether and how it might vary from that of the industrial relations mediator; and even about what constituted success or failure.

The beginnings of ethnic and racial dispute resolution

The first applications of the contemporary public conflict resolution movement occurred in the mediation of community racial disputes. By 1971, there were a dozen or so organizations formed to mediate or to research such disputes.[8] The very existence of these organizations might be taken as an indication of acceptance of the mediation of racial disputes. But there always was considerable skepticism even among these early advocates about whether mediation in situations of uneven power was useful or appropriate.

The Racial Negotiations Project, which began its work in 1968, provides a good example of such concern. The project originally sought, in the organizer's own words, to 'explore whether or not a negotiating process provides a mechanism that can be used by both the black protesters and the institutions to work out their differences in such a way that a satisfactory rate of change is achieved without tearing the nation apart' (Chalmers and Cormick, 1971: 5)

Chalmers and Cormick noted that other social institutions were able to make use of negotiations for accommodating social interests, but that such negotiations are most acceptable when the disputants have some coercive potential relative to one another. The interest in the researchers was directed more towards the negotiation process as a medium of change for the status of blacks in American society than towards a 'peace' which might leave the status quo in place. Their conclusions, upon reporting two cases – the Memphis Public Employees Strike and the Cleveland Water Works Employees Strike – were mixed. It was not at all clear to them that negotiations or mediated negotiations were acceptable to those who desired change.

Many of these organizations left the scene without a trace, and there was little research and writing that outlived them; the anticipated movement was put on hold. It faded along with the decline of civil rights activism, with the increased access by minorities to existing institutions of governance, with the improved capacity of police and other community organizations to handle racial disputes, and particularly with the growth in interest in other areas of intervention, including most particularly the environment.

The beginnings of environmental dispute resolution

The first suggestion for environmental dispute resolution is found in Foster's 1969 article, 'A case for environmental conciliation' (Mernitz, 1980). Mernitz also notes that a number of environmental laws (e.g. NEPA, PL 91–190, 1970; FWPCA, PL 84–660, 1956; FPWCA, PL 92–500, 1972; CAA, PL 91–604, 1970; the Coastal Zone Management Act, PL 92–583, 1972) have what he terms 'clues' to mediable aspects. There are also precedents for negotiated rulemakings in the way manufacturers voluntarily worked for product and fire safety codes (Bacow and Wheeler, 1984). But it is generally conceded that the beginnings of environmental dispute resolution can be traced to a single case. The efforts of Gerald Cormick and Jane McCarthy to mediate a dispute over the construction of the Snoqualmie River dam constitute the first effort to apply dispute resolution techniques to environmental issues (Dembart and Kwartler, 1980; Bingham, 1986). This mediation was part of a deliberate effort sponsored primarily by the Ford Foundation to expand the range of applications of dispute resolution procedures from the labor-management arena to neighborhoods and communities. The mediation resulted in a number of agreements, but some of those agreements were never implemented.

Many of the first applications of environmental dispute resolution were conceived as 'showcase' examples, intended to demonstrate to a variety of interested parties in fields not familiar with its philosophy or practices the feasibility of conflict resolution. These were efforts to introduce the concepts of consensus, participation, integration, and interest-based negotiation to individuals and institutions more accustomed to adversarial modes of thinking and practice.

The National Coal Policy Project of the 1970s was the first effort to bring together business and environmental leaders to attempt to reach consensus on issues of national policy (Bingham, 1986). Under the direction of Francis X. Murray of the Georgetown University Center for Strategic and International Studies, the project involved as many as 105 participants in plenary sessions or task-force meetings grappling with over 200 issues. Although agreement was reached on almost 90 percent of the issues, implementation of those agreements was a problem, and some of the non-participating environmental organizations were critical of the outcome. Bingham suggests that the real contribution of the National Coal Policy Project may have been less any agreements that were reached than the precedent demonstrated by the cooperation among the disparate groups.

The second phase: Institutionalizing a field

The second phase of development of public conflict resolution built upon the first pioneering efforts to develop new forums, gain entry into new arenas, create a track record of success and acceptance, and devise the institutions necessary to ensure the continued growth of the field. This phase included the following components:

- a second generation of practitioners, many of whom received their training within the field;
- the growth of programs within higher education;
- the development of capacity to use mediation and other conflict resolution procedures within the institutions of government, including most prominently the establishment of state offices of dispute resolution and the passage of enabling legislation, including the federal Administrative Dispute Resolution and Negotiated Rulemaking Acts of 1990;
- increasing influence on policymaking and policymakers;
- the spread of practice to other nations;
- increased reflection upon the meanings of practice.

This second phase may be best represented by outlining the institutional structure which developed to guide the direction of the field of conflict resolution and, within that field, the public conflict resolution arena. Four types of organizations took part in this growth: funding; funding and advocacy; federal; and professional associations. Their roles will be examined in turn.

Funding

The funders, those grant-sponsoring foundations which support research, practice, and organizational needs, are of two classes. A few, such as the William and Flora Hewlett Foundation and the Ford Foundation, have had program officers who work closely with leaders of the field in shaping the overall development of the field. The larger class of foundations typically provides occasional funding for specific interventions or problems, or for individual organizations.

As difficult as it is to imagine a field of public conflict resolution without the example of labor-management mediation, it is even harder to believe that the field might have developed as it did without the active interest and support of several highly influential grantmaking foundations. During the 1970s, and even into the early 1980s, most dispute resolution services were offered at low or no cost to the disputants by foundation-sponsored, non-profit private or university-based institutions (Haygood, 1988b). Without the formal connections to government agencies and other institutions (Haygood, 1988b), mediators needed to devote a great deal of time to promoting their services. Entry was achieved on a case-by-case basis, through knowledgeable individuals, rather than through any systematic process of dispute identification and assessment. Foundation support removed the major issue of who would pay for the mediator's services, with its attending complications for the mediator's neutrality.

Primarily responsible for funding of early public dispute resolution efforts and institutions were the Ford and the William and Flora Hewlett Foundations. They were joined by the Rockefeller Foundation; Mellon Foundation; J.N. Pew, Jr. Charitable Trust; Charles Stewart Mott Foundation; Joyce Foundation; and three corporations: Atlantic Richfield, Texas Utilities, and Exxon (Reilly, 1984).

The Ford Foundation was particularly active at the early stages of the development of the field, in the late 1960s and early 1970s, when the venture of transporting dispute resolution procedures from labor-management to the public arena was new. The focus of the program follows: '(1) strengthening the dispute-processing capacity of existing institutions; (2) finding better ways to handle disputes outside of those institutions, and (3) identifying system-wide changes designed to reduce conflicts or to make their handling more efficient' (Ford Foundation, 1978: 63). The Ford Foundation funded such pioneering organizations as the American Arbitration Association (AAA) National Center for Dispute Settlement, New York's Institute for Mediation and Conflict Resolution, the Community Crisis Intervention Center at Washington University in St. Louis, and the Center for Community Justice, all of which were involved in community disputes involving ethnic and racial issues. They supported the first attempts at environmental dispute resolution, including the Snoqualmie Dam mediation, and they provided general support for the Institute for Environmental Studies at the University of Washington in Seattle, and the Office of Environmental Mediation at the University of Wisconsin. They were also one of several co-founders of, and provided continued funding for, the National Institute for Dispute Resolution (NIDR). In 1987 the Ford Foundation established the Fund for Research in Dispute Resolution (FRDR), administered by NIDR, as the first research program devoted specifically to disputing and methods of dispute resolution.

In the environmental arena, the Ford Foundation tended to fund pioneers in more formal dispute resolution efforts (Bingham, 1986). The Hewlett Foundation, on the other hand, tended to fund less formal processes designed to build relationships which could sustain the tensions of subsequent decision-making processes (Bingham, 1986). Hewlett particularly stressed the development of conflict and conflict resolution theory, funding fourteen university centers in a combination of research and practice. It supported conferences (e.g. the Florisant, Colorado meeting in 1982 for environmental dispute resolution; the National Conference on Peacemaking and Conflict Resolution (NCPCR); the 1992 Charlottesville Symposium ('The Cutting Edge', 1994) for senior environmental dispute resolution practitioners, umbrella institutions (e.g. the Society for Professionals in Dispute Resolution, National Institute for Dispute Resolution), practitioner organizations (e.g. CDR Associates, Conflict Clinic, Justice Center of Atlanta) and theory-building institutions (e.g. the Institute for Conflict Analysis and Resolution at George Mason University and the Program on Negotiations at Harvard University).

While most of the practitioner organizations are still non-profit and tax-exempt and thus continue to rely upon foundation support, such support has moved away from the establishment of new institutions and testing new applications and towards support for specific problems and disputes. With increasing acceptance of the need for conflict resolution by local, state, and federal authorities, both elected and administrative, business communities, and advocacy organizations (such as environmental groups), the field in the late 1980s began shifting away from being foundation-directed towards having more of a market orientation (Szanton Associates, 1989), albeit a market dominated by government agencies.

Funding and advocacy

Under the category of funding and advocacy are several organizations which provide significant guidance and support beyond funding. Such support may include introduction of dispute resolution information to different constituencies, convening of conferences, development of educational materials, or sponsorship of journals.

The organization most responsible for establishing and guiding the direction of the public conflict resolution field has been NIDR, founded in 1982. The premier foundation devoted solely to conflict resolution in the United

States, NIDR's stated mission is to 'enhance the fairness, effectiveness and efficiency of the ways Americans resolve disputes. In particular, the Institute supports the development, testing, and expansion of the use of innovative techniques to settle conflicts' (NIDR, 1989).

NIDR began withdrawing from its role as a funder in the 1990s; however, its mandate always went much beyond providing financial support. NIDR's Public Policy Program began two years after the organization's founding. The purpose of the Program is as follows:

> to help build the institutions, the infrastructure, and the methodologies for settling large-scale conflicts involving the public interest. The program includes support for public policy dispute resolution experiments within state and federal government and for the continued use and refinement of public interest mediation in disputes across the country ('Statewide offices of mediation', 1987: 2).

This interest has taken several forms: consultation with leading practitioners about the establishment of a number of programs or practices, most significantly statewide offices of mediation and regulatory negotiations; direct financial support for state offices; a Fund for Public Interest Mediation to subsidize both mediators and participants in mediations; support for education and training, including developing and publishing curriculum materials for use in law and various graduate schools; and administration of the FRDR. NIDR's Innovation Fund, which granted up to $50,000 for developing, testing, and documenting innovative approaches to dispute resolution, was perhaps the most adventurous vehicle within the public arena.

Other foundations have adopted conflict resolution as a significant component of their agenda. The Kettering Foundation does not make outright grants of financial aid, but collaborates with other institutions on various problems of governance, education, and science. In 1978 they moved the field in a new direction, sponsoring the 'Negotiated Investment Strategy', ('NIS') (Kettering Foundation, 1982) to develop consensus agreements about policy on future investments for cities and states. The NIS represented the earliest effort to institutionalize mediation of public policy issues.

The National Civic League has actively promoted collaborative, participatory processes of dispute resolution, including advocacy for grassroots efforts at social change. They sponsor CIVITEX, a computerized database containing several hundred profiles of successful community problem-solving efforts. Their publication *National Civic Review* has a regular department, 'Conflict management', and it often publishes articles about dispute resolution. In conjunction with several other associations, the National Civic League initiated the Program for Community Problem Solving (Carpenter, 1989). The Program is intended to document examples of successful collaborative community problem solving, develop guidelines for community leaders, promote collaborative processes, and build networks within and between communities to support the use of effective problem-solving processes (Program for Community Problem Solving, 1988). In 1994 the Program became part of the National Civic League.

Federal

One indication of the growing interest in conflict resolution in general is the listing of dispute resolution legislation compiled by the American Bar Association (ABA) Standing Committee on Dispute Resolution, which at the beginning of the 1990s stood at just over 270 pages (ABA Standing Committee on Dispute Resolution, 1990). The two most influential pieces of federal dispute resolution legislation were both signed into law at the same time – §303, the 'Negotiated Rulemaking Act of 1990', and H.R. 2497, the 'Administrative Dispute Resolution Act of 1990'.

The federal government was a party to 55,000 civil cases in 1989, with over 100,000 private civil cases involving some federal question (Susskind, 1989). H.R. 2497, the Administrative Dispute Resolution Act of 1990, was an effort to address those numbers. In the words of the act itself, it 'authorize[s] and encourage[s] Federal agencies to use mediation, conciliation, arbitration, and other techniques for the prompt and informal resolution of disputes, and for other purposes.' The Act requires each federal agency to consult with the Administrative Conference of the United States (ACUS) and the Federal Mediation and Conciliation Service (FMCS) about non-litigative means of dispute resolution, appoint a senior official as dispute resolution specialist, and train this specialist and other employees in the 'theory and practice of negotiation, mediation, arbitration, or related techniques' (Sec. 3). The Act guarantees confidentiality. It amends the Contract Disputes Act to allow ADR settlement of contract issues. It increases the role of the FMCS, whose mediators, previously limited to private disputes, may now assist agencies. ACUS will keep a roster of 'qualified neutrals' to distribute to interested agencies.

It is somewhat ironic that the administrative procedures the Act was designed to supplement were themselves, in the Act's words, 'intended to offer a prompt, expert, and inexpensive means of resolving disputes as an alternative to litigation.' But these proceedings 'have become increasingly formal, costly, and lengthy'; hence, 'alternative' procedures, which yield 'faster, less expensive, and less contentious' decisions and can lead to 'more creative, efficient, and sensible outcomes,' are needed. Federal agencies may benefit from these 'techniques' and even 'lead in further development and refinement of such techniques' (Sec. 2). There is some risk, of course, that the institutionalization of these 'alternative' procedures will in due course lead to their becoming 'increasingly formal, costly, and lengthy' as well.

§303, the 'Negotiated Rulemaking Act of 1990,' codified the procedure and encouraged federal agencies to make use of it. According to this Act, current rulemaking procedures 'may discourage the affected parties from meeting and communicating with each other', and may cause parties to 'assume conflicting and antagonistic positions', with 'expensive and time-consuming litigation' over the rules. Adversarial rulemaking deprives parties and public of the 'shared information, knowledge, expertise, and technical abilities' of the parties. Negotiated rulemaking as an alternative may increase acceptability, shorten the time it takes to get a rule established, and improve the rule's substance (Sec. 2). With over 100 federal agencies issuing over 5,000 rules each year, negotiated rulemaking could become a significant factor in producing these rules (Susskind 1989).

Despite these two pieces of legislation, systematic implementation and institutionalization of conflict resolution procedures was relatively slow to develop at the federal level. Nonetheless, various federal agencies have played a significant role in attracting interest and in funding applications. Federal organizations involved in the field may be placed into two categories. Some agencies have been willing to integrate dispute resolution procedures within their own work and to share their lessons with the public conflict resolution field and other agencies. The second category includes agencies whose responsibility it is to study, promote, and educate about conflict resolution.

Most important in the first category is the Environmental Protection Agency (EPA). EPA's administrator at the time of their initial interest, William Reilly, came to the job having been President of the Conservation Foundation and the World Wildlife Fund, a pioneer in the public conflict resolution field. Despite some internal opposition from within the agency and the Justice Department, the EPA has been instrumental in testing the negotiated rulemaking procedure. It has also extensively promoted mediation to settle Superfund (clean-up of toxic waste sites) disputes. The EPA in 1991 established a formal contracting procedure to allow its divisions easier access to, and funding for, a variety of training and 'alternative dispute resolution (ADR)' activities. The EPA has also sponsored educational workshops to introduce its personnel to 'alternative dispute resolution'.

The Army Corps of Engineers (COE) has been another pioneer in the use of dispute resolution procedures, training its own personnel in facilitation and collaborative problem solving procedures and participating in mediations and mini-trials (Dellipriscolli, 1989; US Army Corps of Engineers, 1990). In 1992 they, too, facilitated operational procedures by establishing contractual relations for dispute resolution services with a number of practitioner organizations (Creighton, 1992).

In the second category of federal involvement in public conflict resolution are two agencies: the Administrative Conference of the United States (ACUS) and the Federal Mediation and Conciliation Service (FMCS). These two agencies were given responsibility for administering the 1990 Negotiated Rulemaking and Administrative Dispute Resolution Acts. The primary role of FMCS is to provide mediation for labor-management disputes. But FMCS also provides help for federal agencies, including finding convenors, practitioners, and training. The dispute resolution role of ACUS is to 'establish standards for neutrals (including experience, training, affiliations, diligence, actual or potential conflicts of interest, and other qualifications)' (Sec. 583). Among other implications, the roster of 'neutrals' established by ACUS is likely to impact the field as the only complete 'official' roster or index of practitioners sponsored by a federal entity.

Professional associations

The professional associations are those institutions devoted to serving the interests of practitioners and, presumably, consumers of their services. These include the American Arbitration Association (AAA), American Bar Association's Standing Committee on Dispute Resolution, the National Conference on Peacemaking and Conflict Resolution (NCPCR), the Society for Professionals in Dispute Resolution (SPIDR), the International Association of Public Participation Practitioners (IAP3), and various state networks, such as the North Carolina Public Disputes Network and the Virginia Mediation Network.

In addition, there is an informal network of leading practitioners who present at conferences, train, and otherwise build the field. This network includes institutions such as the Public Disputes Network of Harvard and MIT, RESOLVE (formerly of the Conservation Foundation/World Wildlife Fund), the Institute for Conflict Analysis and Resolution at George Mason University, and, among the religious institutions, the Mennonite Conciliation Service.

The only association devoted specifically to public conflict resolution is the SPIDR Sector on Environmental and Public Dispute Resolution, one of several such SPIDR sectors. The Sector has only a few dozen members, but the 1992 Charlottesville Conference for Senior Environmental Dispute Resolution Practitioners (RESOLVE and Institute for Environmental Negotiation (IEN), 1994) and later annual conferences increased its utility and visibility. The International Association of Public Participation Practitioners, formed in 1990, includes public conflict resolution practitioners among its Board and general membership; it grew rapidly the first few years after its founding.

The past yet to come

The history of public conflict resolution is not static. As the field moves into new arenas, develops new procedures, takes on new meanings, and seeks new outlets, it pursues and discovers complementary historical dimensions as well. For example, there has been substantial interest among public conflict resolution theorists and practitioners in cross-cultural conflict resolution, both domestic and abroad (Moore, 1993). Such interest has led to a new appreciation of conflict resolution traditions of other cultures and other times.

Like a tree whose roots extend underground as its limbs branch outward, public conflict resolution is growing in depth as well as breadth. From beginnings as efforts simply to apply processes which had achieved success in the labor-management arena to public disputes over racial and environmental issues, the field now is an organism encompassing activities such as citizen participation movements, community coalition building, social activism, populism, participatory democracy, and the sustenance of democratic practice. The institutional capacity is increasing correspondingly. The significance of this expansion is an open question.

Notes

1   See, e.g., the Beachey Amish-Mennonites (Dukes, 1987).
2   Among many examples that might be given are the Kpelle moot courts (Danzig, 1973) and the Nuer leopard-skin chief (Kolb, 1983b). For other kinds of procedures see, e.g., Nader (1969), Gulliver (1979), and Abel (1982b).
3   The exception may be those Kpelle courts, whose philosophy of conciliation within the community has served, albeit loosely, as a model for neighborhood justice centers (Harrington and Merry, 1988).
4   See, e.g., Sata (1975).
5   See analysis in Burton and Dukes, (1990).
6   See, e.g., Brown and Mazza (1991), Price (1990).
7   See, e.g., Cormick and Patton (1980), Bellman *et al.* (1982), Harrington and Merry (1988).
8   Laue and Cormick (1973) were able to identify eleven organizations pioneering third-party intervention in community disputes in the early 1970s.

Part II

A portrait of
current practice

4

Mediation and its variants

For the purposes of illumination, the practices of public conflict resolution will be divided into two kinds:

1   Activities directed towards reaching agreement over a specific issue or set of issues. These processes are distinguished particularly by the consideration of how agreements may be implemented, through formal or informal mechanisms and ties to the standard legislative, administrative, or judicial processes. Practices in this category will be termed *mediation*.
2   Those activites which are exploratory, educational, or otherwise directed at gathering information and developing understanding short of agreement. These serve a variety of functions: educating various interested parties and/or the general public, increasing public involvement, demonstrating an unfamiliar process, engaging different viewpoints, or raising consciousness about an issue. They may precede or accompany efforts more directly tied to reaching and implementing agreements. This category will be termed *facilitation*, the subject of Chapter Five.[1]

Both Chapters Four and Five demonstrate the breadth of activities encompassed by the public conflict resolution field. Neither critical nor positive assessment of the field generally acknowledges this breadth, focusing instead primarily on a narrow view of the mediation process.

It must also be emphasized that these chapters present only a snapshot of what is a dynamic arena. The future pace of change within the public conflict resolution field is not likely to match that of the past two decades, but it is inevitable that the evolution will continue.

Mediation and public disputes

The nature of public disputes

Conflict resolution, and especially mediation, is a 'hot' topic. Newspapers and magazines feature stories about divorce mediation; graduate programs in conflict resolution and mediation proliferate. On two consecutive evenings in September 1994, on two different programs broadcast throughout the United States, television viewers saw reports of peer mediation programs in secondary schools. Two separate electronic networks, one a for-fee service (ConflictNet) and one open to anyone with access to the Internet (dispute-res@listserv.law.cornell.edu), offer hundreds of subscribers the opportunities for discussion and debate. The International Society of Professionals in Dispute Resolution has 3,200 members and its membership is beginning to reflect the scope of its title. The fields of community, family, student, and commercial mediation have spawned their own umbrella organizations.[2]

For most of these domains, it is clear what is meant by mediation. Of course, there are significant disagreements within each of these fields about mediation's purposes and goals, and different considerations of what constitutes 'best practices'. But in each of these fields there is a clear distinction between mediation and other types of decision-making forums.

At one time, and not so long ago, it was also clear what was meant by mediation in the public arena. The required formula included clear impasse, distinct parties, defined issues, formal intervention by a 'neutral' third party, and a set of procedures largely borrowed from the labor-management arena. But that formula no longer holds. A single process cannot be discovered for public mediation.

For one thing, the distinction between a private and public dispute is often blurred in practice. Some cases are easy to exclude from the public realm: a couple who are divorcing and who need to work out support, custody, and visitation issues; neighbors whose dogs have been fighting one another; a business suing its supplier for breach of contract. But it is not so easy to keep neat divisions when the disputes widen, as they often do: the divorcing couple owns property which could become more valuable if rezoned; neighbors appeal to local government for an ordinance which would impact their larger community; a business seeks to expand its operations against the wishes of its neighbors.

An example from my own experience illustrates this point. In a predominantly rural county in Virginia, the organizers of the local County Fair became divided among themselves about the future direction and leadership of the fair. The president of the Board was dismissed from his post. At the annual meeting of the fair, the former president's allies took over the meeting and voted in a new slate of officers after the existing leadership adjourned early. Two sets of Board members, each claiming legitimacy, vied for control of the treasury, and each side hired attorneys and threatened litigation. The parties agreed to attend a single mediation session, during which some of the issues were resolved; soon after, one side withdrew from contention.

44

Was this a public dispute, and the mediation a public conflict resolution procedure? The Board of the County Fair is a private organization, and the issues were not a matter of public policy. But there were multiple parties; the impact to the community, given that the survival of the fair was at stake, was both lasting and profound; the mediator (myself) works in the public conflict resolution arena. There is no definitive answer.

Furthermore, there is substantial overlap among other fields and the public arena. Community mediators who normally mediate private, interpersonal disputes have been drawn into issues of a more public nature. Conversely, a number of public mediators also work in the community arena as volunteers, or work professionally in other fields, such as commercial mediation. Practitioners from different fields meet at conferences and other forums and exchange ideas.

But the main reason the old definition of public mediation no longer holds lies in the nature of public disputes themselves. Lentz (1986) contrasts the clearly-defined situations typical of labor-management mediation with the more nebulous issues and contexts that environmental mediators must deal with. The lessons are applicable for other public disputes as well. In labor-management disputes the primary issues are economic and data is therefore readily available. There are two fixed sides to deal with, and each side has at least one common goal, avoidance or end of a strike. The search for a new contract provides a focus for the negotiations, and (arguably) parties have fairly balanced power, at least in most circumstances. In environmental as well as other public disputes, on the other hand, issues are often complex, and can involve mutually exclusive and strongly held values. Data is often complex and difficult to obtain. Numerous separate parties may be involved.

Public disputes bring their own dynamics. They have a complex network of interests (Carpenter and Kennedy, 1988). That is, there are always a number of parties to any public dispute, and these parties themselves are groups and organizations, as well as individuals. New parties often emerge as new issues surface or as negotiations proceed.

The organizations that parties to these disputes represent may have vastly different structures; some are incorporated, others are established government institutions, while others may be ad hoc groups formed in response to the issues precipitating the dispute. Some parties may be represented by an individual who has full decision-making authority, while others must report back to their constituencies before agreeing to any action.

Unlike labor negotiations, there may not be a common deadline, such as a pending strike, to impel negotiations. Goals may be quite different, and, not unrelated to that factor, parties often have greatly different resources and power, including financial, legal, expertise, size of group, and access to decision makers (Carpenter and Kennedy, 1988). Perhaps more impor-

45

tantly, the parties themselves often recognize the obvious power imbalances, and these disparities themselves often are important issues. As Lentz (1986) observes, negotiators on each side of union-management disputes often are experienced with both negotiation and mediation processes, while public issues can involve parties who either have no experience in the public realm at all or, in the case of citizen advocacy groups, are most familiar with confrontational tactics.[3]

Gaining entry into a dispute is a problem unique to the public disputes field. Unlike many other arenas within the conflict resolution family, which have established procedures to create mediated forums, the public arena has few forums readily available which offer the requisite conditions (Laue, *et al.*, 1988). The parties have varying levels of knowledge about what are often complex technical questions or about the political and legal context of the issues. Unlike family or labor-management disputes, many of the parties may have little or no continuing relationship with other parties. There may be no institutional vehicles for resolving disputes, or indeed for adversaries to engage one another in dialogue at all. It may be unclear which, if any, government authority has jurisdiction or responsibility for dealing with an issue (Carpenter and Kennedy, 1988).

The elements of public mediation

The complexity of the dynamics of public disputes is matched by the extraordinary diversity of contentious public issues. To name any one area of public interest – education, environment and land use, health, safety, economic development, agriculture, and more – is to identify a battleground, or, more accurately, a number of battlegrounds in different locations and at all levels of government. This extraordinary diversity in the nature and types of public disputes, combined with the increasing demand for effective and lasting means of breaking impasse and making decisions, has led to the use of public conflict resolution forums of many shapes, sizes, and purposes.

Two cases again from my own experience illustrate the extremes of what may be considered 'textbook' mediation, on the one hand, and the ad hoc, irregular, uncertain nature of other types of intervention. In November of 1994 I began working as co-mediator of the Virginia Mental Health Insurance Parity Task Force. The membership roster had already been completed. The charge to the group was offered by a supervising Commission made up of members of the legislative and executive branches. Funding had largely been arranged. The Task Force was expected to complete its work in time for the 1996 state legislative session, thus presenting a clear and compelling deadline. And the two mediators were introduced to Task Force members by a senior legislator and member of the supervisory commission. All in all, · this mediation began with as neat a package as a mediator could desire.

At the same time, I began working on what became known as the

'Tobacco Communities' project. A coalition of health organizations was seeking a grant from a foundation program designed to promote anti-smoking activities. This coalition requested my assistance in proposing an initiative which would unite health interests with tobacco growers and other tobacco interests to examine the need for agricultural diversification and economic development in tobacco growing communities. Their grant proposal was funded; a certain portion of the money was allocated for my role.

Now consider the circumstances of this endeavor and ask whether this might be considered a mediation. There was no 'dispute,' *per se*, and certainly no impasse, despite the conflict inherent in the activities of the two sides. The parties simply never talked to one another at all. No linkage existed with any body which might be able to implement any agreements the two groups could reach. No deadline compelled action. And there was certainly no demand for discussion, much less negotiations, on the part of the tobacco growing community.

Despite these ambiguities, it is possible to offer some general guidelines to distinguish mediation procedures from other means of creating and enacting policy or settling and resolving disputes and conflicts. As a working definition, the following elements are offered as minimal characteristics of what constitutes a public mediation process.[4] This is a skeletal and somewhat abstract outline which will be enriched by the subsequent presentation of actual processes and the problems addressed by public mediation.

- There are involved two or more groups, such as governmental bodies, public interest groups, civic and neighborhood associations, private corporations, or ad hoc collectivities, engaged in *public* issues.
- These entities are involved in *negotiations* directed towards clarification, understanding and eventual agreement over these issues.
- These negotiations involve a significant component of *direct*, face-to-face discussions among the parties.
- The process is *inclusive*, within the situation's particular context, of affected parties.
- The focus of the interaction is *collaborative* or *non-adversarial* in the legal sense of the term (although much of the interaction may be highly conflictual).
- Decision-making is based on some form of *consensus* (that is, agreement by some substantial portion or even all of the participants, rather than majority vote).
- A *third party*[5] (an individual or organization not involved as direct party to the dispute or controversy) acts to guide the process.

The boundaries between mediation and other types of public decision-making activities are not at all fixed. Indeed, in mediation a particular forum often serves to provide input into the established policymaking appa-

47

ratus, so that the conflict resolution process becomes an integral part of that policymaking procedure, rather than a separate entity. Of course, as practitioners can attest, public officials will sometimes use the language of 'consensus building' and 'conflict resolution' for established legislative or administrative procedures which might have some flavor, but little substance, of conflict resolution.

The variants of mediation

Ad hoc mediation

The term 'ad hoc mediation' refers to the use of mediation for disputes centered around particular circumstances, such as a planned use for a piece of land. Mediation of this sort is typically conducted on a one-time basis.

Madigan *et al.* (1990) offer a credible generic overview of the public mediation process. They identify three primary phases of mediated negotiations: the *pre-negotiation* phase; the *negotiation and consensus-building* phase; and the *post-negotiation* phase.

During the pre-negotiation phase the nature of the conflict is assessed, stakeholders are identified and persuaded to participate in negotiations, and a third party is selected to manage the process. A timetable and ground rules are established, a mutually agreeable agenda is developed, resources are identified, joint factfinding begins, and, sometimes, pre-negotiation training is offered.

In the negotiation and consensus-building phase, the parties work towards a single negotiating text. They explore underlying interests, invent potential agreement 'packages', draft a final agreement, and check with their constituencies before final ratification.

The post-negotiation phase begins with steps to bind the parties to the agreement. The agreement must be linked to formal implementation connections, implementation must be monitored, and provisions for future negotiation or remediation must be made. Evaluation of the whole procedure, while not essential, can benefit future negotiation efforts.

It must be noted that the combination of elements found in public disputes, including high stakes, multiple parties, and high visibility, make for a dynamic situation which rarely follows textbook procedures. Every mediation actually involves several sets of negotiations. In public disputes, most parties are negotiating on behalf of a larger constituency than themselves. Various interest groups – whether they be industry, public interest organizations, citizens, or regulators – often have considerable internal differences. Individual companies may differ in their policies, the types of ownership of property and other resources, and specific organizational interests which may make a common position difficult. Members of the business community are often competitors, of course, but less attention is paid to the fact that public interest organizations, citizens, and regulators are often competing as well for limited funds, status and power. Participants must also satisfy their organizational interests. And their relations with parties not directly involved in the dispute, such as legislators, interested regulatory agencies, and the media, affect the course of the mediation as well.

Example: The Warrenton Land Use Task Force[6]   In the summer of 1992, a small town in Virginia concluded a 'boundary adjustment' which transferred a portion of land from county to town jurisdiction. Most of the annexed area was undeveloped, except for a paving/excavation company and a minority residential neighborhood known as Oliver City. The owner of the paving company supported the boundary adjustment. He anticipated that the town would welcome the expansion of his business because of the taxes that it would provide.

When the Planning Commission held hearings on the requested expansion, neighboring residents of Oliver City and of a historic district on a ridge overlooking the paving company objected. These hearings demonstrated such an intense interest in the issue, with different views about the proper public response to the proposed changes, that outside help was sought to resolve the issues. In an effort to develop community agreement about the use of the annexed area, a mediation group which had helped the town resolve a land-use dispute several years earlier was retained.

After considerable discussions by the mediation team with many of the key parties, these parties agreed to convene what was termed the 'Warrenton Land Use Task Force' to consider these issues. The Task Force included the owner of the business, neighbors from the historic district and the minority community, and a representative of the Chamber of Commerce. This Task Force was expected to report to the Town Council any consensus about land use and the proposed expansion. The Planning Commission deferred any changes in this area pending a report about these discussions.

The mediation team conducted a conflict assessment through interviews with key stakeholders; they provided the logistic services necessary to set time, place, date, and agendas for the meetings; they searched for and provided the information necessary for discussions; and they facilitated meetings. In addition, the mediators conducted extensive discussions with individual parties to clarify concerns and gauge the potential of suggested solutions.

During the series of four meetings of the whole Task Force parties were able to express their desires and concerns. The owner of the business was concerned that the constraints of the exising land-use designation were adversely affecting his business operations. He therefore requested changes that would allow him to increase the size of his building and better accommodate the growth of his business.

The neighboring residents from the minority neighborhood and the historic district opposed any expansion of the operations. They cited nuisance effects from the current operations, including noise, litter, traffic, and safety issues. The neighbors were also concerned with the type of development that would be permitted on the rest of the newly annexed land. Generally, they favored residential rather than industrial uses, and felt that any expansion of the contractor's yard would encourage additional industrial use nearby. They were concerned with how the character of their community might be preserved and enhanced, and particularly whether their concerns would be respected when decisions affecting the community were to be made.

The town initially hoped that through discussions among the interested parties there might be some accommodation of the interests that were in conflict. Since the business operations which already existed would be allowed to continue indefinitely whatever the outcome of the dispute, there was some thought that a tradeoff could be arranged which would allow the expanded operations in return for changes such as increased buffering, improved vehicle access to the site, and other accommodations.

At each meeting the public was invited to make comments or ask questions of Task Force members. Members also met for a tour of the area under consideration. After considerable exploration and discussion it became clear that there was strong opposition to any change in the zoning on the property and any expansion of operations. Attention shifted from mitigating existing site problems or expanding industrial uses to a search for an alternative site in town for the operations. In that way, the tax benefits of the business would continue to accrue to the town and the annexed land could be developed more compatibly with the existing residential uses.

The owner of the site withdrew his request for rezoning and indicated that he would concentrate on finding an alternative location. The owner also agreed that he would take additional steps to mitigate the impacts of his operations on the neighborhood while operations continued at his existing site. The town agreed to work with the minority residents, particularly in obtaining funding for sewer and water services. The town would also assist in finding an alternative site for the contractor's yard, and would undertake additional planning studies before any rezoning would occur.

Was the process successful? The answer to that question depends on the definition of 'success'. The process expanded the range of possible land use choices beyond those being considered initially. The Town Council might have preferred an outcome in which the industrial rezoning and expansion would have been approved with the neighbors' support. But at the end of the Task Force the owner, the town, and the neighbors had changed their goal to finding a new site for industrial use and converting the existing site to residential use.

Regulatory negotiation (reg-neg)

'Regulatory negotiation' ('reg-neg'), also known as *negotiated rulemaking*, is a procedure which supplements existing agency rulemaking by fostering mediated negotiations among parties with a stake in a proposed rule. The genesis of regulatory negotiations was the dissatisfaction of agencies and others with established rulemaking procedures. These procedures, designed in part to prevent agency 'capture' by special interests, had become so formalized and cumbersome that in some circumstances they shut off agencies from real-world constraints and opportunities. In addition, the promulgation of a rule often merely marked the shifting of contention among the affected parties from the regulatory forum into the judicial arena. Bingham (1986) suggests as well that the incorporation of conflict resolution procedures into the administrative rulemaking process was an extension of the example of policy dialogues in areas such as coal and energy policy, toxic substances control, and air quality in the steel industry.

With the assistance of public conflict resolution practitioners such as Susskind and Harter (NIDR, 1986), the Administrative Conference of the United States (ACUS) began to develop and experiment with collaborative, consensual decision-making procedures which would actively involve interested stakeholders in developing the rules and regulations. §303, the 'Negotiated Rulemaking Act of 1990', provides a framework encouraging federal agencies to consider rulemaking by negotiations among the affected interests. The law provides guidelines which include the following considerations: a relatively few parties; a committment to negotiate in good faith; multiple issues, with trade-offs possible; adequate agency resources; agency commitment to the process; and, most importantly, the acceptance of consensus as the decision-making procedure (Sec. 583). While the rules are still subject to judicial review, the agency actions relative to the negotiated rulemaking committee are not.

Harter (1984, in NIDR, 1986) describes the procedures used for regulatory negotiations. The procedure may be initiated from within or outside an agency. If the agency is interested, it appoints a convenor who studies the feasibility of the process by identifying the issues and parties likely to be involved. The convenor uses the following criteria as the basis for deciding whether or not to proceed with mediation:

- no more than twenty-five (preferably fifteen) represented interests;
- interests sufficiently organized such that they can be represented during negotiations;
- parties sufficiently powerful that the outcome of standard rulemaking might be in doubt;
- issues that are ripe for decisions;
- a realistic deadline, which usually means a time after which the agency

will decide the regulations on its own if progress has not been made;
- no party must compromise on issues 'fundamental to its existence';
- the agency supports the process; and,
- the parties will agree to participate in good faith.

If the convenor decides that regulatory negotiations are feasible, the agency may or may not accept the recommendation. If the decision is made to proceed, the agency must publish in the *Federal Register* a notice describing the proposed process, the issues, and a list of parties who have already agreed to participate. It may also invite participation by other unrepresented interests. The convenor may also be chosen as the facilitator of the group. The group will generally be chartered as an advisory committee under the Federal Advisory Committee Act (FACA). Under FACA rules plenary meetings are open to the public, while separate work groups may meet privately.

The goal is to reach 'consensus' agreement on the preamble and all major issues. 'Consensus' is defined as either approval or the absence of active opposition by each interest. What this means in practice is that each represented interest, no matter how much power it may wield outside the negotiations, can veto any proposal.

This process has been encapsulated by Haygood (1988a) into six stages:

1 Identification of a rule that might be appropriate for negotiation.
2 Convening (assessment of whether and how negotiations would be conducted).
3 Notice of proposed rulemaking.
4 Organization of the negotiated rulemaking committee (decisions on committee membership, training of committee members, agreement on groundrules).
5 Negotiations.
6 Publication of proposed rule (p. 79).

Haygood suggests that one of the most important issues is helping the parties make an informed decision about whether or not to participate in the process. She also argues that agreement and implementation is not necessarily the best criteria for judging the success of the process, since even in cases where agreement was not reached the convening agency still can find the process useful in informing the agency of constituent needs.

Of all the procedures examined here, regulatory negotiation has the strongest ties to the formal policy process. But reaching a consensual agreement does not ensure adoption of that agreement by the agency. The proposed rules may be challenged by any party, including those involved in the negotiations who may have a change of mind. In practice, however, it has been difficult to overturn the consensus of a representative group.

Negotiated rulemaking has been used to deal with issues such as flight and rest rules for pilots, handicapped air travel, exposure to benzene, radioactive waste disposal, payment for special education, air quality regulations for oil exploration and production off California, asbestos in schools, emergency pesticide exemptions, farmworker protection standards, performance standards for woodburning stoves, underground injection well standards, and gasoline standards.[7]

Regulatory negotiations have been held at state and local levels as well. These procedures are generally less formal than those at the federal level, although they vary from case to case and state to state. States have used informal negotiated rulemaking for issues such as utility rate setting in New Mexico and tidelands use in Massachusetts (Susskind, 1986). In Virginia alone there have been such procedures resulting in legislation on issues of low-level radioactive waste, groundwater management, nontidal wetlands protection, protection for the Chesapeake Bay, and instream flow.[8]

Example: The sheep scrapie regulatory negotiation[9]   The late 1980s were not a good time for many sheep farmers. Farmers saw the value of their stocks drop precipitously, driving many out of business. Among other problems was an infectious disease of the nervous system, called 'sheep scrapie', which was the cause of considerable concern within the industry. Among those concerns was the fear that the public would link the disease to human health and shun lamb entirely.

The Animal and Plant Health Inspection Service (APHIS) of the US Department of Agriculture was considering how best to combat scrapie. Faced with limited resources and scientific uncertainty, no feasible response was apparent. They decided to explore the negotiated rulemaking process. The experienced mediator who conducted the convening reported favorable conditions for negotiations, and the rulemaking proceeded. Participants in the Scrapie Negotiated Rulemaking Advisory Committee included representatives from the various breeding and farm organizations, veterinarians, and researchers. APHIS agreed that any full consensus reached by the Committee would be adopted as the language for the notice of proposed rulemaking.

As is typical of mediated processes in public disputes, not everything went by the book. At the initial meeting of the Advisory Committee one participant touted the promise of a vaccine under development and insisted that the responsible researcher be included at the table. As it turned out, the vaccine was only in the preliminary stages of development. More significantly, a representative of the meat processing industry who addressed the Committee during the time reserved for public comments made it clear that the processors would not be afraid to stop slaughtering sheep if the sheep industry could not deal with the scrapie problem. The membership, sensitive to the consequences of this potential loss, added this representative to the negotiation group.

Negotiations conducted during five two-day meetings of the Advisory Committee did produce a consensus plan featuring a scrapie-free certification program and research. The final rule followed the recommendations of the Committee.

Policy dialogue

Sometimes called 'research' dialogues (Office of Policy, EPA, undated) or 'roundtables' (DeLong and Orenstein, 1990), *policy dialogues* bring together government agencies and representatives of interested groups to, in the words of the EPA, 'fully explore the various forces shaping a policy and discuss the effect of the policy on the regulated industry and the public' (Office of Policy, undated: 3).[10] These dialogues do not have the direct tie-in to policy apparatus that regulatory negotiations do, and might therefore be thought of as exploratory or 'facilitative' in nature. However, these dialogues are typically conducted over issues for which policy action is being considered. Furthermore, the level of participation in these dialogues is such that agreements are expected to have a significant impact on such policy.

Bingham (1986) suggests that the use of policy dialogues can be traced to a late-1970s forum designed to build consensus on coal policy. The National Coal Policy Project, which lasted for five years, was a massive undertaking involving 105 participants in plenary and task-force sessions who reached agreement on nearly 90 percent of the more than 200 issues they addressed. However, few of these results were implemented. But, as Bingham points out, the precedent of face-to-face negotiations may have been more important than the success or failure of the actual dialogue.

Initial policy dialogues were sponsored by independent, nonprofit institutions such as the Conservation Foundation and the Keystone Center. Later, such dialogues were sponsored by agencies such as the EPA and the Forest Service (Ehrmann and Lesnick, 1988).

Ehrmann and Lesnick (1988) describe the typical policy dialogue process. Participants, who may number from a dozen to more than fifty, are selected for their scientific or political credibility and representation of a particular interest. They may be members of citizen or environmental organizations, regulatory agencies, corporations, congressional staff, academic institutions, labor unions, and lobbying organizations. Although selected on the basis of this representation, participants are usually asked explicitly to represent themselves rather than their organizations, thus mitigating somewhat the complexity of issues and the difficulties of binding an interest group to particular outcomes.

Ehrmann and Lesnick (1988) identify three phases of the policy dialogue process:

1 entry;
2 designing and initiating the intervention; and,
3 conducting intervention and settlement.

Entry is often aided by an advisory committee which assists in the formulation of questions and selection of the participants and other key issues of entry. Dialogue design must address questions of location, an effective process, the agenda and schedule, and the third-party structure. In order to reach an agreement satisfactory to all the parties, Ehrmann and Lesnick contend, a third party must address documentation of issues and extent of consensus, maintenance of continuing focus, reaching closure on specific issues, and implementation of any agreements.

Bingham (1986) and Ehrmann and Lesnick (1988) note the difficulties involved in implementing consensus agreements without a secure link between the dialogue process and established policymaking apparatus. Early dialogues excluded representatives of government agencies, on the basis that their absence would encourage freer discussions between business and environmental leaders. The assumption was that agency involvement was unnecessary because administrative agencies are looking for policy options with broad support. Contemporary dialogues are designed with implementation more clearly in mind, and are thus more likely to have agency and legislative participation or representation.

Example: The Chesapeake Bay land use roundtable[11]   A 1983 EPA study of the Chesapeake Bay, the largest estuary in the United States, indicated that continuing business as usual would destroy the Bay. Damage to the Bay and other large bodies of water often comes less from actual discharges into the water than from the impact of land use around the water: septic and sewer drainage, pesticide use, nutrient (fertilizer) runoff, and so forth. But changing land-use policy is almost always controversial because of the financial impact imposed on landowners by restrictions on their use of the land.

In Virginia, as in other states, authority to regulate land use rests almost exclusively with localities. Local authority added to a strong tradition of property rights made state-wide land-use legislation to protect the Bay problematical; indeed, no such legislation had been introduced because of anticipated overwhelming opposition any land-use restrictions would engender.

In an effort to overcome these obstacles, the state General Assembly appropriated funding to convene a policy dialogue about Bay protection. A mediation team helped assemble a representative group which included two state legislators, a timber-harvester, a commercial oyster-harvester, marina and land developers, a ship-builder, a local government official, four citizen and environmental activists, and two businessmen. A team of land use and water resource professionals provided technical assistance. As is typical of policy dialogues, members participated not as official representatives of their organizations but as individuals representing the major interests and perspectives affected by the issues under consideration.

The Roundtable spent eighteen months identifying problems, reviewing approaches used by other coastal states, and debating the role of state and local governments in land-use regulation. Agreement was reached about recommendations including new legislation which granted localities greater regulatory authority to protect natural resources, minimum state standards for designated areas of shorelands, wetlands, sand dunes, and barrier islands, and state financial aid and technical assistance to localities. The consensus reached by this representative group enabled the legislature to overcome opposition by various farming and development interest groups and enact the recommendations without significant changes in the Chesapeake Bay Preservation Act of 1988. One of the most important results of the Act was the creation of the Chesapeake Bay Local Assistance Board specifically to help localities develop and implement preservation regulations.

Negotiated investment strategy

One of the earliest efforts to institutionalize the mediation process for public issues is the Negotiated Investment Strategy (NIS). Founded by the Kettering Foundation (1982), the NIS was intended as way of coordinating national urban policy with community needs (Carlson, 1985). Originators of the process believed that the best way to address the complex problems unique to urban jurisdictions was to bring together the parties interested in the future of the city to negotiate long-range strategies and to coordinate their investment of time and resources (Moore, 1988).

Moore, with experience as evaluator of the first four applications of NIS and facilitator/mediator of three others, suggests three reasons why the cities needed this kind of planning help. The assistance available from the federal government was usually in the form of categorical grants, which were not easily adapted to local needs; many uncoordinated programs duplicated services; and cities were not profiting from their existing resources, including facilities, infrastructure, and public and private sector commitments. In addition, there were inadvertent impacts from federal policy, such as effects of public work projects and investment tax credits, which NIS might help avoid (Carlson, 1985).

The NIS required an impartial mediator to guide the process and representative negotiating teams who would meet, exchange information, adopt a written agreement with mutual commitments, and undertake public review before adoption and monitoring of implementation (Carlson, 1985). Moore (1988) argues that there are four key elements required to make productive decisions in NIS:

1 all affected parties participate;
2 negotiating teams represent affected interests;
3 differences are identified through negotiation; and,
4 there is effective mediator assistance.

The NIS was used in the cities of Hartford and Bridgeport, Connecticut (Miller, 1989b) to develop regional housing plans. Statewide in Connecticut, the NIS was used to devise principles for the allocation of federal block grant funds (Carlson, 1985). It has also been used in Malden, Massachusetts; Gary, Indiana; and other areas for issues such as future development, city services, and budget priorities (Moore, 1988; Carlson, 1985, Madigan *et al.*, 1990).

Example: Gary, Indiana[12]   Gary, Indiana was one of three midwest cities selected by the Chicago Federal Regional Council, representing major federal agencies, for the experimental NIS process. Representatives were appointed from three teams: city, state, and federal governments. Also included were 'observers' from the giant corporation US Steel. The city prepared a draft statement of a proposed investment plan for Gary which served as the basis for discussions. The first meeting consisted of an exchange of information. Subsequent negotiating sessions, held every two months, lasted several days each to allow time for caucusing among individual teams and reconvening with the entire group.

The result was a plan for investing almost $250 million in improvements to Gary's downtown commercial district, nearby residential neighborhoods, and transportation, housing, and health care facilities. The agreement was signed by the mayor of Gary, the governor of Indiana, and the chair of the federal regional council. Despite the high-level buy-in on the part of the public officials and commitments on the part of team captains to work for implementation with the assistance of the mediator, changes in administration made the implementation difficult. Cutbacks in federal programs and a tight financial situation for the private sector meant that not all the anticipated money was available. Nonetheless, observers noted substantial improvements in both physical infrastructure and in the relationships among city, state, and federal authorities as well as with the private sector.

System design

An increasingly popular form of intervention which has engendered a new conception of the third party's role in a variety of fields is that of dispute resolution and settlement *system design*. The theme of a popular book (Ury *et al.*, 1988), system design is as much a conceptual aid for the analysis of disputes as it is a dispute settlement or resolution process. Instead of seeing a series of disputes within a particular institution or relationship as individual incidents, a systems approach recognizes the connections among those disputes within that institution or relationship. System design suggests that many of the costs associated with intractable disputes can be avoided by removing systemic elements which encourage dysfunctional disputing, and instituting in their place more productive mechanisms to address differences.

Ury *et al.* (1988) suggest several fundamental principles crucial to the design of any dispute system:

- focus on interests rather than positions;
- institute 'loop-backs' to negotiation;
- allow for inexpensive back-ups to the system, based on determination of rights and power;
- allow for consultation before disputes occur and feedback after;
- arrange procedures sequentially by expense;
- provide necessary motivation, skills, and resources.

Example: The South African election process[13]   During the critical time preceeding the first all-race elections in South Africa, the Independent Electoral Commission faced many extraordinary challenges. Among those challenges was the anticipated high level of election-related conflict. A conflict resolution structure was set up to deal with issues falling under the terms of Electoral Act 202 of 1993. Several hundred mediators worked mediating disputes between and among election officials, party representatives, rival constituency groups, and other parties to the electoral process.

Issues covered by the Electoral Act included biased voter education, intimidation of voters, relations between security forces and political parties, and the conduct of voting officials. For example, mediators helped resolve controversy over the protection of Inkatha Freedom Party supporters by the Kwa Zulu police. The Mediation Department also mediated disputes which fell outside the boundaries of the Act. As the election neared and the speedy resolution of disputes became ever more important, the mediator was sometimes asked by the parties to offer their solution to the dispute.

There were extraordinary difficulties attending the election process. The dispute resolution mechanism was new and untested. Mediators often found themselves working in unfamiliar areas with very high stakes and little or no guidance. There were conflicting lines of authority in the administration of the conflict resolution mechanisms, the Electoral Act was unclear, and there were less than four months to implement the system. Despite these obstacles, the dispute resolution mechanism played an important role in allowing the democratic process to move forward.

Process design

A number of public conflict resolution practitioners identify themselves as consultants in *process design* (Dukes, 1992). In effect, a process designer consults with an organization about their needs for handling a particular issue or project, but does not serve as the actual mediator or facilitator responsible for overseeing the entire project. Training in negotiation and consensus-building may be a part of the consultative process.

Example: Durham city-county school merger[14]   In the late 1980s a prosperous southern county and the small city which served as its capitol faced the usual consequences of decades of white flight: well-financed and increasingly white suburban schools contrasted with a growing concentration of minorities and declining financial support in the city. A number of city residents and others believed that a fair and logical response to this decline was a merger of the two systems. However, significant opposition from county residents made such a merger problematical.

A task force to study the improvement of the school systems, including the potential of school merger, was proposed. It was thought that the ordinary task force process would be insufficient to respond effectively to the anticipated conflict. The area supported a successful community mediation center which was interested in assisting the process; however, the scope and level of controversy was beyond anything the center had ever managed. A mediator from a prominent public conflict resolution organization was invited to assist in the design of the task force process.

The mediator recommended an 'accordion' process involving a sequence of full task force meetings followed by committee meetings and public outreach. Each meeting was facilitated by one of a team of facilitators, many of them drawn from the community mediation center's corps of volunteers. This sequence would be repeated as each group went through the stages of issue identification, education and data gathering, developing problem statements, identifying options, and developing recommendations.

The process went through nine months of intensive and exhausting activity. The Task Force then reported a long list of recommendations, including steps which ought to precede merger of the schools. The County Commissioners held a series of facilitated public discussions during which a number of concerns about merger were addressed. When the question was put before the electorate for a vote, both the City and County approved merger by a wide margin.

Notes

1   Many writers have offered their own typologies of processes. Cormick (1987), for instance, suggests these three types of intervention processes:

Consensus-building is a problem-solving approach grounded in small-group process that emphasizes the common interests of disputants in jointly defining and solving problems. *Mediation* is an approach adapted from labor relations that seeks to identify – through negotiation – the limited but real cooperative actions possible for mutually interdependent parties having different long-term interests and objectives. *Policy dialogues* are a problem-solving and negotiation approach developed on a pragmatic, ad hoc basis by leaders of environmental groups and representatives of industry. Dialogues are intended to identify joint positions that can be advocated in the public policy arena by interest groups that are normally opposed to one another (p. 29).

Others adopt a broader view. For instance, Gray (1989) offers the following typology of process: exploratory, advisory, confederative, and contractual. The SPIDR Law and Public Policy Committee (1990) classifies practice by the mode of interaction. They define three types of intervention: *rights-based*, with a goal of settling a dispute on the basis of the parties' legal rights; *interest-based*, 'with a focus on the interest or compelling issue of the dispute' (p. 27); and *therapeutic*, which 'focuses more on the problem-solving skills of the parties involved' (p. 27).

2 For example the Association of Community Mediation, the Academy of Family Mediators, the National Association for Mediation in Education, the International Association of Commercial Mediators.

3 As Ehrmann and Lesnick (1988) note, however, with mediation becoming more common, many parties to public conflict are becoming experienced participants in direct negotiations.

4 See Carpenter (1989) for the components of what she terms 'consensus decision-making'; Madigan *et al.* (1990) for elements of 'mediated negotiation'; Gray (1989) for characteristics of 'collaborative processes'; and Potapchuk (1988) for keys to the 'collaborative problem-solving' process. As may be imagined, many of these elements are honored more as an ideal than in reality.

5 See Laue (1990) for illumination of third party roles. This definition does exclude from the mediation category efforts by non-'neutral' parties such as planners, administrators, and elected officials. This exclusion does not denigrate these efforts, and in fact they are becoming increasingly common. See, e.g., Goldmann (1980), Forester and Stitzel (1989), and Dotson *et al.* (1989).

6 This case is from my own experience at the Institute for Environmental Negotiation. The lead mediator was Richard Collins.

7 See Harter (1984; 1988), NIDR (1986), Gray (1989), Haygood (1988a), Susskind (1989), 'Cleaner air, by consensus' (1991).

8 See, respectively, Haygood and Orenstein (1988), Mealey (1988), DeLong (1991), Chesapeake Bay Land Use Initiative (1987), Collins and Dotson (1990), DeLong and Orenstein (1990).

9 The negotiations were mediated by Howard Bellman. Information was obtained through observation of the negotiations and discussions with participants.

10 Ehrmann and Lesnick, mediators from a leading convenor of policy dialogues,

the Keystone Center, define policy dialogues as 'complex, multiparty discussions aimed at clarifying policy questions and developing agreements relating to broad public issues rather than site-specific disputes' (1988: 94).

11 The Roundtable was mediated by the Institute for Environmental Negotiation. The primary source of information about this case is McCubbin (1989).

12 Information is drawn from 'Public decision making' (1984) and Moore (1988). Lead mediator was Jim Laue.

13 Information about the Independent Electoral Commission's conflict resolution system came from Hayter (1994), Nupen (1994), Ngwenya (1994), Collins (1994), and Visser (1994).

14 Information about this case was provided in conversations with the consultant, Bill Potapchuk, and in discussions occurring at a de-briefing meeting attended by Potapchuk and the volunteer facilitators from the Durham Dispute Settlement Center.

5

Facilitation of dialogue[1]

The search for productive dialogue

The range of individuals and institutions calling for strengthened public dialogue is extraordinary.

- In an unprecedented event, an unpopular President of the United States and the acerbic opposition Speaker of the House repeatedly compliment one another as they engage in a forum intended to demonstrate common ground and civility.[2]
- A sociologist argues the need for dialogue between various sides of the cultural divide 'before the shooting begins' (Hunter, 1994).
- A Catholic pro-choice group newsletter features a remarkable series of dialogues between pro-choice and pro-life advocates (Becker *et al.*,1992).
- The first initiative of the new director of the National Endowment for the Humanities is a call for a massive public dialogue about what it means to be an American.
- One of the leading black intellectuals of our time accompanies a scathing critique of contemporary liberalism and conservatism with statements about the importance of caring for one another and the need for a new language of empathy and compassion (West, 1993).[3]
- The tobacco industry bases a public relations campaign on the search for dialogue, understanding and common ground, with language such as 'we believe that common courtesy and mutual respect are still the best ways for people to resolve their differences,' and 'Through dialogue and discussion, we can agree on solutions without resorting to Government intervention.'[4]

This extraordinary recognition of the importance of dialogue comes in good part because of the obviously sorry state of contemporary public discourse. The most common forums for public discussion of social problems and controversial issues rarely lend themselves to developing understanding and solving problems. The stream of invective which emanates from the radio and television airwaves does much to agitate but little to educate. And matters may be no better in the executive, legislative, and judicial arenas, where procedures for debating and adjudicating public concerns are often inflexible, stilted, adversarial, episodic, and generally intimidating for non-professionals.

Consider a typical public hearing. Speakers stand with their backs to the audience. They face an array of microphones on an unfamiliar podium. Speaking time is restricted and carefully monitored. The authorities hearing comments, seated behind their own desks and their own microphones, look down on the speaker from an elevated stage. Little or no response by these authorities is offered to the comments. If there is any negative response by following speakers there is no further opportunity for rebuttal, much less engagement in dialogue.

Accompanying this sterile and intimidating setting is the often well-founded suspicion on the part of the public that the entire process is a charade. Are the authorities listening? Have they already made up their mind? Have those who believe that rules are for others already exerted their influence on the authorities in private? Who knows? – one certainly cannot get answers from this type of hearing.

Nor are matters much better in other forums for public dialogue. The public discussion mediated through contemporary vehicles of communication, such as television, radio, and newspaper, is generally sensational, shallow, adversarial, personal, and entirely unproductive of understanding. 'Talk' shows are aptly titled: they are all talk and little or no listening.

Public engagement in discussion over controversial issues certainly precedes the public conflict resolution field. But the same two decades which saw the explosive development of mediation also saw an increase in the efforts to address the problems just enumerated by enhancing and even institutionalizing dialogic processes. There have been within the past few decades a host of new developments for dealing with differences within the public domain, the common thread being the perceived need for increased capabilities of dialogue, reflection, and understanding. Older forums such as study circles and salons have been revived. New forums offered by organizations such as the 'Search for Common Ground' and 'National Issues Forum' have been developed. And new varieties of public participation such as 'community visioning' reward stakeholder involvement with real change.

Unlike other types of forums and practices which seek agreement and decision, these 'exploratory' processes have more circumspect goals. Purposes may include any or all of the following:

- educating disputants, stakeholders, and/or the general public about the issues under consideration;

- discovering public interest in, concern with, and ideas about particular issues;
- raising the level of awareness among a particular audience about an issue;
- demonstrating to adversaries that even on the most divisive issues there are items which can be discussed and people on the other side(s) worth talking to;[5]
- reducing the risk of violent confrontation;
- building public support for consequential decisions.

Public participation processes

There is substantial interaction between public participation processes and public conflict resolution. Indeed, much of public conflict resolution may be seen as one component of the larger field of public participation. The International Association of Public Participation Practitioners has a number of public conflict resolution practitioners on its Board of Directors and in its membership. Organizations which provide mediation services often also assist government in the design and facilitation of public participation processes. Such facilitation in controversial situations may even require informal mediation between and among the government agency or agencies and interested stakeholders.

There are perhaps as many different models of public participation processes as there are public initiatives put out for review and comment. Most, if not all, public institutions have standard if not codified procedures for getting information to the public and receiving input back. Some circumstances, such as the promulgation of regulations, have very detailed requirements for public participation. Other issues may offer discretion as to the quality or even the use of public participation. Creighton (1992) notes that criteria such as the impact of a forthcoming decision, the effects on particular populations, the impact on a vested interest, the level of controversy surrounding an issue, or the need for active support in order to implement a decision, may be used to gauge the need for public participation.

Potapchuk (1988) describes three common types of citizen participation, ranging from the least participation by general citizenry to the most such involvement:

1 the 'Blue Ribbon Panel,' made up of leadership from various organizations;
2 the 'Public Hearing Model,' in which government authorities consult with residents, hold hearings, and present recommendations; and,
3 the 'Community-Based Working Group,' which has broad participation from the citizenry.

Yet another continuum is offered by DeSario and Langston (1987) for deci-sion-making techniques offering maximum citizen participation, but based on the proportion of the role of experts. These range from virtually unas-sisted processes such as initiatives, referenda, and citizen courts; to those requiring moderate assistance, such as neighborhood councils, citizen advi-sory councils, mediation councils, and public hearings; to those dominated by experts, such as councils of information, science committees or courts, and professional bureaucracies or commissions.

The most important typology concerns the legitimacy of public participa-tion processes, which vary considerably in the consideration they offer to public views. Arnstein's classic 'A ladder of citizen participation' (1969) is still current in the distinction she makes between participation which offers real influence and procedures which pose only an empty ritual. Qualities which determine the legitimacy of particular public participation processes include adequate time for consideration of the issues, free exchange of infor-mation, visibility and outreach to the affected and interested public, open-ness of the decision-making procedures, and commitment on the part of the authorities to use the product of the process.

Ad hoc public participation

'Ad hoc participation' refers to the design and facilitation of public partici-pation processes beyond standard requirements. Most public decisions are made using required forums of participation, including notification, public hearing, publication of intended decision, opportunity for appeal, and so forth. There are issues, however, which by virtue of their innovation or scope either are not covered by these requirements, or, more commonly, are judged to call for more than standard procedures.

Example: Berlin-Brandenburg International Airport[6]   A preeminent showcase project for the application of innovative public participation for contentious public issues has been the siting of the proposed Berlin-Brandenburg Inter-national Airport in Germany. As is not uncommon for public conflict reso-lution efforts, the methodology is a mix of process design, mediation, public participation, and facilitation of dialogue between and among the various stakeholders and government representatives.

Siting any airport is a complex endeavor. The planning for an airport of the scope of Berlin-Brandenburg, with capacity estimated at 28 million pas-sengers per year and total cost estimated at 10 billion Deutschmarks, is almost beyond imagination. Each consideration such as infrastructure needs (e.g. major roadways, hotels, and other enterprises associated with major airports), tangential development potential, public–private interactions (the airport is planned to be a privately funded project), and inter-governmental relationships, brings its own set of issues and its own stakeholders.

The environmental considerations are equally complex. The three existing airports currently located in Berlin are not expected to be able to handle future air traffic demands, and there is hope among some citizen and environmental groups, based on indications offered by authorities, that a new airport would allow the closing of each of the other three. Thus the environmental impact of the project involves not only the land at the airport site, a vast expanse of roads and other development, and noise and safety considerations, but clean-up and conversion of the other three airports as well.

Planners for Berlin-Brandenburg had the advantage of the example of the Munich airport, a saga which lasted nearly thirty years from the time of its proposal to its opening in 1992. Among the reasons for delay was the exclusion of the public from the siting process, an exclusion which led to extensive conflict and political and legal resistance. Given this example, and given the high stakes of the Berlin airport, it is not surprising that the ministers of transport and of environmental affairs for both Berlin and Brandenburg agreed on the importance of active citizen participation in planning.

At an early public meeting in Berlin the facilitator proposed the basic ideas of what increased public participation would mean. Elected and administrative officials as well as representatives from business and environmental groups endorsed the concept, and the facilitator was charged with the task of designing an appropriate public participation plan. The plan was itself discussed by public officials, industry, labor, and citizen and environmental organizations.

An initial task was deciding which publics required what level of participation. The facilitator distinguished between the general public, the organized public, and the local public. The general public is considered to be those people not yet having a specific, identified stake in the decisions relating to the airport, who have jobs and responsibilities unrelated to the project, and who therefore do not have the time or motivation to attend meetings or conduct research or otherwise participate in an active way.

The organized public consists of members of groups such as business, labor, and environment, who have the interest, knowledge, and time to devote to active participation. This latter group includes both paid staff and citizen activists.

The local public includes those individuals who might be directly and significantly impacted by a proposed action and who take an intense interest in the decision-making process. They often coalesce into one or more groups, sometimes on opposing sides, which remain active only until the outcome has been decided.

The design of the participation strategy reflected the different capacities and needs of these three publics. An on-site office was opened in Brandenburg to allow individuals to see and read information about the project and raise questions with the full-time staff member. A facilitated 'Airport Forum,' consisting of about thirty individuals representing a wide range of perspectives (including two of the existing airports), served as the core advisory group. Each of the three sites had their own facilitated 'community liaison' group of twenty to thirty people.

The public involvement process began with the development of the criteria used to identify potential sites for the airport. Along with the private airport company and the state representatives, the Environmental Advisory Council of the Ministry of Environmental Affairs, Nature Conservation and Land Use Planning (MUNR), which included representatives of labor, business, farm, church, and environmental organizations, each had a say in what criteria would be used. Three potential sites were eventually identified from an initial list of ninety-three.

Public meetings were held both centrally and near each of the three potential sites. These meetings, which took place every four to six months, included both plenary sessions and smaller working groups. The results of these meetings were then considered by the core airport forum and the three community liaison groups.

As this book goes to press, the process is still underway. A decision on the site is expected to be announced some time in 1996.

Visioning[7]

'Visioning' is the term used to describe a process which involves substantial portions of a community in imagining their desired future and in setting goals for how that future might be attained. Typically, the process begins with the recognition of the need to move beyond existing processes to build community-wide consensus for change.

Setting goals and planning for the future is not unique to the visioning process; communities and planners do this all the time. But visioning differs from the traditional planning process in many ways. Visioning is typically focused on the long term, twenty or more years in the future. The emphasis is on community members and their values and goals rather than the interests of elite citizen leadership or professional planners.

Like other forms of public participation, visioning can be manipulated as a public relations exercise. But when done with the commitment of community leaders to openness and change, visioning can provide many benefits. The visioning process itself enhances public participation in governance. It allows members of a community to identify shared values and recognize areas of common concern; these commonalities are often forgotten in the rancor which accompanies contentious issues. It affords an opportunity for citizens to serve the community. It encourages new ways of thinking beyond immediate problems. And it educates participants, including elected and other public officials, about what makes a successful community.

The visioning process also contributes to efforts to inform and educate citizens about the planning process, including legal requirements and constraints, administrative capabilities, and fiscal considerations. It thus helps develop public expertise about public issues, and involves interested parties in the planning process at a time when their efforts can still effect real change.

With full participation, visioning helps legitimize decisions about the comprehensive planning process. It can help prepare the community and build support for difficult change. Participants in the visioning process provide an engaged citizenry who will demand accountability for the goals which are set. And the visioning process itself can set the tone for continued planning – clear, inclusive, thoughtful, comprehensive, and responsive.

Communities have been using visioning processes as a keystone for long-range planning since the mid-1980s (Thomas *et al.*, 1988). A number of smaller cities, such as Winston-Salem, North Carolina, and Santa Clara, California, have used variations of the visioning process with inclusive participation and consensus as the basis for decision-making to strategize for the future (Bradley, 1991). Their example has inspired major cities to explore these processes as well. Baltimore, for instance, had a massive project with some forty people overseeing the project, ten facilitating the process, four hundred citizens and officials involved, at a total cost of around $400,000 (Bradley, 1991).

Example: Chattanooga, Tennessee[8] In the early and mid-1980s Chattanooga, Tennessee was a city in decline. The chemical and manufacturing industries which had provided the major portion of the tax and employment base had declined significantly, leaving behind a legacy of toxic air and waste. Racial divisions dominated political issues. Civic leaders watched in frustration as the energy and economic renewal which was vitalizing other Southern cities left Chattanooga behind.

Chattanooga, like all cities, continues to have problems. But the city is now held up as a model of how people, including many ordinary citizens, can work together to transform their communities. This transformation was initiated by a massive community visioning process entitled 'Chattanooga Venture,' begun by the local Chamber of Commerce and funded by a local private foundation. Over 1,700 people were involved in setting 40 goals for the city, goals which were to be accomplished by the year 2000. These goals focused not only on substantive elements such as the downtown area, public transportation, and jobs, but on less tangible aspects such as creating a positive image for the city.

Many of these goals have been accomplished. Almost a decade later, when Chattanooga decided to assess its accomplishments and renew its vision, they found that an estimated $739 million in new investment developed directly from Chattanooga Venture. Improvements have been made to economic, civic, and cultural life. The downtown area is vibrant. Minority concerns are taken seriously, and race relations are improved. ReVision 2000 generated an additional 2,559 suggestions which were refined into 27 goals. And Chattanooga, a city that nobody would have envisioned in the early 1980s as a model of anything but failure, is now being studied by other cities seeking means of addressing their problems.

New modes of facilitated dialogue

Dialogue

We all know the characteristics of an all-out, knock-down, drag-out debate. Opponents line up against one another to seek (or invent) the weaknesses in others' statements. Nobody ever admits wrong or uncertainty. Everyone begins with the answer and defends that answer against all attack.

Tactics typically include verbal and physical intimidation, name calling, labeling, and stereotyping. Deception and deliberate distortion of the opponents' words are also often accepted as part of the game. Supporters of each side rally around their own afterward. And observers who do not share the fervor of the true believer turn away in despair at ever figuring who to believe.

But rancorous personal debate does not have to be the only accompaniment to contentious issues.

Think of the qualities most appreciated in a good discussion:

- an opportunity to be heard without interruption or distortion of one's views;
- an assumption that one is speaking honestly, without a hidden agenda;
- an interest in understanding one's views and to seek agreement where agreement exists;
- an acknowledgment of the importance of one's feelings about this issue;
- an opportunity to share doubts about one's own positions without that ambivalence being marked as a sign of weakness;
- a readiness on others' part to admit doubt, to learn, to change;
- a recognition that difference does not mean enmity.

The question then becomes how to create a forum which nourishes this type of productive dialogue rather than debate.

Work which is creating forums which nourish this type of productive dialogue is being done in many contentious areas, including not only environmental issues but such hot topics as gun control and abortion policy. While actual processes will vary depending upon issues, participants, and setting, it is possible to identify a number of key elements to such dialogues.

Productive dialogue does not just happen, even when good will is present.

The goals of the dialogue and the groundrules for discussion must be developed. Participants must be selected and recruited. All parties must have a clear understanding of the purposes and processes of the dialogue.

Potential participants ought to be willing advocates for their perspective. They must be free to discuss, within the context of the intended forum, their own personal views about the topic. In practice, this may present a difficulty for individuals who represent an institution or constituency or who aspire to public office. Again, participants must understand the purposes and groundrules of the dialogue.

The tendency in debates is for participants to play to the audience. That tendency can be mitigated by briefing the audience, by ensuring that participants understand the dialogue goals, and by reminding them of those purposes as necessary.

Informality and comfort are conducive to productive discussion. Depending upon the issues and other circumstances, a private setting, such as a living room, a church parlor, or a classroom, may help foster an atmosphere conducive to productive talk.

An audience which appreciates and honors the goals of the dialogue can enrich the quality of that dialogue. Written questions submitted to the facilitator before or during the discussion avoid unforeseen provocative tactics by uncooperative audience members. However, 'live' questions, when consistent with the spirit of the dialogue, allow for more fluid interaction and help remove the focus from the facilitator.

Example: The classroom as dialogic forum[9]   Four guests enter a classroom at the University of Virginia. Two of the guests, a man and a woman, are friends and ardent advocates for protection of the environment. The other two guests, both women and also friends, have led the development of a state-wide movement for protection of property rights, primarily in response to the perceived encroachment of those rights by environmental regulations. Neither pair has met the other. Two of the four, one on each 'side', are outspoken and even combative in their advocacy; the other two, while less vociferous, are equally determined advocates for their views.

The mix might seem designed as a recipe for explosive confrontation. But such confrontation does not occur. The parties have been invited to participate, not in a debate, but in a dialogue. They have been asked not to defend their own views or attack those of their 'opponents', but to explain the basis for their own perspectives and to understand those with whom they disagree. They come not as representatives of the organizations they have founded but as individuals who speak only for themselves.

The facilitator introduces the process: 'We see the dialogue as an educational opportunity for participants and audience to gain an understanding of the issues and, most importantly, the people behind the issues – their real beliefs, values, goals, and fears. We hope that it is an opportunity for the participants to deepen their understanding of their own and others' perspectives. And we hope that we can demonstrate the benefits of creating a safe climate for dialogue, even in situations where parties hold (and will continue to hold after the dialogue) very different views on divisive issues.'

A few basic suggestions for the process are offered to all parties by the facilitator.

- This is not a debate; participants are not being asked to defend their own views or to find the weaknesses in the others' positions, but to explain their own perspectives. Participants are invited to ask questions of others, and any participant is free to 'pass' on any questions, without explanation.
- Parties speak for themselves only, not as representatives of a group. In addition, individuals do not characterize the beliefs, values, or motivations of others unless requested to do so.
- Participation in dialogue requires a commitment to candor, to considerate language, and to purposeful listening.

The discussion is initially tense. Suspicion as to the motivations of the other participants and the moderator, who is also teaching the class, is evident. But as each party in turn describes why these issues are important to them and what is personally at stake, the tension dissipates. After an opening round of questions, participants are invited to ask each other questions of clarification only at first. Questions intended to elicit understanding then follow. The members of the audience then join the discussion, asking further questions of the parties. The invited participants find that they have much in common, including an aversion to suburban sprawl and a love for nature. Two of the participants are able to admit to uncertainties about their positions, admissions which class evaluations later reveal generate sympathy and respect from the audience.

Participant evaluation of the process can help with the design of future dialogues, and is an important part of any dialogue. Audience feedback about the process is particularly useful. Observers tend to credit behavior consistent with the groundrules and reject typical debate behavior.

Search for Common Ground

One approach designed not so much to forge agreements as to promote the possibilities of finding common ground in intense public conflicts is that used by the group, 'Search for Common Ground'. A television series (described in McDaniel, 1990c), hosted by National Public Radio's Scott Simon, spotlights that approach. Typically, Common Ground invites the participation of leading proponents of both sides of a highly polarized issue, such as gun control or abortion, and a moderator guides them through a highly controlled discussion about that issue. The end product is a series of points upon which the two sides do find themselves in agreement. However, there is no mechanism for translating that agreement into action; rather, the expectation is that wide use of the format would lead to a change in consciousness about the way society deals with these issues.

National Issues Forum

The National Issues Forum (NIF) was initiated to increase public awareness of and participation in major public policy issues. Sponsored by the Kettering Foundation and administered by the Domestic Policy Association (DPA), these forums each year focus on three topics of current public concern. The DPA publishes issue books and discussion guides, which are used in community discussions held across the country twice yearly. Representatives of these local forums convene in a yearly National Forum where they report to members of Congress and the Administration.

An intriguing corollary to the NIF is the National Issues Forum Literacy Program, which is designed to involve adult non-readers in the public discussion. The Forum materials are designed so that they can be incorporated into adult basic education curriculum. Workbooks are written at a fourth to sixth grade level, and each topic is also covered by a videotape. Issues are as varied as drugs, the environment, day care, and racism.

Study circles

Emulating the Swedish model of study circles, the Study Circles Resource Center (SCRC) distributes, at no charge, materials about various matters of public concern, including foreign policy issues such as the Gulf War (Emigh, 1991). Typically, they present a variety of opinion, attempting to be non-partisan and balanced. Information is also provided about how to facilitate effective group discussions. The basis for study circles is the conviction that knowledge and participation are forms of power, and that opportunities for both will tend to equalize power (Corson, 1991). The study circle is thus intended as one means of fostering deliberative democracy.

The SCRC has focused in recent years on deep problems, including community violence and race relations. Organizers have also begun working with newspapers as advocates of 'public journalism'. The *Hartford Courant*, for example, helped organize interested readers into study circles, and coordinated various features, including essays, letters, and interviews, with the discussions.

Policy juries

The concept of a 'policy jury' was developed by the Jefferson Center for New Democratic Processes. Policy juries are made up of citizens who hear substantial testimony about prominent issues and make policy recommendations. The process begins as a randomly selected list of citizens is generated. Organizers then seek volunteers from that list to sit on the jury. The citizens are paid a stipend for the time they give to the project. Once the jury is seated, members hear arguments from experts about various policy options. They then take time to discuss among themselves the merits of these options before voting on specific proposals.

The jury process provides an opportunity for average citizens to educate themselves about particular issues and affords them the opportunity to have input into the policy process. It also gives public officials an opportunity to hear from citizens who have become knowledgable about a particular issue about their concerns and ideas about policy options. Policy juries have been used for issues such as farming, water quality, and public health (Miller, 1989a).

Example: School-based health clinics   In one such effort, each congressional district in Minnesota formed twelve-member panels of 'jurors', chosen through random polling. Members were paid $75/day for four days of hearings on the topic of school-based clinics for prevention of teenage pregnancies, AIDS, and venereal disease. Each congressional district issued its recommendations, and sent three of its members to a state-wide policy jury. The state-wide jury rejected mandatory clinics by a vote of 13 to 11, but did offer some other recommendations for consideration by the legislature.

The Listening Project

The Listening Project is the innovation of a grassroots peace organization in North Carolina, Rural Southern Voice for Peace (1993). Volunteers who are trained in conflict resolution and communication skills conduct surveys of people in their own communities about a particular issue of controversy. These volunteers are generally advocates for a particular perspective, but they approach the community surveys with the idea that they must first understand community concerns and needs before taking action. It is when people's concerns are heard and understood that they are most open to the possibility of dialogue and even change.

The goals of a Listening Project are to identify and develop community-based leadership, clarify community needs, increase understanding and identify common ground among people in conflict, and empower people to work towards solutions. Listening Projects have been used for many issues, including church responses to homophobia, economic conversion, and sustainable agriculture.

Diversity training and prejudice reduction

One response to racial, religious, or ethnic tensions which merits additional attention has been the revival of 'sensitivity training' or 'encounter' type activities as a response to public disputes. Thought during the 1960s and early 1970s to offer promise for intra- and inter-group conflict resolution at levels ranging from organizations to the international arena, interest in these processes had waned during the 1980s. This occurred at least in part because of criticism about the durability of results and possible manipulation of participants.[10]

But a number of individuals and organizations have revived the practice, in modified forms, for use in communities and, notably, college campuses. The activities now occurring under the titles of 'diversity training' and 'prejudice reduction' (Brown and Mazza, 1991) range from one or two hour lecture and question-and-answer formats to workshops occupying several days of intensive confrontation. The goal of these workshops is generally not to develop agreement on specific issues; rather, it is to develop insight about the origins and power of one's own identity, and understanding of and respect for the identity of others.

Miscellany

Other programs designed to encourage public discussion and debate of national issues at local and national levels exist as well. Gurwitt (1991) describes a town using a public lecture series as a vehicle for resolving a local environmental conflict. White (1991) offers a portrait of 'decision conferencing', a process for bringing decision makers together in relatively informal settings, developed by the University of Georgia's Institute of Community and Area Development.

'Community Building Workshop' is the innovation of the Foundation for Community Encouragement, headed by the best-selling author of *The Road Less Travelled*, M. Scott Peck. Over 200 individuals have been trained to facilitate three-day forums where members of a community engage one another about the meaning and worth of community. This process has also been used within a number of corporations to develop trust and a shared sense of purpose.[11]

Some of these other programs have developed without leadership or deliberate direction. *Utne Reader* sponsored an issue devoted to the revival of salons as vehicles of public discussion and debate (Mills, 1991). The *Whole Earth Review* collection of articles entitled 'Electronic Democracy' (1991) asserts the importance of electronic communication and conferencing. Indeed, there has even been a kind of national-level 'policy dialogue' on the issue of abortion conducted via electronic mail and facilitated by a veteran mediator, Robert Coulson (Western Behavioral Sciences Institute, 1991).

Conclusion

The search for productive public dialogue, both within and outside formal policy settings, shows no signs of abatement. Conflict resolution conferences feature seminars describing innovative dialogic forums to address such controversial issues as abortion, sexual orientation, race relations, and violence. Organizations devoted to developing such dialogue proliferate. Membership in the International Association of Public Participation Practitioners continues to increase rapidly. With the global advent of electronic conferencing, innovations will undoubtedly continue.

Notes

1   The term 'facilitation' is being used in a broad sense to refer to the category of processes which are exploratory, educational, or otherwise not directed specifically toward reaching an agreement.
2   As broadcast on many public radio and television stations on 11 June 1995.
3   West (1993) argues that 'The vitality of any public square ultimately depends on how much we *care* about the quality of our lives together' (p. 6). He continues: 'Either we learn a new language of empathy and compassion, or the fire this time will consume us all' (p. 8).
4   The first is from a flyer entitled 'Courtesy' published by Phillip Morris, a large American tobacco manufacturing company. The latter is from a paid advertisement in the Richmond-Times Dispatch, November 1994, by R J Reynolds Tobacco Comopany.
5   See Kelman (1990) for discussion of this point.
6   The sources for information about this initiative are an unpublished and undated paper by Horst Zillessen, mediator for the project, entitled 'Public Participation in Airport Siting in Germany – Berlin-Brandenburg International Airport', and discussions in 1993 and 1994 with Zillessen and his associate Thomas Barbian.
7   For a good overview of community visioning, see 'A Guide to Community Visioning' (Oregon Visions Project, 1993).
8   Information about Chattanooga Ventures can be found in many sources; see Walljasper (1994).
9   This example is based on my own experience. Inspiration for this and other dialogues has come from the Public Conversations Project, an extraordinary experiment in bringing therapeutic skills into such contentious public issues as abortion and environment. The process described here is adapted from their model as described in Becker *et al.* (1992) and Roth (1994).
10   For an introduction to these processes see Doob (1970) and Doob and Foltz (1973; 1974). For critique, see Laue and Cormick (1973) and Kelman and Cohen (1976). See also Chapter Six for a brief description of an encounter process used for Northern Ireland.
11   Radio interview with facilitator Carol Langton, 5 June 1995, station WINA.

6

Practitioners: The United States and beyond

Practitioners[1]

Public conflict resolution is not the province of any single group of professionals or experts. Citizens leading neighborhood discussions, public officials working through controversies to develop consensus, teachers demonstrating how informed dialogue can lead students to see public problems in a new light – each is doing the work of public conflict resolution.

But there is a core of individuals and institutions who contribute to research and literature, who create practices and institutions, and who are engaged professionally in the field, whose activities bear closer examination. These practitioners are drawn from a variety of sources, including attorneys, environmentalists, planners, social service providers (primarily in the nonprofit organizations focused on community disputes), and scholars and teachers.

A substantial number of them began their involvement in conflict resolution working in positions such as community organizers, VISTA and Peace Corps volunteers, or staff for the Nuclear Freeze campaign. A few have worked for environmental advocacy organizations. Many claim to have been using consensual problem-solving procedures well before they ever heard of the terms 'mediation', 'consensus', 'conflict resolution', and so forth.

The terms these practitioners use to identify themselves vary considerably. Many use different terms depending on the audience; some find it easier to describe in some detail what they do than to place an identifying label upon their work. Practitioners identify themselves by terms such as 'convening interviewer', 'consultant', 'trainer', 'negotiator', 'process advisor', 'process designer', 'consultant in conflict management and democratic decision making', 'conflict resolution professional', 'conciliator', 'coordinator', 'broker', and 'problem-solver'. Contrary to what might be expected from the experience of related areas of mediation, the terms 'neutral' and 'third party', so common in the popular and research literature, receive minimal attention. One individual who does use these terms nonetheless describes them as 'nauseating'!

Several who clearly practice what is usually termed mediation avoid the term entirely. Some practitioners suggest that disputants do not like the term 'mediator', especially in the areas where it is associated with unions, or because officials and others may not want to admit to the kind of problem which requires mediation.

The field is divided between specialists, who affiliate themselves within one particular substantive area, and generalists, who practice in a variety of settings. This split parallels the division between those who advocate experience within their field of practice and those who favor procedural expertise, an ongoing debate which has been muted somewhat in recent years. For example, a number of practitioners work entirely within the environmental arena, while others may include the environment as one component of a much broader arena of multi-party public disputes. Some work exclusively within a particular level of government, such as community or local government, while others have a state, national, or even international practice.

The growth of the field and the blurring of distinctions between environmental and other public issues means that many other individuals and organizations, some of them doing quite a bit of other kinds of work, are also entering the field. At a 1992 conference for senior environmental practitioners (many of whom work in other areas as well) there were thirty-one organizations or sole practitoners represented. As of March 1995, 122 members of SPIDR listed the Environment and Public Dispute Sector as their main interest. There is no certification organization, and these associations are entirely voluntary; there is no way to know exactly how many practitioners there are working in public conflict resolution.

The organizations

Several classes of practitioner organizations exist. Private organizations encompass both for-profit and nonprofit groups. Academic institutions attached to universities may operate with some independence and responsibility for their own financial support. The federal government has some capacity. There are several state initiatives, including state offices of dispute resolution, most of which have a public component and three which focus solely on public disputes. And, in a different class entirely, some organizations are developing an internal dispute resolution capability, an effort with its own set of advantages and difficulties.

Private

The private organizations have a variety of formal and informal affiliations. Some are associated with universities, others are tied to court systems or groups of corporations. Some are components of larger entitites; e.g. until 1995 RESOLVE was a part of the World Wildlife Fund, for whom conflict resolution was only a small part of their overall mission.

The most recent assessment of the field in the United States occurred as part of a 1992 Symposium for senior practitioners, as documented in 'The Cutting Edge' (1994). While the Symposium was centered around environmental issues, many of the individuals and organizations practice in a variety of other public settings as well. The profile indicates a field in transition and growth. No longer is nearly every organization operated on a not-for-profit basis. And no longer is it even possible to clearly identify the field, given both the diversity of settings and practices.

Academic

At least three universities have been providing conflict resolution services, including practice, research, theory, and education, for over fifteen years. The MIT-Harvard Public Disputes Program, the University of Michigan School of Natural Resources, and the Institute for Environmental Negotiation of the University of Virginia have each graduated a number of students now in substantive positions within the public conflict resolution field. The prospective student can choose from several dozens of universities offering public conflict resolution classes, and there are at least ten universities offering advanced conflict resolution degrees of various sorts.

Federal

The Federal Mediation and Conciliation Service, founded through the Department of Labor in 1917 as the US Conciliation Service, was revamped in 1947 as an independent federal agency. At one time devoted only to labor-management disputes, its jurisdiction now includes other federal agencies, federally funded programs, and private nonprofit health facilities. It mediates all complaints brought under the Age Discrimination Act of 1975.

It also is moving into a proactive mode, which includes negotiation training, preventive mediation, funding for joint labor-management committees, and arbitration services. In the public arena, it now offers service to disputes involving public employees. With the passage of the two federal dispute resolution acts of 1990, FMCS is likely to provide increasing consultation, training, and mediation services to other agencies. Since 1990 it has also increased its contact with other nations, including the republics of the former Soviet Union (Swanson, 1991).

The Community Relations Service (CRS) of the Department of Justice was created in 1964 in response to the racial disorders of the 1950s and early

1960s. Its mandate, according to Title X of the Civil Rights Act of 1964 (42 U.S.C. 2000g), is to 'provide assistance to communities and persons therein in resolving disputes, disagreements, or difficulties relating to discriminatory practices based on race, color, or national origin'. Since 1983 they have also had responsibility for the 'care, processing, and resettlement' of Cuban and Haitian refugees in the United States (Community Relations Service, undated).

Their services include conciliation, mediation, and technical assistance. Their stated priority is 'always to help communities and their residents settle their differences in a way that is fair and just for everyone' (Community Relations Service, undated: 2) – a tall order! The essential premise of their work, according to Taylor (in 'Mediation by and for minorities', 1990), is to help people of good will in distressed communities. They work with these people, including public officials and community leaders, first through informal conciliation, entering into more formal negotiations if conciliation is inadequate. They can enter a case either upon request or upon their own initiative. They are involved in many kinds of cases, from school desegregation problems in numerous communities and the major riots of the 1960s, to single incidents such as the Miami riot of 1980, the Nazi march in Skokie, Illinois, and the Wounded Knee violence. Because they are mandated to work in confidence and without publicity, they have had a lower profile than the impact of their activities might deserve. CRS now has approximately 120 employees distributed in ten regions (Klugman *et al.*, 1990).

State initiatives

The states have served as laboratories of innovative organizational structure. There are at least four kinds of state-sponsored conflict resolution organizations. A number of state universities sponsor conflict resolution programs combining research and practice. Several states have programs focusing on a single particular issue, such as annexation or hazardous waste facility siting. There have been almost a dozen NIDR-assisted state offices which focus solely on conflict resolution; some of these do not emphasize public disputes. And a number of states have also sponsored state-wide growth-management programs which include some types of conflict resolution procedures.

A brief sampling of state laws demonstrates a variety of applications. Negotiation over hazardous waste facility siting disputes is mandated or encouraged by law in Massachusetts, Rhode Island, Texas, Virginia and Wisconsin (Haygood, 1988b). The state of Washington provides grants for mediating natural resource disputes (Haygood, 1988b). Virginia law mandates negotiation and mediation of city-county annexation disputes (Richman, 1983a; 1983b; 1985; Richman *et al.*, 1986). Virginia's annexation program represents perhaps the first example of institutionalized dispute resolution procedures for intra-government disputes. The state's Commission on Local Government, established by statute in 1979, has sponsored since 1980 an 'interjurisdictional' system which 'brings political, administrative, and legal professionals together in structured negotiating environments to deal with complex political and technical issues' (Richman, 1985: 510).

Anecdotal and other evidence suggests that a number of community mediation centers, whose focus has traditionally been on interpersonal disputes, are moving into the public arena. For instance the Orange County, North Carolina mediation center includes a public component, with its own program director, corps of volunteer facilitators and mediators, and development manual (Sachs, 1988; 1989).

State offices   The best known and, arguably, most successful component of NIDR's public policy program is their effort to establish and evaluate state offices of dispute resolution. In order to ensure the success of these programs, NIDR developed a number of criteria for selection. These included a highly placed sponsor, the official sanction of state government, an appropriate institutional affiliation, matching funding, policy negotiation experience, and acceptance by the local dispute resolution community (Haygood, 1988b). Programs also needed to focus on a wide range of significant public disputes, offer state-wide services, and create referral mechanisms for private mediators (Drake, 1989).

In 1984 NIDR provided matching grants ranging from $10,000–$50,000 to New Jersey, Massachusetts, Minnesota, Hawaii, and Wisconsin. Of the original five states selected for the program, only Wisconsin's program did not survive beyond the first years. Each state's public policy program is structured differently. For instance, the New Jersey Center for Public Dispute Resolution is in the Department of Public Advocate's Division of Citizen Complaints and Dispute Settlement. The Massachusetts Mediation Service is under the Executive Office for Administration and Finance. The Minnesota State Planning Agency hosts their Office of Dispute Resolution.

The Hawaii Program on Alternative Dispute Resolution, hosted by the Administrative Director of the Courts, is one of two state offices in a judicial setting. The other office, in Virginia, has no public dispute component. But each of the offices inevitably has developed relationships with the judiciary in their state (Carlson, in 'Statewide offices of mediation', 1987).

Members of Ohio's independent Commission on Dispute Resolution and Conflict Management are appointed by the governor, the chief justice and the legislature. Oregon's office is funded by the state Department of Land Conservation and Development. The Florida Growth Management Conflict Resolution Consortium is a part of Florida State University. The North Dakota Consensus Council (Levi and Spears, 1994) is unique in that it is a private, not-for-profit organization focused on public policy but without formal ties to the state's administrative, legislative, or judicial branches.

A brief survey of several of the state offices will give some sense of their diversity.

The Massachusetts Mediation Service performs direct mediation services, identifies and appoints mediators and arranges for funding. It also helps design dispute processing administrative procedures for public officials, provides education and training for public officials, and helps the courts set up dispute resolution programs ('Statewide offices', 1987).

Minnesota's Office of Dispute Resolution (Minnesota State Planning Agency, 1989) is the smallest of all the surviving state offices, being essentially a one-person operation. It acts as a training and referral center for state agencies, brokering mediation of public disputes and informing state agencies about dispute resolution (Williams, in 'Statewide offices', 1987). Among its activities are help for planning and implementing Minnesota's farm credit mediation program. The office has also provided assistance in siting, social service, regulatory, land use, resource management, and administrative disputes. It trains public employees in conflict management skills, including both mediation and negotiation. It also facilitates meetings intended to prevent disputes.

New Jersey's Center for Public Dispute Resolution trains public managers, public interest lawyers, law students, planning board officials, probation officers, and community mediation volunteers (Haygood, 1988b; 'Statewide offices', 1987). It has served as a special master appointed by the state court and has been consulted on issues such as state emergency medical service system, Superfund site clean-up, and construction of public housing ('New Jersey Center', 1989).

Ohio and Iowa are special cases ('Statewide offices', 1989), since neither was part of the original NIDR program for state offices, and in both states the public policy component is only a small portion of the overall program. Ohio's Peace and Conflict Management Commission (Governor's Peace and Conflict Management Commission, 1988; 1990; Harbert and Pollack, 1990) has a broad mandate, which includes a public disputes component. For example, each department within state government is encouraged to develop negotiated rulemaking procedures.

Ohio's mandate also includes development of elementary and high school conflict management programs (where students mediate disputes among their peers), support for court-annexed mediation/arbitration projects, training for non-violent family living, and other components. It is the first of the state offices to begin with statutory authorization and to be an independent agency, and the first as well to offer school, community, higher education, and peacemaking programs (Drake, 1989). It is worth quoting the language of their mandate as an example of the advocacy which accompanies these agencies:

In an effort to enable individuals and institutions to more fully exercise their power to create a more peaceful society, we have:

- promoted the widespread use of mediation and other non-judicial dispute resolution techniques which can help lessen tensions and reduce the threat of violence in our homes, our communities and the world.
- urged our educators to introduce the concept of peace and conflict management to our children at an early age and to give them tools for dealing with conflict constructively and non-violently throughout their lives.
- encouraged our colleges and universities to expand the world's understanding of peace and conflict management through study, experimentation, research and practical application.

(Governor's Peace and Conflict Management Commission, 1990: 2).

The Iowa Peace Institute focuses on global education and international trade and development as well as conflict resolution. Besides offering training in school and business conflict management and serving as a resource for neighborhood dispute resolution centers, it has been asked by the governor to take responsibility for environmental conflict resolution within Iowa and it hopes 'to provide broadly-defined public policy conflict resolution, training and technical assistance services throughout the midwest region' ('State support for peace education', 1989: 3).

Oregon's Dispute Resolution Commission is the only office with a designated environmental component, although other offices incorporate environmental issues in their practice. The Oregon office mandate includes a charge to assist all state agencies in developing their own dispute resolution programs (Dawkins, 1991).

Susskind (1987) suggests that these offices have not been entirely successful in overcoming resistance from within the executive branch and state administrative agencies. He notes that key officials often fear a loss of authority and are concerned that asking for outside help amounts to an admission of failure.

State growth management programs   Between 1985 and 1990 seven states established state-wide growth management programs, with other states considering comparable legislation (Innes, 1991). Besides Florida, these were Georgia, Maine, New Jersey, Rhode Island, Vermont, and Washington. Innes notes that each state offers some final arbiter of disputes, but they also have intermediary steps of 'interactive group processes at all stages of the development and implementation of plans, policies, and regulatory standards' (p. 3). Some states move beyond that to include, and even require, informal types of conflict resolution and provide negotiation and mediation training not only for public officials but interest group representatives as well (Innes, 1991).

The Florida Growth Management Conflict Resolution Consortium, a public service institute at Florida State University in Talahassee, is unique. It has received some NIDR funding, but it is a 'dedicated' institution, concerned only with a single issue, albeit one which encompasses many areas. Its mandate includes providing education and training for public and private sectors; delivery of services in anticipation, management, and resolution of environmental and land use disputes; research; and promoting legislation to reduce disputes and encourage 'alternative dispute resolution' (Jostes, 1989).

Innes cautions that while the principle of dispute resolution is popular, the level of its acceptance is not decided. Nonetheless, she evaluates these programs very favorably. Decision-making groups formed by these agencies to deal with difficult issues, unlike other such groups, have more than a minor role in decision-making. They are instead 'integral' to the policy and program processes (Innes, 1991: 4). Not only do they involve in meaningful ways more players than in past comparable efforts, they are a significant innovation in land-use planning and intergovernmental relations.

Internal services

'Internal service' is intended here to refer to the capability of an organization, institution, or community to improve their own capacity for handling or preventing disputes, using the methodology of conflict resolution, without the assistance of an independent third party. There are at least three dimensions to this capability, which might be ranked according to the degree to which these capabilities are integrated within an institution. These dimensions are:

1   Institutionalizing procedures for selecting third-party assistance, rather than relying on ad hoc requests for assistance by individuals who might be familiar with the field. This is the stated intention of the Administrative Dispute Resolution Act, which mandates that each federal agency appoint a senior official responsible for overseeing the use of ADR procedures within that agency.
2   Training individual members of an organization or community in the methods of conflict resolution. Community in this sense is not limited to its geographical meaning, but extends to any formal or informal association of both individuals and organizations. These trained individuals are then used in various circumstances outside of their normal responsibility.
3   Adopting institutional reforms such that the entire organizational culture is transformed in ways consistent with the public conflict resolution philosophy of inclusion, openness, and consensual decision-making.

There are a number of exceptional examples of this form of internal empowerment. Fonte (1991) of the Maverick Institute instituted a project in which youth hired by the University of Arizona are trained to facilitate focus groups on health needs of their peers. Medical ethics committees have begun to adopt facilitation and mediation skills and values in their decision-making procedures (West and Gibson, 1992). The National Association of Counties created a Select Committee on County/Native American Relations to deal with local county-tribal disputes through negotiation (McDaniel, 1990d). The organization 'Americans for Indians Opportunity' has trained tribal and community leaders to participate in issue management teams. These teams use both traditional tribal consensus-building processes and other methods to intervene in intra- and inter-tribal disputes as well as disputes between tribes and other jurisdictions (Public Disputes Network, 1991).

The NIDR Innovation Fund funded a project established by the National League of Cities and Lorain (Ohio) County Community College Public Services Institute. This 'Council Collaboration' program invites elected officials to serve as dispute resolution mentors and facilitators for cities and counties. The program has trained elected officials from cities and towns of various sizes and localities in conflict management and dispute resolution processes. These officials can be called into a locality to help deal with difficult issues (McDaniel, 1990a).

Interest in developing an in-house capacity occurs as an organization whose activities regularly impact the public, such as the Army Corps of Engineers (US Army Corps of Engineers, 1990), the US Forest Service, or perhaps a locality's Department of Planning, become sensitized to the need for inclusive, proactive, problem-solving approaches for recurring problems which are inherent in their operation. While this interest may lead to any of the three responses listed above, the third may have the most significant implications for transformations in governance.

The Minnesota Office of Dispute Resolution is a state office designed primarily to encourage this responsiveness. The office is designed to increase the capacity of state agency managers to act as dispute resolvers (Haygood, 1988b). Agency familiarity with non-litigative processes is intended to lead them to develop procedures themselves for negotiating solutions at various levels throughout the organizational structure and such procedures will become incorporated as part of everyday operations of agencies ('Statewide offices', 1987).

Wondolleck has suggested that some federal agencies are effecting such changes (in Bellman *et al.*, 1990). This is occurring at least in part because of their experience, either as one of the disputing parties, or as convening sponsor, in numerous mediations, policy dialogues, and other public conflict resolution forums. Wondolleck suggests that both the Forest Service and the US Fish and Wildlife Service are setting the stage for this transition. There are three components to this involvement:

1 *Training.* Managers receive training in people skills and public involvement.
2 *Facilitation/mediation.* While primarily using outside facilitators/mediators, they are developing their own in-house capability.
3 *Self-recognition.* They are taking greater notice of their own people with skills in this area.

Wondolleck is most pleased with the proactive measures. The Forest Service adopted a plan, entitled 'New perspectives', intended to incorporate 'social values' into their decision-making apparatus. She suggests that they want to integrate what makes conflict resolution work, not so much through institutionalization of facilitation or mediation, but by fundamentally changing the ways in which they do business. Their focus is to deal with the public in ways which will build trust and relationships. The analogy used by Wondolleck to describe this transformation is that of a physician who recognizes the need for disease prevention rather than simply treating the symptoms.

What will make these changes succeed? Wondolleck's observations are pertinent beyond the Forest Service. She suggests that success will be a function of the legitimacy of these efforts, in particular rewards and promotions. The comfort of decision-makers in no longer operating under a command and control mindset is another important variable. And the level of awareness in the agencies of the roots of their problems, and the options available to them, will have a significant impact on the success or failure of this initiative.

Susskind *et al.* (1993: 70–2) suggest five ways agencies might improve their dispute resolution capacities, in particular in making the Administrative Dispute Resolution Act more effective. These five recommendations are:

1 Increase information dissemination (particularly results of pilot projects) within and among agencies.
2 Evaluate the viability of 'inside' neutrals; stay open to the possibility of increasing the use of outside neutrals.
3 Change the culture of federal agencies, so that good settlements are valued over winning or 'being right'.
4 Commit to systematic evaluation of all ADR efforts.
5 Encourage the use of dispute systems analysis and design.

The spread of the field: Public conflict resolution around the world

The focus of this work has necessarily been on the United States, where the field of public conflict resolution developed and gained capacity the earliest. However, it is worth noting that the field is expanding internationally in two other directions. Public conflict resolution procedures are now being applied to a significant number of transnational concerns, such as debt-for-nature swaps (von Moltke and DeLong, 1990). And there are also a number of other nations developing public conflict resolution capabilities for both intra- and trans-national problems.[2]

While there has been considerable use in other nations of public conflict resolution procedures developed in the United States, there is some question about their applicability (Moore, 1993). The rapid development of the field in the United States has much to do with many conditions particular to American society. Where a nation does not have the particular confluence of social, political, and institutional arrangements which allowed public conflict resolution to garner such a strong foothold in the United States, there is a natural and considerable question about whether these procedures would, or should, have equal applicability (Zillessen, 1991).

These countries looked to the United States conflict resolution field during the 1980s and 1990s for inspiration, for training and trainers, for literature, and even in many cases for funding. Yet the benefits of this exchange did not run in a single direction. Many Americans returned from overseas inspired by their encounters with those in other countries doing difficult work with limited resources. The field as a whole benefitted from the critical reflection attendant to cross-cultural practice, as well as the cross-fertilization of ideas about purposes and processes.

A very brief survey of practices in other nations leading the development of public conflict resolution will give some flavor of work outside the United States and indicate the potential for future interaction.

Canada

Canada has been a global leader in several areas of innovative conflict resolution, including victim-offender, gender discrimination, inter-cultural, and environmental issues. One such innovation originated in Quebec, where provincial officials from the Bureau d'audiences publiques sur l'environnement (BAPE) mediate disputes involving environmental impact assessments (Renaud, 1994). In another enterprise, the Canadian Centre for Management Development, a federal agency, has been seeking to change the culture of public service by bringing to public employees an understanding of and capacity for cooperative conflict resolution.[3]

Perhaps the most far-reaching of Canadian public conflict resolution efforts has been the National Round Table of the Environment and the Economy and the Provincial and Territorial Round Tables set up to chart a course for sustainable development (McDaniel, 1990b). Key to finding the path to sustainability has been the consensus-building process devised for the round tables. The National, Provincial, and Territorial Roundtables developed guidelines to assist Round Table members in seeking consensus about issues concerning economic and social development and environmental protection, to provide a tool for assessing the progress of the Round Table, and to serve as a common baseline linking consensus builders throughout Canada (Field, 1993). The ten guiding principles for consensus processes included such key elements as inclusion, voluntary participation, self design, flexibility, accountability, and implementation (*Building Consensus*, 1993).

United Kingdom

The United Kingdom has seen a good deal in the way of commercial, peer, community, and victim-offender mediation, but somewhat less in the public arena save some environmental mediation (England, 1992). The Centre for Dispute Resolution (CEDR), with a roster of several hundred members, has been particularly active in promoting mediation and other conflict resolution procedures. In 1993 CEDR received a grant from the Commission of the European Communities to establish a European Network for Alternative Dispute Resolution Development.[4]

MEDIATION UK is a very active network of community-based organizations and individuals whose interest groups include such diverse arenas as divorce, gender issues, and environmental issues and public policy.[5] Environmental Resolve, which is a branch of the Environment Council, offers training in environmental mediation. Public Voice International focuses on the relationship between citizens and government, advocating public partnerships which encourage effective public participation.[6]

Some UK-based organizations focus primarily on work overseas. For instance, Conciliation Resources offers services to local organizations in nations struggling with violence.[7] The group Responding to Conflict offers consultation and training in conflict handling skills for organizations and individuals working in the area of human rights and development.[8]

In Ireland alone there are some one hundred organizations working in the area of peace and reconciliation in community relations (Hinds, 1994). One of the most prominent is the Mediation Network of Northern Ireland, founded in 1991. Members received initial training from American community mediators, but soon thereafter developed conflict resolution procedures based on practices appropriate to the Northern Ireland context. The Network asserts that the major conflict in Northern Ireland is over how to accommodate those with a British identity and those with an Irish identity, and that this conflict manifests itself in many ways. The Network addresses this conflict with seven programs: family and child care, neighbourhood, churches, justice system, training, support for the field of conflict resolution (administration), and political affairs.[9]

South Africa

The legacy of South African apartheid continues to bring pain and tragedy. Yet despite lingering violence and economic disruption, despite significant continuing animosities between and among blacks and whites, despite threats of retribution and revolution, the worst fears held by both supporters and opponents of the transition to majority rule have not been realized.

Credit for this extraordinary achievement may be distributed among many leaders and organizations working for a peaceful transition to a just majority rule and reconciliation. Among these organizations have been a number of groups who promoted the resolution of conflicts through mediated negotiations (see Chapter Four). Ron Kraybill, an American mediator and researcher who formerly headed the Mennonite Conciliation Service and then worked for the Centre for Conflict Resolution, suggests that South Africa is the world's leading user of and advocate for the mediation and facilitation of public conflict.[10]

The Centre for Conflict Resolution (formerly the Centre for Intergroup Studies) in Cape Town has been a leader in theory building as well as practice. They facilitated a forum in the Western Cape between police and community members designed not only to build trust but to negotiate police access to areas previously designated as 'no go'. A key issue was how a new police station would be used. The township had blocked access to the police; eventually, an agreement was reached which involved the community in selecting the commander of the station, and made other government services available from the building as well. The Centre mediated a variety of land and housing issues, particularly those involving squatters and local authorities. They also mediated a 'taxi war' which had taken over a hundred lives.

Australia[11]

Many types of conflict resolution initiatives have been developed in Australia. A number of Australian law firms have ADR sections, and several retired judges practice mediation. Several jurisdictions have in place various types of ADR legislation. The Dispute Resolution Centres Act 1990 offers privileges and responsibilities for all types of mediation, including public.

Wright[12] suggests that Australia has begun to recognize the potential of public conflict resolution, including in the environmental realm. The adversarial nature of the merit appeals system, lobbying, and public meetings may encourage officials to use a variety of public conflict resolution procedures for environmental disputes. Herriot[13] argues that it is issues of involvement, empowerment, and quality of decision-making which underpin the use of dispute resolution in public policy and public interest disputes. Governments are considering how best to incorporate mediation and other forms of dispute resolution into planning and environmental decision-making procedures.

The Alternative Dispute Resolution Division of the Department of Justice and Attorney-General, Queensland, has expanded its services into the arena of public policy. The Division has been involved in several different types of public conflict resolution procedures. For instance, in 1991 they mediated discussions of a Zoning Working Group which made recommendations to a Consultative Committee examining the Conondale Ranges in South-west Queensland. Again in 1991 they mediated a consultative process between Brisbane City Council and the local community in Paddington; a representative working group formed after a number of contentious meetings agreed upon a Development Plan and an Action Plan after some fifteen meetings held over a six month period. They have been involved as mediators in discussions in a country town between white elected and police officials and representatives from the Aboriginal community.

The Accord Group, a private mediation firm, designed and facilitated the largest community consultation project ever conducted in Australia.[14] Thirty-five community consultation committee meetings and six public meetings attended by hundreds of people led to a reorganization of the services of six public hospitals in Sydney.

Germany[15]

Germany, like other Western European nations, has a tightly structured and formal policy decision-making process. There is thus a strong tradition of participation, but one which may not allow the flexibility necessary to use mediation. Furthermore, the standing of the Green Party means that environmental conflict often has a partisan emphasis. And there is much greater acceptance, indeed expectation, of the strong role of government in public affairs. Most mediation is conducted on an ad hoc basis. The Wissenschaftszentrum Berlin fur Sozialforschung Institute is examining the foundations of public policy mediation.

Yet despite the theoretical obstacles, the practice is growing. Indeed, the united Germany has developed a competitive public mediation field. Some organisations which provide environmental consultation have expanded their scope to include mediation services as well.[16]

The most visible public conflict resolution process in Germany has been the siting of the planned Berlin-Brandenburg International Airport, described in Chapter Five. A different type of case involved the closure of a hazardous waste disposal facility in Muenchehagen. The use of mediation in this case came from outside the government. The organization Our House is part of the Evangelical Methodist Church effort to promote dialogue on contentious public issues. They served to mediate the dispute and seek additional opportunities for intervention.

89

The future

The extraordinary variety of individuals and institutions practicing in the field of public conflict resolution suggests several trends which promise to have a significant impact upon the field. The development of academic centers for the study and practice of public conflict resolution will likely enhance the legitimacy of the field, bringing about an increase in research and drawing the attention of foundations, upon whose support these centers are in great part dependent. The numbers of private organizations are likely to increase, making the field more sensitive to market forces of supply and demand. The state offices, which have moved beyond the stage of experimentation, will bring awareness of conflict resolution to increasing numbers of government and other institutions. Government agencies as well as other associations will look closely at organizations such as the Forest Service to judge the impact of the changes they are attempting. And work now being initiated in other nations has undoubtedly already enhanced the development of theory and practice far beyond what might have been expected by the United States alone.

Notes

1   Information in this sub-section is based on interviews conducted by the author with two dozen leading practitioners between 1989 and 1991 (Dukes, 1992).

2   See, e.g., McDaniel (1990), Trolldallen (1991), International Environmental Negotiation Network (1991), and Moore (1993).

3   From an article by Joseph Stanford, 'Changing the Bureaucratic Culture: ADR in the Canadian Public Service', written 12 January 1994 on ConflictNet by peg:adrd.

4   In 'Network News', *Consensus*, January 1994.

5   Information about MEDIATION UK is from their newsletter *MEDIATION*.

6   This information is based on an electronic mail message from Karl Berger, 17 May 1995.

7   This information is based on promotional material.

8   This information is based on promotional material.

9   This information is based on promotional materials and discussion with staff.

10   Electronic mail communication, 1994.

11   Most of the information for Australia was derived electronically, through the resources of ConflictNet, an interactive computer network designed for the broad conflict resolution field. ConflictNet provides a forum allowing for exchange of views among practitioners, students, researchers, and a variety of interested participants who subscribe to the service. Subscribers may send electronic mail, or 'e-mail', to one another, or they may 'visit' and contribute to 'conferences' on a variety of topics, including environment and public policy, community mediation, training, and research.

    Among the conferences is one devoted to conflict resolution journals, including the *Queensland ADR Review*. The *Queensland ADR Review*, a newsletter published three times per year by the ADR Division of the Department of Justice and Attorney-General, Queensland, Australia, is one of several periodicals which are made available electronically. Information about the Queensland cases comes from an article entitled 'Public Policy Disputes – The Alternative Dispute Resolution Division's Experience', written 8:05 p.m., 26 August 1994 by Marg O'Donnell.

12   In Ian Wright, *Mediation of Planning and Environmental Conflicts*, written 5:03 p.m., 11 August 1994, ConflictNet.

13   On ConflictNet: in 'Alternative Dispute Resolution: Participatory Democracy in Action', written 5:24 p.m., 11 August 1994; reprinted from the *Alternative Law Journal*, April 1994.

14   From 'The Network News', *Consensus*, January 1994.

15   Except where stated, this information is derived from an interview with Michael Elliott in the January 1994 newsletter *The Consortium on Negotiation and Conflict Resolution*, of the Georgia Institute of Technology. Elliott believes that the Canadian experience with public policy mediation may be more applicable to Germany than that of the United States, given the greater similarity of formal methods of public participation.

16   Thomas Barbian, personal communication, September 1994. Among the competitors are public relations firms.

Assessment

The goals[1]

While proponents of the merits of conflict resolution procedures often advocate the savings in costs and other burdens relative to litigation, they have not shied away from claiming benefits beyond agreements and costs. Carpenter (1989) suggests that in face-to-face interaction participants learn from one another how they perceive the situation and what concerns and needs they have, as well as their ideas about possible solutions. She claims as well that diverse participation can lead to better decisions, greater acceptance of the outcome, and faster implementation of any agreements.

One ancillary benefit she claims is the creation of new networks of constructive relationships. Another practitioner echoes that claim, suggesting that people not only get better solutions, they can work for their community in better ways and treat each other more humanely. These relationships make more likely joint efforts when new issues arise. Yet another practitioner claims that conflict resolution procedures can create a sense of inter-relatedness. She speculates that what the field is really doing is helping build citizens and citizenship.

According to Susskind and Ozawa (1985), mediation removes many of the constraints imposed by the formalities of adjudication. Those parties most affected by an issue can participate in the search for solutions. These stakeholders themselves can adopt procedures suitable for their needs. Another practitioner notes that when important ideas clash (e.g. when environmental values clash with property rights, or when there are conflicting standards for quality of life), a third party can create a 'discourse' which helps advocates to be persuasive, to articulate important understandings, and to gain credibility.

Susskind, Bacow and Wheeler (1983) contend that mediation attenuates the risks which accompany the winner-take-all format of litigation. Consensus agreements also increase the stability of the outcome. The critic Amy

(1987) acknowledges that the power mediation brings is the legitimacy of decisions, a legitimacy engendered by mediation's participatory nature. Because of this legitimacy, decisions reached during mediations are less likely to be challenged than those produced through conventional means. Another practitioner notes that as the legitimacy of the law becomes increasingly eroded the importance of this role increases.

Another practitioner claims that the mediation process opens up options for people who don't see or refuse to see them. This individual noted that it can also lift from unconscious to conscious, from the invisible to the visible, the message that process is important. Along similar lines, Bellman *et al.* (1982) suggest that the act of mediation, of bringing disputants together, can serve to legitimize the conflict itself. More significantly, in their words, it can 'provide an arena within which shifting social priorities and power centers can interact to ensure that the social fabric may yield to and reflect social changes rather than resist and be torn apart' (p. 6).

Additional benefits are claimed by The Report of the Ad Hoc Committee on Dispute Resolution and Public Policy ('Paths to justice', 1983). These include the opportunity to deal with underlying issues which might be ignored by other forums. Negotiations may relieve tensions and build acceptance of one another and ownership of solutions among participants. And by avoiding the adversarial legacy of adjudication, productive negotiations may model a path for future controversies.

An important theme which is beginning to intrigue many practitioners is the role public conflict resolution can play in democracy-building, a question to be addressed in the remaining portion of this book. One component of that role is increasing access to government. One practitioner focuses on the empowerment brought by increased participation, wherein people are offered an opportunity to solve problems by themselves without a helper. Others see the opportunities public conflict resolution provides as a means of educating public officials, of changing their behaviors, and of creating new norms of participation. Yet another practitioner speaks of alleviating the deep problem of alienation of the public, who are deprived of a channel to their government. And another speaks of providing processes for informed public decision-making. These processes empower people to take a role in that decision-making, something many people are discouraged from by the distance between their votes and decisions.

A more subtle argument in favor of consensual processes is offered by Bacow and Wheeler (1984), for whom the mediation process serves as a forum for education in 'realpolitik'. While their focus is the environmental arena, their eloquent description of the realities of negotiation is applicable to other public issues:

Negotiating the resolution of the same controversy lays bare all of the uncertainties and complexities that render environmental policymaking so difficult in the first place ... The pulling and hauling that is the essence of bargaining forces the parties to recognize that there are no right answers – only compromises worked out on intermediate positions. Instead of creating the illusion of truth, bargaining embraces the accommodation of competing interests. Moreover, the process of compromise forces each side to acknowledge the legitimacy of the claims of the opposition (p. 365).

Evaluating success

The search for agreement dominates the field; the movement is from conflict to resolution, dissensus to consensus, disagreement to agreement, breakdown to order, gridlock to movement. A practitioner whose record included few agreements would soon stop being a practitioner. Yet agreement is not always seen as the sole, or even the most important, goal of intervention.

An impressive early study by Buckle and Thomas-Buckle (1986) of eighty-one proposed mediations of site-specific conflicts uncovered some startling information which still gives fruit for reflection. Fifty of the eighty-one cases in which mediation was proposed rejected the idea immediately, seven soon after. Of the remaining twenty-four cases, sixteen rejected mediation at the first joint meeting. Two of the actual convened mediation efforts failed to reach agreement, three reached unstable agreements, and only three reached what were considered stable agreements. The mediators of the cases they examined admitted 'unaminously' they felt 'largely unsuccessful'.

One might conclude from these numbers – eighty-one attempted mediations and only three stable agreements – that, at best, mediation has an extremely limited role, at least in site-specific disputes. But Buckle and Thomas-Buckle's research did not end with a count of agreements. Even when the mediation itself did not result in agreement, participants in these mediations claimed a variety of other benefits. Thus, Buckle and Thomas-Buckle contend that agreement or disagreement is only one of a large constellation of desired outcomes of mediated negotiations. The other benefits participants in 'failed' mediations found included the following:

- helping the parties clarify their own interests;
- generating new options for solutions;
- demonstrating good will to judges and regulators;
- providing service as a virtual staff resource for regulators; and,
- educating the parties about effective procedures of negotiation.

The assessment of Buckle and Thomas-Buckle was used as a point of departure by Dotson (1993), who reviewed the caseload of the Institute for Environmental Negotiation at the University of Virginia. From its founding in 1981 through 1993, the Institute served a mediating role in over sixty cases. These cases varied in scope from local to federal issues, in duration from one day to eighteen months, and in expense from pro bono to $100,000.

What Dotson calls a 'conclusive' or 'classic' success is demonstrated by a documented agreement among the participants in the negotiation, validated by authorities, and implemented as envisioned. Of the sixty cases reviewed by Dotson, sixteen came to this conclusive end.

In thirty of the cases Dotson examined the objective never was a viable agreement; these situations include informal strategic planning workshops, conflict assessments, and facilitation of meetings among scientific experts to develop consensus of opinion on policy issues. Dotson suggests that success of these types of interventions ought to be judged on the basis of their own expectations. In fourteen cases the mediator sought the classic success but failed to meet that expectation. Dotson argues that factors external to the negotiations themselves are most often responsible for lack of formal agreement. These factors include the following:

- preference for litigation: when parties are already engaged in litigation they may not be willing to engage in good faith negotiations;
- inadequate pressure to implement an agreement: an agreement may be declined or postponed by authorities responsible for implementation;
- unwillingness to negotiate: parties may be willing to discuss issues but reluctant to negotiate when negotiation is seen as giving up decision-making authority or the opportunity to appeal;
- changing political and legislative arena: pending elections or anticipated legislation may leave parties reluctant to agree to a course of action when the context of the issue under consideration might alter significantly;
- power imbalance: parties may agree to negotiate for a variety of reasons but have little incentive to alter their positions;
- shifting issues: new issues uncovered during the negotiations may alter the dynamics of the original dispute.

Part of the difficulty in evaluating mediation cases is divining the role mediation may have played in reaching agreement. The mediation process is not always, or even often, as cut and dried as textbooks or the expectations derived from family or community or labor mediation might lead one to believe. Even in the six cases which reached agreement in the Buckle and Thomas-Buckle (1986) study, the parties expressed ambiguity about how the case was processed. As the researchers explain, '... the relationships among mediation, direct negotiation among themselves, legislative politics, regulatory process, media-based efforts at persuasion, litigation, and many other events influencing the outcome of the conflict are typically complex, constantly variable and mutually interactive' (p. 64).

As the foregoing discussion demonstrates, and as has been suggested by several other observers,[2] there are a considerable number of products of conflict resolution procedures which lie beyond the instrumentalities of time, cost, and even agreement, which are very difficult to observe, and which are even more difficult to measure. Evaluation of conflict resolution procedures can, and ought, to move beyond these questions.

Dotson (1993) offers three categories in which gains may be made despite the failure to achieve the classic standard of success. These categories are content, relationships, and process. As for content, negotiations may stimulate change outside of the negotiating process itself, as parties take actions independent of any agreement and as institutions examine their own shortcomings. In situations where antagonisms have divided parties for many years, or perhaps where parties simply would not otherwise be brought together, building relationships may be an important first step in long-term interactions. And the mediation process, if conducted fairly, can shape the manner in which future differences can be managed. Perhaps the most accurate way of evaluating a mediation, Dotson argues, is to order a hierarchy of goals, with a 'degree of difficulty' rating which would acknowledge accomplishment in relative rather than absolute terms.

Lee (1982) contends that it is important to move beyond the interests of the disputants and the mediator and attempt to answer the question of how well the public interest is served. While parties and the mediator may equate an agreement with success, it may mark only an 'uncertain beginning' for the parties involved in forging that agreement. He suggests several more complete indicators of success, including how well the agreement was implemented; the extent necessary changes are made in programs and procedures; the ability of the parties to work together on implementation problems; and the continuing satisfaction of the parties that their interests were advanced.

Talbot (1983) agrees that evaluations based on agreement or agreement and implementation are inadequate to assess results of those cases which reach neither stage. He suggests that it is misleading to make mediators accountable for outcomes beyond their control while overlooking other gains which can be credited to mediators' efforts. He notes that disputants do not only want agreement; in fact, what they want most from mediation is to learn more about their interests, to identify available options, and most important of all, to learn how to negotiate.

He suggests, then, that the mediator's efforts be evaluated by the degree that the parties increase their awareness of both their relationship and the disputed issues. Mediators would be viewed as teachers of negotiation, and each stage of the mediation process would be evaluated on the basis of how well the disputants gained an understanding of their own and each others' situation.

The Report of the Ad Hoc Committee on Dispute Resolution and Public Policy ('Paths to justice', 1983) suggests several criteria for judging conflict resolution mechanisms. These are accessibility, including affordability; protection of rights, in particular when there is a disparity of power; cost and time efficiency; fairness to the parties, consistent with societal expectations of justice; ensuring finality and enforceability, while providing a means for reviewing the decision; and credibility. Finally, these processes 'should give expression to the community's sense of justice through the creation and dissemination of norms and guidelines so that other disputes are prevented, violators deterred, and disputants encouraged to reach resolution on their own' (p. 17).

The most consequential criteria for success are offered by Susskind (1981), who argues that the public conflict resolution field needs a definition of success broad enough to encompass the interests of all segments of society. The vehicles available for ensuring practitioner accountability in other fields, including moral, legal, and economic pressure, are not present in the public disputes arena. Labor mediators, for example, can measure success by whether or not an agreement is reached and maintained. But in public disputes, agreements among disputants which don't maximize joint gains, which set dangerous precedents, or which fail to account for impacts on unrepresented interests, including those of future generations, may lose natural resources, jeopardize public health and safety, and, for environmental issues, ignite an 'environmental time bomb'.

The implications of his analysis led Susskind to a conclusion which was quite controversial at the time: practitioners needed to take an active role in meeting responsibilities to the public interest in terms of precedents and the impact on under- or un-represented groups. For many of those coming from a labor-management background or adopting that perspective, what Susskind and his supporters were suggesting was heretical, unworkable, and damaging to the profession as a whole.[3] The debate centered around the question of mediator accountability for results, and involved issues such as the mediator's role in balancing power, the substantive knowledge and experience of the mediator, and the mediator's impact on any agreement.

The arguments were more intense in practice than might be gleaned from reading the literature. At a 1992 conference for senior environmental dispute resolution practitioners ('The cutting edge', 1994), attendees ruefully recalled the passions these differences engaged. But the debate never really concluded. It was simply put aside, lost to the demands of practice, while attention moved to other issues. Current practice indicates that Susskind and his supporters have had the better of it, although important questions of ecological effects, community acceptance, and representation remain in many cases unanswered and even unasked.

Critical assessment

Advocates of conflict resolution, including practitioners, do not claim its utility in all situations, although upon reading the promotional literature of the field's practitioners and organizations one might think otherwise (Forester, 1992). The Report of the Ad Hoc Committee on Dispute Resolution and Public Policy ('Paths to justice', 1983) cautions that negotiations can be time consuming and lack a sturdy enforcement mechanism. They may depend upon a good-faith willingness to negotiate and, as ought to be obvious, they do not always reach agreement.

The Panel suggested several concerns about conflict resolution procedures relative to litigation. These procedures may not actually save money; indeed, negotiations may continue indefinitely without the authority of judicial decision to end process. Access to negotiating forums may be denied to interested parties either because they do not know about them, or they are too expensive. Their informal nature means there is no guarantee of due process, or power to induce settlements or enforce decisions.

In reaching settlement without lawyers or counselors, negotiations may lead to poorly informed choices. This is of particular concern for sometimes disenfranchised groups who might be less powerful or less experienced at negotiation than their opponents. A settlement which may appear to resolve a dispute may leave fundamental issues unsettled or ignore potentially extensive liability. Others have suggested that participation in negotiations might mean forfeiture of legal rights (Ury *et al.*, 1988). And the skills and strengths which make for successful mobilization and organizational efforts of advocacy groups are not conducive to bargaining (Sullivan, 1984).

Certainly practitioners admit to the risks inherent in negotiations. Cormick (1985) notes that there might be inadequate support for negotiators within the organization or constituency they represent, which can result in difficulty in implementing any agreement. Parties might misuse the process to delay opponents. And negotiations, he claims, may increase misunderstandings and distrust.

Cormick (1987) also contends that there are many misconceptions about conflict resolution. For instance, despite popular claims to the contrary, mediation does not resolve basic differences; nor is it a process where participants learn to like, trust, and agree with one another. Indeed, he warns that if they were to do so they might forge solutions that are not politically viable. Rather, mediation allows parties to agree on accommodations for coexistence in situations where their continuing differences prevent the parties from achieving their goals unilaterally. And rather than mediation being an alternative to litigation, he continues, it actually relies on the courts for its viability.

In an argument which receives both support and dissent from several practitioners, Cormick (1987) cautions that the field now faces a danger of overselling the process. He claims that mistakes by inexperienced mediators will discredit the entire field. This is a warning that Kaplan (1988) contends is already too late. He maintains that mediation threatens to become a public policy fad as it spawns weak graduate school classes and weaker mediators.

The critiques presented to this point focus on what might be termed the 'microanalysis' of conflict resolution (Bacow and Wheeler, 1984). Important questions, they nonetheless admittedly give short thrift to the broader implications of mediation as a vehicle for policymaking.

Examples of these broader concerns are offered by the Report of the Ad Hoc Committee on Dispute Resolution and Public Policy ('Paths to justice', 1983). By providing alternatives, instead of making the courts face their own weaknesses, conflict resolution may weaken needed court reform movements. The Committee also notes that increasing numbers of agreements may be a poor argument for the resulting privatization of public disputes. The risk is that people would make deals which benefit the negotiating parties at the expense of society (Fiss, 1984; Bacow and Wheeler, 1984), in what might be termed a 'win/win/lose' solution.

There is a substantial critical literature along these lines for other arenas of conflict resolution, particularly community mediation.[4] The thrust of the critical argument is that 'informalism', the term provided for procedures developed in reaction to the 'formalism' of adjudication, legislation, and administrative decision-making, is an undesirable extension of state control, offered without the minimal advantages of state protection. The criticism, in a nutshell, is unequivocal: 'The informalism of dispute resolution extends the power of the state while decreasing its public accessiblity, visibility, and accountability' (Ellison, 1991: 247).

Lederach (1989) signifies the 'deep' critique of conflict resolution as the tension between activism and mediation. The themes of this critique include mediators with a superficial understanding of structural problems, a reduction of social conflict to matters of miscommunication, and solutions of mediocrity. The conclusion of this argument is that there is an 'unspoken, but powerfully manipulative, ideology of harmony that ultimately benefits the rich, powerful and conservative' (p. 12).

Amy (1987) has provided the most developed critique of conflict resolution in the public domain. His focus is on the environmental arena, but he extends his observations to other fields as well. Using the Mansbridge (1983; 1984) studies of interaction at town meetings and workplaces, he suggests that apparent consensus is often the product of powerful pressures applied in political forums. He argues that powerful groups use this pressure to maintain their advantages.

In a chapter provocatively entitled 'Mediation as seduction', Amy points to the corporate funding for mediations, and suggests that negotiators for environmental organizations are coopted by the process. Bringing parties face-to-face and cooling down hot emotions, he argues, may encourage trust but it also may open a path for abuse of that trust.

Amy suggests that past innovations in citizen participation have not resulted in true power-sharing, and he warns that conflict resolution might have similar limitations. The business community can use conflict resolution to distract environmentalists from other political strategies, to distort the nature of the issues at stake, and to give the illusion of legitimacy to development projects. Those in government can use mediation to give the appearance of public participation and to undermine public opposition to controversial policies, what might be called 'participating the public'.

He suggests that the market offers a fair basis of comparison of the choice between courts and mediation as means of dealing with differences. In his view, the absence of any great demand for mediation is de facto evidence of its weaknesses. He concludes that mediation ought to have only a relatively small role, and at that only when approached with caution and skepticism.

More recently, Ellison's (1991) analysis of dispute resolution in legal and public policy processes offers the same general conclusion. His 'central claim' is that it 'inadequately analyzes the problems of democracy', that it 'embodies processes that are generally not consistent with democratic principles', and that it 'may, therefore, contribute to, rather than lessen, the legitimation problems of American democracy' (p. 243). It is worth quoting at length his defense of adjudication vis-à-vis negotiation:

> Adjudication's public purpose is to articulate and interpret the rights, principles, and rules that help to protect individuals and groups. Rights can enable suppressed voices and conflicts to surface and can restrain and compel state justification of acts of power. Rights discourse enables members of a political community to live together with conflict (p. 248).

The weaknesses of critical assessment

Public conflict resolution is ripe for healthy reflection and criticism. Many practitioners themselves suggest that there is a substantial need for research, evaluation, and documentation of the various practices of the field.

But the existing critical assessment misses the mark by a considerable margin. A substantial amount of the analysis of conflict resolution in general, and public conflict resolution in particular, is either unsubstantiated, inaccurate, or misleading. Ultimately, it is quite unproductive. With few exceptions, the analysts demonstrate an inadequate knowledge base of actual practice from which to inform their decisions.

A typology of common faults is all too easy to construct.

Blanket and unproven generalizations   Some of the most telling indictments of public conflict resolution are either speculative or based on undocumented practice. For example, Ellison's (1991) claims about the undemocratic nature of dispute resolution are based primarily on selective quotations from other observers. And witness the claims of a usually perceptive critic and analyst of the field of conflict resolution that 'most third party ADR and CI [conflict intervention] efforts are or end up reducing, avoiding and neutralizing social protest, and retaining dominant power and privilege in the hands of elites and powerful stakeholders' (Chesler, 1989: 2). This critique is an important and valid perspective when presented as a cautionary tale; but is there any empirical basis for these claims? None is offered.

Such statements, offered without substantiating evidence, are essentially opinion. Yet because they originate from respected and persuasive sources, they are all too easily adopted as doctrine.

Straw men[5]   Lentz (1986) divides environmental mediators into 'traditionalists' and 'revisionists'. Ellison (1991) divides mediation practice into 'rational-choice' and 'cultural' perspectives. Stephenson and Pops (1989: 463) offer a portrait of dispute resolution advocates as politically unsophisticated, having 'pursued their interests with little regard to the policy context in which conflicts occur'. As ideal types, such representation can serve useful purposes by pointing to significant patterns of thought and behavior. But it is all too easy to step over the edge of characterization into caricature, and create images of practice and practitioners which those in the field are not themselves able to recognize.

Critics such as Ellison and Amy see that problems such as cooptation and abuse of rights disadvantage the activist participants in conflict resolution, who are portrayed as naive innocents with a 'tendency to be too trusting' (Ellison, 1991: 261). The image is one of naifs entering the lion's den unaware of the pitfalls planned by the rapacious corporate spoilers of the environment. Never is it imagined that corporate or state representatives in dispute resolution processes might be subject to the same influences offered by the intimacy of face-to-face interaction, although such a view is offered by some who think environmentalists have too much influence (see, e.g., Brookes, 1991). It is a gross distortion to label the representatives of contemporary public interest movements, with decades of experience in the policymaking arena, as unsophisticated, naive or malleable. And anyone who has worked with grassroots groups activated by a threat to their children, communities, and livelihoods is unlikely to envision them as too trusting.

The courts as hallowed gatekeepers of justice   Some critics of conflict resolution retreat to a vision of the law and its protection so idealized as to create wonder that anyone could have ever doubted its primacy. The refusal to admit the value of a strong role for mediation and other 'alternatives' within the legal system is not shared by the legal profession as a whole; indeed, attorneys and judges have been among conflict resolution's strongest advocates. But there are those[6] who appear to confuse what they want from the law – protection of public interest, champion of the powerless – with what the law actually is, and does.

Sacrificing the victim   When solutions to problems which disproportionately affect the less powerful stress what these individuals and groups can do to address those problems, they are sometimes said to suggest unfair culpability. These kinds of solutions are termed 'blaming the victim' (Ryan, 1971). There are those whose aversion to any insinuation of 'blaming the victim' leads them to denounce any program which does not offer more complete structural transformation.[7] Yet is it appropriate for outside critics, who may not share the circumstances of those they are attempting to protect, to prevent what may indeed be only incremental improvements when the prospects for structural transformation are remote? This practice may well be termed 'sacrificing the victim'.

Exaggeration   This category is reserved for those who exaggerate the importance of real difficulties and concerns. It is all too easy to develop scenarios about the potential problems with conflict resolution vis-à-vis adjudication. While there are dangers to conflict resolution, the existing critical literature makes extravagant leaps of conjecture in order to transform these concerns into arguments against any but the most modest use of conflict resolution procedures. Bacow and Wheeler (1984) provide a pointed and straightforward response to these criticisms: 'Negotiation does not eliminate the possibility of serious mistakes – but neither do other processes' (p. 363).

A flawed conceptual framework

There is another problem with contemporary analysis for which the public conflict resolution literature alone cannot be blamed; that is, it is a condition common to the complete body of research and theorizing within the larger field of conflict resolution, and not simply that portion within the public arena. The problem is this: questions that critics and analysts together attempt to answer have been constructed within a conceptual framework that ignores many important aspects of the conflict resolution movement.

Like community mediation (Dukes, 1990), public conflict resolution research and analysis is dominated by the focus on dispute processing.[8] The goal of this research is to assess the viability of the varieties of conflict resolution procedures as they are applied to different kinds of disputes. Esser (1988) details the conceptual framework implicit in this research. A number of types of procedures are used for settling and resolving disputes. Each of these procedures has distinctive characteristics which makes it appropriate for certain types of disputes and inappropriate for others. Research can demonstrate which processes fit which disputes, while ineffectiveness can be explained and reforms derived from the resultant theory.

Others have recognized the problems with this conceptualization. Sarat (1988) criticizes what he terms its 'new formalism'. It is inadequate, he claims, because it ignores the dynamic nature of conflict, it fails to recognize the flexibility and adaptivity of dispute processes, and it implicitly accepts the 'conflict is bad' paradigm. In brief, this 'new formalism' is criticized as a conservative view of disputes, disputing, and dispute resolution, that inherently favors the status quo to the detriment of legitimate challengers and challenges.

This conceptual framework is reinforced by, just as it in turn reinforces, a limited range of accepted research methods. Problems are to some extent defined by the questions asked about them, and these questions are themselves guided by the means by which answers can be found. What is studied may be studied not because of its import but because it is easier to study it than other, more important questions. The methodology most researchers are trained in and use is inappropriate for studying questions which are outside of the accepted framework. It follows that there is the predominance of studies assessing processes in terms of cost, time, and disputant satisfaction, in part because these factors can be operationalized and analyzed relatively easily.

When referring to issues such as the impact of conflict resolution, both promotional and critical literature are based more upon fancy than research; they each share the same blinders. There is no doubt that it is important to learn about factors such as efficiency, cost, and disputant satisfaction. However, the field might be better served by also addressing in research the kinds of questions and problems which do not readily lend themselves to the most popular tools of empirical investigation, instead of leaving them to the airy conjectures of critical analysts or the wishes of promoters.

This framework is inaccurate, and hence inadequate, because it does not encompass the full scope of these organizations' activities. There is an entire constellation of beliefs, practices, and organizational action, of which intervention is merely one component, which has been ignored in the discourse of assessment and critique. These institutions are not solely places where people come to have their disputes processed. Each has its own history: the goals and ideology which inspired its beginnings; the people who came together to create it; the drive for economic viability and, often, institutional affiliation; and the relationships with its own network of funders, allies, competitors, and other institutions in its orbit of practice.

Each practice has staff who are socialized into the ideology and practices of their own particular program, as they are recruited, trained, and given opportunities to work with disputants. Many of these organizations affect other organizations and communities through training, publicity and public education. Most also provide opportunities for employment and advancement for those interested in pursuing various kinds of careers in the field. On the debit side of the ledger, they may coopt activists whose energies would otherwise be put to better use. Or they may divert scarce funds from programs whose benefits are more established.

Many conflict resolution practitioners have branched out into other areas. More and more handle a wider range of disputes than was part of their original mandate. Others specialize in certain kinds of programs, such as mediation of Superfund cleanups. Many do training in negotiation, conciliation, and mediation, for the general public as well as specified populations, including businesses and government personnel. There is a whole range of practices – dispute system design, policy dialogues, and the entire domain of exploratory processes – left out of current conceptualizations of what public conflict resolution is about. Until the conceptual framework by which conflict resolution is understood moves beyond dispute processing to include these other elements, its actual influence and import will remain undiscovered.

Conclusion

It is one thing to recognize the wide range of elements of public conflict resolution which impact the public domain; but assessing that impact is another question entirely. The growth of the field can perhaps be documented in several ways, including the number and size of practitioner organizations ('The cutting edge', 1994), the amount and relevance of state and federal legislation, the number and quality of publications, the development of practice in other nations (Moore, 1993), and the growth of university programs and courses. But measuring the impact of that growth is another matter. As one practitioner remarked, the effects of public conflict resolution are somewhere between 'inconsequential' and 'radical', an evaluation less useful as an indicator of impact than as a reflection of the ambivalence many practitioners and observers maintain about the field.

Other practitioners observe that there are individuals, in both the public and private sectors, who discover that what conflict resolution offers fits well with what they have been doing independently of any training or formal knowledge. Many individuals and institutions are eager to be trained, and many agencies request assistance. More public officials are beginning to consider dispute resolution as a major part of their role. There are a number of new models of governance appearing which reflect the lessons of collaboration and consensual problem-solving. These include public-private partnerships, task forces, and citizens' groups (Kunde and Rudd, 1988).

Many key personnel in private sector, government, and public interest organizations who have participated themselves in public conflict resolution forums become advocates for conflict resolution processes, as participation and success change their views about how to conduct business (Susskind and Cruikshank, 1987). And it may not take actual participation in such a forum to create change; followup interviews to a Department of Energy training found that more than half the participants intend to behave cooperatively in future siting controversies (Rundle, 1986).

Can a new 'spirit of cooperation' be found, as is claimed by some (Buntz, 1989)? There clearly is an increase in the attention paid to conflict resolution by journals and foundations (Bosso, 1988). And there is much talk of collaboration and cooperation. For instance, one observer of African-American leadership finds a new breed of black politician who formulates 'coalition politics', who focuses on 'common difficulties', and who trumpets the 'quietly potent theme of inclusion and racial unity' (Gurwitt, 1990: 29). And Peter Harkness, the publisher of *Governing* magazine, finds himself encountering in his travels around the country a consensus that business, government, and academia need to work together in partnership, the particular combination of cooperation and pragmatism (Harkness, 1990).

One practitioner sees a broad movement from a rights-centered dialogue to one that is interest-based. But others caution that the jury is still out; the vocabulary has increased, but it remains misunderstood. Several caution that a lot of people use the words in a 'trendy' way, with phrases such as 'win/win' becoming trite.

It is impossible to measure the responsibility borne by public conflict resolution for these changes, if indeed these changes are occurring. The size and nature of that impact will remain a subject for debate, in great part because at least for the time being such an assessment is mainly subjective. At a soft level, there is some shift in norms and in language, and even a change in the corporate culture among the different players in the public arena. The consensus among practitioners themselves is that there is some impact upon policymaking and policymakers, but that it is spotty, that the use of feel-good language sometimes substitutes for a real understanding of the practice, and that the true impact is impossible to measure accurately.

Notes

1   Practitioner comments not otherwise identified were taken from interviews the author conducted from 1989 to 1991 (Dukes, 1992).

2   See, e.g., Susskind (1981), Lee (1982), Talbot (1983), Sullivan (1984), and Bush (1984; 1988).

3   See Stulberg (1981) and McCrory (1981).

4   See, e.g., Abel (1982a, b), Harrington (1985), Hofrichter (1987), Sarat (1988), and Nader (undated).

5   I am aware that my own typology of 'management' and 'transformation' may be criticized for this fault. I wish to emphasize once again that these characteristics are not found in any individual practitioner, but in the cumulative effects of many practices within the entire field, including research, writing, and caseload, of which technique or process is only one component.

6   See, e.g., Fiss (1984), Rodwin (1982), and Ellison (1991).

7   See, e.g., Abel (1982a, b), Hofrichter (1987).

8   For examples of this research see, e.g., Wall (1981), Kolb (1983b), Pruitt and Kressel (1985), Kressel and Pruitt (1989), and Kolb and Rubin (1989).

8

The ideology of management

In Chapter One, I suggested that public conflict resolution risked becoming another minor element in a consensus set of explanations and justifications offered for public problems and their solutions. This consensus, as popularized in mainstream media and in fields such as planning and public administration, was termed the 'ideology of management'. The main components of this ideology, as enacted in public conflict resolution, were sketched:

- The problem public conflict resolution is designed to address – the 'crisis of governance' – and the accompanying intended audience/consumers of the product: authorities in the executive, legislative, and judicial branches of government at local, state, and federal levels.
- A vision of human nature and society, and a conception of how government fulfills this vision consistent with this 'crisis of governance'.
- Key components of the public conflict resolution practice, including most importantly a prevailing explanation of disputes, conflict, and dispute resolution, a singular view of the third party role, and distinctive goals and objectives consistent with these two components.

Each of these themes will be developed here in greater depth.

The role of ideology

The role of ideology has generated considerable interest within certain elements of the conflict resolution field. This interest may be surprising to some, particularly American readers. Unlike much of the West, the United States never experienced the overthrow of a well-defined aristocracy, with its particular constellation of 'ideological and symbolic justifications' (Lea, 1982: 37). Therefore the prevailing beliefs and symbols common to the nation are not perceived as an ideology. Yet there certainly exist national beliefs, defined by special symbols and protected by implicit rules, which are ingrained as ideology within the American psyche (Lea, 1982). Like the fish who do not realize that they are swimming in water, for most Americans these rules and symbols are an unseen component of their natural environment.

Folger and Bush (1994) clearly articulate the basis and role of ideology in mediation. Ideologies are frameworks used to interpret and judge people's surroundings. Supporters and critics of mediation base their views upon their beliefs about what should happen in mediation, and why. Concepts of conflict and approaches to intervention evince broad ideologies which both reflect and shape their owners' views of human nature, relationships, and society. These ideological foundations may be so deeply rooted in culture that they exist unexamined.

While the ideology of management emerging within public conflict resolution has its own distinctive characteristics, it is consistent with earlier, more influential traditions in fields such as planning and law. Imagine a continuum of social change, ranging from accommodation to existing social relations, at one end, to radical transformation at the other. Friedmann (1988), a planner, describes how those who accept what I term the 'management' end of this continuum seek 'the confirmation and reproduction of existing relationships of power in society ... Expressing predominantly technical concerns, they proclaim a carefully nurtured stance of political neutrality. In reality, they address their work to those who are in power and see their primary mission as serving the state' (p. 8). At the other end of the spectrum are those who seek to transcend and even transform existing relationships of power. The client is not the state, but individuals, their communities, and civil society as a whole. This continuum will provide the basis for contrasting the management ideology with the vision of a transformative practice to be offered in later chapters.

The research questions identified by Adler *et al.* (1988), developed as part of their analysis of the community dispute resolution field, are particularly useful in exploring the ideological basis of public conflict resolution. For them, the visions of reality which are at the root of ideologies are fundamental to social reform movements. Ideologies determine how reality is conceptualized, they defend or attack particular institutional interests, they justify commitment, and they provide the basis for the organization of problems and their solutions. It is particularly important, they argue, to define the importance of defining the purposes of conflict resolution organizations. What is the perceived social or political problem to which these organizations are responding? How is that problem defined and articulated? In short, who determines what are compelling problems, using what criteria?[1]

The management problem: a crisis of governance

Within the public conflict resolution field, the answers to those questions are mixed. Many practitioners speak of the need to address the deep-rooted problems of injustice found in societies where there are great inequities of power and resources, and they are equally aware of how these inequities play out along racial, ethnic, and gender lines. But note the implications of the Credo statement from the Public Disputes Network *Consensus*, a quarterly publication well-known within the field, which provides stories of successful cases for public officials and practitioners: 'All too often, public policy initiatives are stalled by opposition from organized groups, which seem to have formed to block every action of government'.

Are initiatives truly stalled 'all too often'? Are these groups really formed in order to 'block every action of government'? Are public policy initiatives the sole province of government authorities? Could not other credos, identifying other problems, be equally or even more appropriate? For instance, is it not equally true that 'All too often, government initiatives are bulldozed through citizen and community concerns'? Or, perhaps, that 'All too often, citizen initiatives are stalled by opposition from organized government'? Or that 'All too often, citizen concerns are discounted by public policy initiatives'?

The primary problem reflected in this Credo, and the problem which the ideology of management offers to address, has been termed the 'crisis of governance'. The main theme of this problem, dramatized by the attention of government officials, the media, and academia, is the inability of authorities to govern: legislative, judicial, and administrative gridlock.

There is a strong litany of criticism along these lines.[2] These critics speak in terms of a society 'paralyzed by special interests and shortsightedness', mired in 'gridlock', stifled by 'government paralysis', where government has taken on the form of a 'bloated, inefficient, helpless giant' (Cloud, 1989: 32).

There are three main strands to this defined problem, strands which are woven together in an interdependent web:

1 the decline of the United States and, indeed, much of democratic society in general, relative to both its own halcyon past as well as new international competition;
2 disengagement of an uninvolved and apathetic citizenry;
3 the inability of government to govern: gridlock.

Decline

The dominant image of the United States today, a view which is echoed to different degrees in other democratic nations, as proclaimed in popular periodicals, books, and radio and television talk shows, is that of a powerful but troubled nation. The current thesis is that this is a period of general moral, economic, and political decline relative to the past and to other powers. This image is shaped by terms and phrases such as 'crumbling infrastructure', 'inefficiency', 'transformation from world's largest creditor to largest debtor', and 'loss of competitive edge'.

There is a cottage industry of books with this theme.[3] These books, despite their different levels of pessimism or optimism, present similar pictures: a struggling but still powerful nation leading the world. The country needs 'more effort', 'greater effort', 'new leadership', 'fresh purpose', 'willpower', 'improvement', all in order to accomplish the main goal (destiny?): the return to the nation's bygone rightful place of world leadership.

The management ideology within public conflict resolution is not just a product of this image; it contributes its own spectres of decline. In their (unsigned) lead story of the July 1991 issue, 'Collaborating on Growth Management', *Consensus* editors speak wistfully of a time when 'life was simpler' and 'working relationships permeated local governments'. Farmers and 'preservationists' worked together as a 'strong coalition'. Public hearings were marked by 'cordiality and respect for neighbors' and 'trusting relationships'. Life, it appears, was better then.[4]

A disengaged citizenry

The second component of the 'crisis of governance' is the failure of individual citizens to fulfill their civic obligations. They have newly become, it seems, a passive, indifferent, and uninvolved citizenry. The *prima facie* evidence for this apathy is abysmally low voting levels (National Civic League, 1991). And the implicit acknowledgment by political leaders of this uninvolved citizenry is the apparent disdain with which it is treated as audience to the games of politics, in which issues substitute for problems, partisan finger-pointing for debate, and power plays for legitimacy.

The inability to govern: gridlock

In one of the most popular public conflict resolution works, theorists and practitioners Susskind and Cruikshank (1987) articulate the notion of a world become ungovernable. They speak of the 'paralysis' of government, of how policymaking has come to an impasse. Leaders cannot lead: 'Public officials are unable to take action, even when everyone agrees that something needs to be done' (p. 3). There is a sense of inevitability about this situation: 'Whenever community leaders try to set standards, allocate resources, or make policy in contemporary society, we can expect a fight' (p. 8).

The 'gridlock' thesis is buttressed by three essential propositions:

1 the erosion of government authority, a product of the proliferation of single-issue groups and resultant special interest politics, as well as the accompanying decline of party power;
2 administrative overregulation and incompetence; and,
3 judicial abuse and overload.

Erosion of authority   A main plaint of the 'crisis of governance' is that a proliferation of powerful single-interest groups has caused a paralyzing diffusion of power.[5] This argument, as descriptive statement, may or may not be accurate, although single-issue politics is nothing new to this era: witness abolitionism, anti-Masonry, temperance, and a host of other movements and issues from the past. But the conclusions drawn from this observation are another matter. These new players on the political arena are viewed with great suspicion, if not downright hostility. For instance, Olson (1982) argues that 'special-interest organizations and collusions reduce efficiency and aggregate income in the societies in which they operate and make political life more divisive' (p. 47). Fiorina (1980) fears that 'the simple proliferation of special interests with their intense, particularistic demands threatens to render us politically incapable of taking actions' (p. 25). Staub (1980) is particularly critical. He argues that the very core of democracy – majority rule, minority protection – is threatened. In his opinion, minorities 'dominate, tyrannize, or terrorize the majority, which appears principally as a conglomerate of constantly changing minorities' (p. 159). These minorities not only include ethnic and national identity groups such as the Basques and Welsh, but interest groups such as the environmentalists.

The explanation given for their behavior is often psychological, a response to personal, individual deficiency. The threat is palpable: 'active, influential, and demagogic minorities are able to play a dominant role and exert a decisive influence on the sound instincts of the people' (Staub, 1980: 166). And the outlook is grim: impasse leading even to anarchy.

Overregulation   The case against administrative regulation is a familiar one. It is, in brief, that productivity and initiative are strangled by overregulation and the growing bureaucratization of an inefficient state administrative apparatus. Handler (1988) summarizes the argument:

> The 'crisis' in regulation is that too many aspects of society, especially the economy, are overregulated. There are too many regulations, they are too detailed, technical, and legalistic ... unnecessary costs are imposed on industry, innovation is stifled, and regulatory goals are not accomplished (p. 1022).

Perhaps the culminating expression of frustration with this impediment to economic productivity is the moratorium on new regulations imposed by politicians without consideration of either public risk or economic benefit.

Judicial abuse and overload   The theme of this plaint is that the legal system is overwhelmed by an abundance of litigation, a recent phenomenon which demonstrates an unprecedented societal preference for litigiousness (Galanter, 1983). The litany of dissatisfaction with the legal system includes displeasure at a 'growing philosophy of entitlements', an 'expanded set of claims for which people seek legal redress', 'new classes of plaintiffs', 'swelled' court dockets, and ballooning backlogs (Gray, 1989: 48).

Worldview: Human nature, the ideal society, and the role of government

The justifications for particular political views, including ideals, values, and beliefs, are built upon conceptions of human nature, society, and the role of the state (Lea, 1982). The ideology of management is no exception. The society implied by this ideology is made up of an aggregation of individuals whose main pursuit is to maximize their self-interest: the 'possessive individual'. The right to individual freedom is the preeminent social value, and the preservation of that right the predominant function of the state (Clark, 1989). In this view, the natural human condition is independence and solitude (Barber, 1984). It is, as Lea (1982) describes, a 'largely unchallenged neo-Madisonian perspective on man, politics, and society which stresses human selfishness, materialistic urges, competitiveness, natural inequality, and man's apolitical and privatized nature' (p. 212).

The model of society implied by this ideology is familiar as the 'order' or 'consensus' theory of society. That which contributes to harmony and productivity is good, and that which challenges that harmony is bad. Dahrendorf (1959) summarizes the underlying assumptions of this model:

1 Every society is a relatively persistent, stable structure of elements.
2 Every society is a well-integrated structure of elements.
3 Every element in a society has a function, i.e., renders a contribution to its maintenance as a system.
4 Every functioning social structure is based on a consensus of values among its members (p. 161).

The kind of government implicit in the ideology of management is in the tradition of the views offered by John Adams, Alexander Hamilton, and James Madison. The 'Madisonian' or 'Federalist' perspective conceives of human beings as motivated by material needs rather than ideals and reason (Lea, 1982). Conflicts between individual and social interests, in this view, are settled by natural tendencies which are essentially 'predatory and anti-social' (Lea, 1982). Thus, society must be protected from popular rule by concentrating power and authority within a limited elite. Governance is the province of this elite, whose power and legitimacy is maintained by their sense of duty, their superior capacity for reason, and their moral authority.

The public conflict resolution field

How is this ideology of management constituted in the public conflict resolution arena?

It cannot be stressed enough that the components of this perspective are not found in any one practitioner or in any single organization. The scope of the ideology of management encompasses, but is much broader than, the practices of intervention. And the course of the field is not necessarily driven by the conscious ideals or intentions of its practitioners, funders, and consumers, alone or together. Harrington and Merry (1988) suggest that ideologies of mediation are constituted by both social action and structural constraints. They note the importance of resource mobilization, which is the process by which mediation proponents gain legitimacy as they attract funding, institutional support, and cases, in shaping and constituting such ideologies. This is an important point: structural relations cannot be explained by individual intentions, whether these intentions be good or bad (Weedon, 1987).

Handler (1988) reveals in generic terms how ideologies are produced and reproduced. Human service organizations are dependent on their environment for legitimacy and clients. In order to obtain some measure of control over their environments, organizations engage in image building: 'they adopt a system of ideas, hold them with fervor, look for self-confirming results, and resist change or re-appraisal. Since ideologies are self-confirming, practitioners can reify their models of human behavior with self-fulfilling prophecies' (p. 1054). While these images are more than invention, they remain less than the truth.

This ideology permeates an essential core of public conflict resolution. It is implicit in the appeal to authorities made by its advocates. It is implicit in the predominant sources of funding for the field's institutions. It is implicit in the scope of research. It is implicit in the types of issues addressed by the field. And it is implicit in the absence of any compelling counterargument.

A service to authorities

Consistent with the identification of the problem public conflict resolution is intended to challenge – the 'crisis of governance' – is the identification of the audience or consumer of the public conflict resolution product. Appeals are made to authorities who might avail themselves of these services – in particular, to those who can afford to pay for them, which increasingly means agencies of government at all levels. These appeals are framed in terms of the use these authorities may make of these services, in the language of management.[6] This audience, in brief, is the state and its institutions of governance: administrative agencies; federal, state, and local executives; representatives of the judiciary; elected officials at all levels; and, finally, the non-governmental organizations (NGOs) which are tied inextricably to this governing apparatus.

The belief prevails that the role of public conflict resolution is to provide one additional tool in the arsenal of public officials, one additional means of problem-solving. It is, in one practitioner's words, merely a 'reconfiguration' of existing negotiations (Dukes, 1992). In appropriate circumstances it offers a useful, efficient way to resolve disputes.

Thus, not only are authorities wooed with promises of efficiency and reduced costs; they are reassured that conflict resolution will not mean a challenge to their power. For example, Susskind and Cruikshank (1987) offer repeated reference to 'restoring the credibility of government' and assurances about how public conflict resolution does not supersede official authority. Bellman and Drake (in 'Statewide offices', 1987) reassure state executives that conflict resolution can 'broaden and strengthen their leadership roles', and that it 'does not mean relinquishing the authority or power granted to a leader'; indeed, its use 'is often politically advantageous' (p. 4) Consensus propels decisions but does not relieve officials of their control.

Neither need the authorities fear that dispute resolution might supplant traditional processes. In this view, public conflict resolution will not, and ought not, have a very large role to play relative to the legitimate institutions of governance. Kaplan (1988) counsels that not only should mediation not be 'oversold', it ought not to be 'allowed to compete with more important management processes' (p. 294). Bellman and Drake ('Statewide offices', 1987) again reassure public officials that the tools of dispute resolution 'are not intended to replace traditional legislative, regulatory, administrative or judicial mechanisms' (p. 4). Susskind (in Staff, 1982) suggests the subordinate role of the field by asking how the three basic decision-making and dispute resolution mechanisms of legislative, judicial, and executive/administrative processes may be 'supplemented' (p. 30).

The meaning of disputes and dispute processing

Within the ideology of management, the range of issues considered suitable for intervention is sharply limited. Problems or disputes which fall outside the domain of responsible governing bodies remain invisible. The implication is that public disputes predominantly arise out of opposition to policy. By restricting consideration of public disputes to policy issues, there is thus drawn a sharp dividing line between certain public concerns, which are considered government responsibility and hence amenable to intervention, and other concerns, which, since they are not brought under government control, are considered private matters.

This approach began early. The Ford Foundation (1978), influential in the early development of the field, identified three types of public conflict. Each of the three involves 'complex public policy disputes' which 'arise out of government regulation of the economic and social systems' (p. 3). The three are:

1 social policy disputes which arise when government objectives 'involve or impinge on many interests and groups, such as racial equality and economic opportunity, environmental protection, income security, and public health and safety' (p. 3);
2 regulatory disputes; and,
3 disputes arising out of social welfare programs.

The ways in which disputes might be managed follow, naturally enough, from the understanding of the meaning of conflict and disputes. Within this narrow range of policy conflict, it is primarily in the distribution of resources that the ideology of management locates the sources of public disputes. For example, Susskind and Cruikshank (1987) specify differences over allocation of funds, setting standards, and siting facilities. Note their language: 'Regardless of which interest groups are objecting, they do so in the hope of affecting the distribution of gains and losses' (pp. 17–18). Nearby residents protesting siting 'may make reference to questions of legality or fundamental rights, but what they are really contesting is a specific allocation of gains and losses, and not the government's right to site facilities' (p. 18).

Others offer a similarly fixed view. Bacow and Wheeler (1984) state that the sources of conflict are different stakes in the outcome, different assessments of probabilities and different tolerances for risks. For Madigan et al. (1990), conflicts involve disagreements over policies and/or budget priorities, fixed resources (e.g. land and water use or development), and standards for facility design and siting. Building upon the work of Susskind et al. (1978), Sullivan (1984) finds four issues at stake: policies and values, distribution of costs and benefits, protection from harm to environment and health, and use of fixed resources. Parties seek to maximize their individual gains, and thus compete for fixed portions of the pie.

When disputes are seen as static clashes of interests, then negotiation will be a process primarily of bargaining and exchange within a power framework. And it is the labor-management practice which serves as the model for the practice of bargaining and exchange. In the labor-management conception, the relative power of the parties is the primary determinant of the settlement (Bellman et al., 1982). The third party's primary role is to get an agreement (Cormick and Patton, 1980), which they do by applying 'pressure toward settlement' (Bellman et al., 1982: 22). Practitioners 'constantly remind ... negotiators that they were in trouble if they did not reach a settlement' (p. 22). The goal of dispute resolution is clear: it is a 'method for constructively channeling conflict into compromise' (p. 6).

It is the methodology of game theory, decision analysis, and multi-attribute analysis which provide the scientific rationale for bargaining.[7] These operations depend primarily on the assumption of fixed parties whose goal is the maximization of their self-interest. This self-interest, which is static throughout negotiations, can be traded and compromised. Successful negotiation is a matter of technique and choice of the right process: 'the difficulties associated with mediation can be overcome with the application of innovative techniques' (Susskind and Ozawa, 1985: 145).

Neutrality

The mantle of the labor mediator weighs heavily in conceiving the third party's role. 'Neutrality', implying value-freedom, is considered a virtue to be cultivated. Questions about the kinds of problems being tackled, the scope of representation in conflict resolution forums, and the impact upon different communities of the agreements emerging from these forums, are ignored or addressed instrumentally, in terms of how they affect the task of reaching agreement. The management practitioner will 'hold the parties to the negotiations – not the mediator – responsible for serving the groups they represent' (Lentz, 1986: 134).

Goals and objectives

One of the 'ideological projects' of mediation identified by Harrington and Merry (1988) they term the 'delivery of dispute resolution services'. It is this delivery of services which chiefly concerns the ideology of management. Within the management ideology, the most prominent goals are saving money (Susskind and Ozawa, 1985; 'Paths to justice', 1983), reducing court loads, eliminating delays (Susskind and Ozawa, 1985; Susskind *et al.*, 1983), and reducing demands on government. The ideal is 'to resolve the disputes faster, at less cost, and with greater satisfaction to the disputing parties than more adversarial methods' (Gleeson in 'Statewide offices of mediation', 1987: 5). Acceptance will come when dispute resolution programs 'save the public money in the long run; reduce demands on the courts and government personnel; reduce the time and overhead costs required to settle disputes; and increase public satisfaction' ('Paths to justice', 1983: 20).

It is the practitioner's role to settle, not resolve, disputes (Cormick, 1982).[8] Agreement is the measure of success, management of conflict the optimal achievement. Disputant satisfaction, justice, and equity are generally ignored or assumed to be a by-product of an efficient governing apparatus.

The failures of critical analysis

One element contributing indirectly to the maintenance of the management ideology is the absence of any clear and persuasive countervailing argument. The critical literature of conflict resolution in general and public conflict resolution in particular is inadequate and easily dismissed by practitioners and others familiar with the field and its practices. Either the critic creates 'straw men' to make a point (e.g. Lentz, 1986, who divides environmental mediators into 'traditionalists' and 'revisionists'), or dispute resolution is contrasted with an illusory ideal (e.g. the courts as the hallowed gatekeepers of justice), or real difficulties and concerns are granted exaggerated importance.[9] While the critical literature offers valid concerns, it takes rather extravagant leaps of conjecture to transform these concerns into the blanket indictments offered by these critics.

Conclusion

There are many reasons for the advancement of the ideology of management. It is consistent with widely held beliefs about human nature, society, the proper role of government, and the nature of problems which face contemporary democratic society. It offers itself as a solution to problems with the existing order while remaining essentially loyal to that order. For public conflict resolution practitioners, it promises to offer a growing source of continuing work and revenue.

It is also evident that the problems addressed by the management practice are present to some considerable degree. Overburdened courts, complicated administrative procedures, special interest politics, citizen withdrawal, gridlock – these are all valid concerns. And certainly the techniques of the management practice can be one part, and even an important part, of the repertoire of dispute resolution practitioners.

There is, however, a risk in accepting the terms of management. That risk is that the field might become so much less than it could be, and far less than democratic society needs. Bacow and Wheeler (1984) ask in the final two pages of their epilogue, 'Has our concern for process efficiency and the interests of particular parties obscured larger social objectives'? (p. 362). The clear answer is still, 'Yes'. Public conflict resolution can be about much more than settling disputes. It can be more than helping authorities maintain power. And it is certainly more than one small tool for returning a nation to an illusory past.

Those who are concerned for the future of public conflict resolution can and should have larger ambitions. Public conflict resolution can be about how individuals relate to one another, how communities sustain themselves and their members, how governance earns and maintains legitimacy. After all, the methods a society sanctions for the resolution of disputes 'communicate the ideals people cherish, their perceptions of themselves, and the quality of their relationships with others ... the most basic values of society are revealed in its dispute-settlement procedures' (Auerbach, 1983: 3–4). And if public conflict resolution is to be expected to embrace a vision of its possibilities consistent with those ideals, it must be offered a portrait of its meaning that its members can identify as their own, a portrait firmly rooted in a genuine understanding of its practice.

Notes

1 According to Reich (1987), political culture is permeated by 'myth-based morality tales' (p. 6) that frame the debate over public problems: they shape how both problems and solutions are viewed. And the most important aspect of political discourse may be defining the problems themselves.

2 See, e.g., Crozier *et al.* (1975), Staub (1980), Olson (1982), and Cloud (1989). For a survey of such literature, see Kennedy (1990).

3 Titles include *The End of the American Century* (Stephen Schlossstein); *Can America Compete?* (Robert Z. Lawrence); and *The Overburdened Economy* (Lloyd J. Dumas). A second wave of books focused on answers to these problems. These include *The Myth of America's Decline: Leading the World Economy into the 1990s* (Henry R. Nau); *America's Economic Resurgence: A Bold New Strategy* (Richard Rosecrance); *Peril and Promise: A Commentary on America* (John Chancellor); and, *Bound to Lead: The Changing Nature of American Power* (Joseph S. Nye, Jr.).

4 I do not wish to pick on a publication which serves an invaluable educational purpose and which is intended not as a critical review but as a practical source of information for elected and administrative officials and public conflict resolution practitioners. *Consensus* is not alone in this depiction; however, as the only periodical devoted to public conflict resolution it is representative of much of the field's thinking.

5 Crozier *et al.* (1975) articulate the issue: 'political competition essential to democracy has intensified, leading to a disaggregation of interests and the decline and fragmentation of political parties' (p. 161).

6 See Forester (1991) for an assessment of the language of promotional material of public conflict resolution organizations.

7 Raiffa (1982) has had the most influence upon the conflict resolution field. See also Nagel and Mills (1991).

8 Settlement, in Cormick's (1982) words, occurs 'when the parties find a mutually acceptable basis for disposing of the issues in which they are in disagreement, despite their continuing differences over basic values' (p. 3).

9 See, e.g., Rodwin (1982), Fiss (1984), Amy (1987), and Ellison (1991).

Part III

Developing a
transformative practice

9

The challenge for a
transformative practice

Challenging the 'crisis of governance'

The construction of a legitimate, effective and transformative practice of
public conflict resolution begins with a challenge to the assumptions underlying the ideology of management. The 'crisis of governance' as presented
within that ideology is an unconvincing and indefensible representation of
the problems of contemporary democratic society. Recall the three themes
of this problem:

1   the decline of the United States relative both to its own, halcyon past as
    well as new international competition;
2   disengagement of an uninvolved and apathetic citizenry;
3   the inability of government to govern: gridlock.

A different interpretation of each of these propositions is offered for consideration. These suggest a rejection of the prevailing conception of the 'crisis
of governance' as a superficial, incomplete, and ultimately unproductive
analysis.

Decline

The thesis of decline offered by the prolific literature on this subject depicts
democracies struggling against one another in international economic competition. Recall the terms used in this argument: 'more effort', 'greater
effort', 'new leadership', 'fresh purpose', and 'willpower'. What the men[1]
proffering this argument fail to recognize is the unquestioned, yet highly
debatable, presumption underlying this thesis: that achieving distinctions
such as highest per-capita income, or largest military, or fastest-growing
GNP are the desired (and only) benchmarks of greatness. Is the real problem how to get richer than others, or is it to become as good as is possible,
and better than now, in deficient areas such as homelessness, poverty, education, and crime (Stein, 1990)?

121

As for the wistful longing for a return to a less-troubled past, there are any number of vehicles available to rebut that illusory, if common, image of history. Societies, like individuals, tend to forget their past troubles in favor of their former triumphs. The United States has certainly always had its share of both. It is a striking, if unnerving, exercise to recall the actual record of civil strife in the United States. It includes:

> Native American uprisings, white settler–Indian conflict, and state violence against American Indians; farmer revolts, including the Wars of the Regulators, the War of the New Hampshire Grants, Shays Rebellion, and the Whiskey, Fries, and Green Corn Rebellions; civil strife associated with the American Revolution; slave revolts, white Southern rebellion, and civil disorders associated with the Civil War; the successful campaign of terrorism waged by white supremacist groups in the Reconstruction South; riots, lynchings, mob actions, and abuses of power connected with nativist–immigrant conflict; 60 years of intense labor-management violence; a century of racial conflict, ranging from lynchings and pogroms to intercommunal riots and anti-authority uprisings; civil strife associated with foreign wars; and state violence directed against ethnic, racial, and political minorities (Rubenstein, 1988: 5–6).

History provides a powerful rebuttal to consensus theory, which tells us that the latest rebellion or abuse of power was the last, and that current consensus is permanent (Rubenstein, 1988). The myth of a peaceful past proves to be little more than a nostalgic exercise of historical amnesia.

Gridlock

The 'gridlock' hypothesis articulated in the previous chapter has three components:

1 the erosion of government power, a product of the proliferation of single-issue groups, special interest politics, and the decline of authority;
2 administrative overregulation and incompetence; and,
3 judicial abuse and overload.

Erosion of power There are several objections to be made against these propositions. The first challenge to the gridlock hypothesis rejects the argument that the recent diffusion of power represents some sort of ominous regression to nihilism. Birnbaum (1986) offers an ironic and biting dissent to this view. He suggests that 'The proliferation and fragmentation of issues has produced a literature on the difficulties, if not the demise, of democracy – by which these critics mean, the recalcitrance of modern populations to treat elites with deference and to take their orders' (p. 35).

The argument that citizen participation groups such as grassroots, public-interest, consumer, and voluntary service organizations are primarily negative and obstructionist is another mythical embellishment of the facts

(Langton, 1978a). Yes, some of these groups are decidedly parochial, disruptive, fickle, antagonistic and adversarial. But the onus for this behavior falls at least in part on the failure of the institutions of governance to recognize their standing, to invite their participation, and to address their concerns. And many of these oppositional groups, often labeled with derogatory terms such as 'NIMBY' (Not In My Back Yard), in fact provide a vehicle for bringing individuals into the democratic process. Indeed, one public conflict resolution practitioner uses the spelling 'NIMBI' rather than 'NIMBY': 'Now I Must Become Involved' (Richard Collins, personal discussion).

Furthermore, there is a significant distinction between those groups representing a narrow (and generally economic) self-interest, which coalesce around a single issue only to disband, and broad-based and lasting movements, including consumer, environmental, peace, and women's rights. As Birnbaum (1986) notes, these broad-based movements offer 'complex approaches to complex questions, not symbolic reduction of complexity' (p. 35).

Indeed, independent organizations are essential to a healthy democracy. Among other virtues, they help avoid domination by a select few. And it is as well to remember that the only alternative to significant public participation in public issues, and the disarray which participation necessarily brings, is a hierarchy which invites domination by those who control the state (Dahl, 1982).

Overregulation   The 'overregulation' theme is a familiar one. A faceless bureaucracy and anonymous rulebooks are easy targets for scorn.

There is no argument with the empirical observation that contemporary society faces increasing influence and intervention by the state. And administrative procedures are clumsy, time consuming, expensive, and often ineffective. Yet is the prevalent interpretation of this reality accurate – that regulations themselves, rather than the behaviors which led to the imposition of the regulations, are the sole locus of the problem?

There are good regulations and there are bad ones, and there are perhaps undesired effects from good ones and positive effects from the bad. Another depiction of the problems of the bureaucratic state will be offered in a later section. Suffice it to say here that responsibility for the expanding role of federal, state, and local regulation may be shared by those who are responsible for the Thalidomide babies, the Love Canals, the Exxon Valdez's, the leaking silicone implants, and the many other abuses to the environment and the human beings who inhabit it.

Judicial abuse and overload   The theme of judicial abuse and overload is indeed a partial truth (Nader, undated). The decades when public conflict resolution was first being developed certainly saw an increase in the trappings of litigation. The number of cases filed in federal courts increased 80 percent between 1960 and 1975 (Ford Foundation, 1978). In the 1970s civil suits in federal courts rose 55.3 percent, the number of lawyers 52.6 percent, pages in the Federal Register 344.2 percent, from under 45,000 pages/year to 90,000 in the four-year Carter administration alone ('Commerce Department Federal Courts Management Statistics', in Brookes, 1991). The United States in 1991 had 70 percent of the world's lawyers serving 5 percent of the world's population (Brookes, 1991).

But those offering this complaint are often the most powerful members of society, who are also most threatened by judicial intervention. Reform groups which turn to the legal system do so because they do not have the political and economic power or administrative connections of those who do not need the courts (Handler, 1988). And, in fact, the empirical evidence does not fully support these claims of a system at breaking point. In a seminal article by Galanter (1983), comparison of past and current levels of litigation show present levels which were not historically unprecedented. The fact is that only a small proportion of troubles and injuries develop into disputes, that a similarly small proportion of these disputes are litigated, and that the 'vast majority' conclude before full adjudication.

Galanter provides an alternative explanation for this sense of litigiousness which pervades our culture. He contends that it is a product of increasing sensitivity to disputing and the various formal means (legislative, administrative, and judicial) of processing disputes. He suggests that 'contemporary patterns of disputing should be seen as a relatively conservative adaptation to changing conditions, including, for example, changes in the production of injuries, knowledge about them, education, and so forth' (Galanter, 1983: 5). While his argument is not entirely convincing – after all, the emergence of the field of conflict resolution owes a great deal to the disenchantment of members of the legal system – it does temper somewhat the distortion brought by disaffection for the judicial system. At the least, these 'elite perceptions of an eruption of pathological litigiousness' (p. 5) do point to the weaknesses of legal scholarship.

The argument of judicial overload can mask the greater significance of the increased litigiousness. The most important issue is how this dependence on the courts demonstrates evidence of increased polarization within communities, an increased sense of individual grievance, and the inability of traditional mediating institutions to resolve these differences peacefully and fairly.

An apathetic citizenry

Nobody argues with one portion of the thesis of an apathetic citizenry – the disaffection of citizens with the institutions of governance. This disaffection is continually reflected by the relatively low voter turnout in all but the most hotly contested elections. However, there is a strong counterargument to this thesis: voter turnout is not necessarily a good indicator of citizen interest, or even involvement (*Citizens and Politics*, 1991).

Low voter turnout disguises the extraordinary growth of an active core of citizenry, those who follow the news and who get involved in political campaigns (Walker, 1988). There is, in fact, what Langton (1978a: 1) calls a 'passivity-participation syndrome', the paradox by which alienation and mistrust are accompanied at the same time by an explosive growth of citizen and public interest organizations. There is a critical difference between apathy and a sense of impotence of a citizenry which wants to participate but often cannot (*Citizens and Politics*, 1991). Citizens become engaged in the areas of public life in which they believe that they make a difference.

The problems of the democratic public domain: The real crisis of governance

If the ideology of management is derived from unfounded premises – in particular, if the account of problems the public conflict resolution field is supposed to manage, the 'crisis of governance', is suspect – what better explanation of these problems is available?

There is indeed what may be termed a crisis of governance; witness the problems articulated in Chapters One and Two. But this crisis does not follow from the decline of centralized power, or the demands of aggrieved citizens, or from political gridlock. These are not causes but symptoms of the ineffectiveness of public institutions and practices. These problems cannot be solved by individuals alone. They cannot be solved by legislation and enforcement alone. They cannot be solved by the agencies of government alone. They require collaboration by many diverse groups of people, a collaboration which can only occur in a civic arena where people care about one another. They require legitimized institutions of governance which invite real and effective public participation. And they require individuals working to achieve justice and solve problems rather than to demand entitlement and conquer their opponents.

I will argue that a real crisis of governance is manifested in three key areas. These are as represented in Chapter One:

1 the disintegration of community and of the relationships and meaning found in community life;
2 alienation from the institutions and practices of governance;
3 the inability to solve public problems and resolve public conflicts.

I do not pretend that these three elements are the sources of all contemporary problems, or that they are exhaustive of all plaints about the public domain. Just as no single practice, whether it be science, public administration, social movements, planning, Marxism, capitalism, democracy, or, for that matter, conflict resolution, can address all difficulties, neither is any single critique of democratic society sufficient. There is not available the luxury of reducing the meaning of society and its governing institutions to one or two primary variables, whether they be the state, class structure, gender relations, economics, language, freedom, or human needs.

I am willing to argue, however, that any democratic society which aspires to develop and sustain itself must develop the capacity to address these challenges, and that the ability to deal with the most serious and persistent social problems, whatever their sources, depends on the response to these challenges.

While these elements are closely tied to one another, for analytical purposes they will be considered in turn.

Disintegration of community and civic life

The meaning of community and civic life   Tocqueville (1969) was the first, and remains the best known, of the many observers who have linked the prosperity and vitality of democracy to community and civic life. As he noted, democracy depends not only upon the strength of its formal institutions but upon the communal and civic ties among its people: 'Amongst the laws which rule human societies there is one which seems to be more precise and clear than all the others. If men are to remain civilized, or to become so, the art of associating together must grow and improve, in the same ration in which the equality of condition is increased' (vol. 1, 2nd book, ch. 5).

Persistent social, economic and physical problems, such as destructive poverty, violence, and environmental degradation, are unequivocally tied to such intangibles as community, affiliation, and compassion, the basic elements of social capital (Putnam, 1993a; 1993b). It is impossible to deal with these problems without addressing those intangibles, within the family, community, place of work, and society at large (Waskow, 1990).

But there is very little of public policy which acknowledges the need to strengthen community or compassion (Waskow, 1990). And many of the dominant social forces particular to contemporary life undermine community. The same extraordinary mobility of the population which allows individuals to seek work and housing also makes for a transient population with little stake in long-term thinking, planning and action. Unprecedented accessibility for a significant portion of the population to a house and plot of land has also meant ugly suburban sprawl, traffic congestion, poisonous air, and the segregation of work and home and market. Roads which maximize individual freedom of transportation at the same time divide long-standing communities. The communication revolution which offers unprecedented access to information and which allows easy and inexpensive communication across vast physical distances also means that more and more people find work and entertainment in physical isolation from one another.

Part of the responsibility for this state of affairs rests on the giant economic and political bureaucracies which dominate society. The lives of individuals and their communities have become dominated by decisions made outside their dominion (Birnbaum, 1986). While contributing to efficiencies of scale, these top-down systems encroach upon the community humans need (Clark, 1989). Clark (1989) detects a direct link between competitive materialism, increasing alienation, and shattered social cohesiveness. She suggests that there are three interacting primary components of a culture: material culture, which depends directly on the ecosystem; social culture, the culture of kinship and family groupings and political and economic arrangements; and the sacred or ideological culture, the belief systems and myths which give lives meaning. These components are interdependent. Yet short-sighted thinking and planning ensures that the importance of cultural integrity and its accompanying social stability are ignored.

The consequence of the dissipation of community and the devaluation of relationship is far more serious than individual alienation. When social bonds are threatened the result is violence. When the bonds disappear, the violence becomes institutionalized (Clark, 1989) and nihilism ensues (West, 1993).

Social change movements have been slow to recognize this. Lerner (1990) argues that advocates for such change are isolated and confused in part because they do not recognize that society suffers from more than mere economic or physical problems. There is a moral and spiritual environment whose health is essential to the development of human life. The destruction of this environment appears as personal failures: failure to find work, failure to maintain relationships, failure to develop nurturing families. Attention is diverted from the political to the individual realms, and the weight of these larger social processes falls upon local communities and families. But these traditional mediating institutions are no longer embedded in larger communities of meaning, and they cannot shoulder the burden of providing life's meaning.

Lerner became a casualty of partisan political competition after Hillary Rodham Clinton endorsed his call for a 'politics of meaning'. Lerner's proposal was derided by some as a typically soft liberal response to times which require tough talk and hard choices. But while the term 'politics of meaning' may not endure, the principles which underlie this concept are timeless. And they are, in fact, not inconsistent at all with needs recognized by observers across the political spectrum. Thoughtful communitarians (Etzioni, 1991; 1993), politicians (Kemmis, 1990), advocates for social justice (West, 1993; Lappé and DuBois, 1994), children's advocates (Edelman, 1992), academics (Bellah *et al.*, 1985; 1991), and many others return again and again to the same themes: the pressures of contemporary life have diminished values essential to sustaining civil society, values such as caring, trust, honesty, tolerance, and cooperation. Without these values there can be no sense of community, no understanding of the common good, no viable public life at all. And these values can only be inculcated in relationships: with one another, with community, with place.

Indeed, it is a testament to the importance of community life that individuals persist in finding the time, place, and interest to come together as much as is done. Schools, churches, sports, Scouts, as well as political, social and civic organizations continue to flourish in many places despite the obstacles they confront. But there are other places where these institutions have little strength. And there are many places where they serve more to accentuate divisions such as class, race, and gender than to bridge those differences.

The distortion of public discourse   In democratic society public life is at once fragile and volatile. It is periodically threatened by events such as the beating of Rodney King and the subsequent responses, by the deceit of public figures, and by the aggrandization of self-interest. It is continually reaffirmed by innumerable daily acts of virtue and responsibility. And the quality of public discourse is a good gauge of its health, of community and civic viability.

The elements of discourse – language, speech, listening, audience – play powerful roles in constructing social relations. Indeed, postmodern theorists such as Foucault (1986) argue that power is enacted through discourse, through 'localized transactions' (Gordon, 1988: 6) in which one group dominates another.[2] Thus, the lives of citizens in industrial societies are shaped by systematically manipulated communications (Forester, 1985). Some argue that in situations of unequal power discourse is necessarily distorted; other theorists see that such power may be productive as well as repressive (Fraser, 1989). While everyone is subject to this form of domination, everyone is also potentially an 'agent of liberation' (Gordon, 1988: 6).

One does not need to accept this analysis to acknowledge the deep problems with contemporary public discourse. There exists great dissatisfaction with the status of speech. At the same time, however, such contributors to its demise as polemical radio talk shows and deceptive political attack ads are more successful than ever.

A Kettering Foundation survey of citizens found complaints about a 'public discourse that remains cast within narrowly defined boundaries, where rhetoric can easily get out of hand and make the situation seem hopeless, and where the very nature of the debate closes off independent thinking' (*Citizens and Politics*, 1991: 2–3). Citizens complained about how most public issues are discussed by leaders, the media, and others such that they 'neither connect with the concerns of citizens nor make any sense to them' (p. 4). Because of the breakdown of political discourse, 'a bond of trust has been broken, a relationship perilously near to being severed' (p. 33).

Consider the spate of a certain type of political talk show which currently dominates the airwaves. The hosts make little pretense of objectivity. They rarely allow opposing opinions a voice. Their interpretations of events are filtered through lenses of suspicion and distrust; the actions taken by those they oppose are always motivated by ill-considered thinking and corrupt, deceitful, and immoral purposes. They substitute labels for analysis, sensationalism for consideration.

These shows have other, more invidious faults. They play on disaffection with private circumstances by blaming all social ills on monoliths of conspiratorial power, a power directed at the radio listeners. They view disagreement as obstructionism, personal failing, and moral weakness, instead of as an opportuniy to learn, to expand options, to involve, and to educate. They justify behavior by the right to exercise that behavior, a message which denies responsibility for the consequences of one's actions. They divide the world into two camps, those who are with them and those who are against them, shutting out any possibility for other voices and other views. They appeal to selfishness, to suspicion, to prejudice, to over-simplification, to meanness, to ignorance.

The strongest message conveyed by these shows is not in the substantive positions taken about issues such as welfare, health care, and other public issues. Their chief message is conveyed in the way they portray those who disagree with their views. Labeling (e.g. 'feminazis', 'liberals', the 'Christian right') and polarizing dehumanizes the opposition with this message: 'People are either for me or against me. Those who are against me are not like you and me. They are less than real humans. Since they are less than real humans, they are not worthy of any respect. Since they are not worthy of respect, we can speak of them and treat them as we desire. It is more than okay to do this: it is necessary to advance our cause'.

The impact of this distorted discourse begins with determination of the political agenda, an agenda dominated by 'issues' more than actual problems, an agenda limited by a narrowly defined range of potential solutions. This agenda is hardly reflective of an informed public debate. Along these same lines, the press as a medium of public dialogue has become the mass media. And the media dependency upon sound bites and negativism mutates citizens' interactions with public officials (*Citizens and Politics*, 1991). Media manipulation of mass consciousness proves individual freedom an 'illusion of choice within a reality of compulsion' (Lerner, 1990: 75).

Why is this the case? Much of public discourse is shaped by reliance on the Anglo-American adversary system. This system encourages speaking and penalizes listening (Barber, 1984). The goal of adversarial proceedings is not to develop understanding, not to find constructive solutions, and not even to discover the truth. The goal of speech in these situations is to win. Indeed, in adversarial systems, Barber (1984) claims, speech is another species of aggression and power.

A last offense to public discourse can be attributed to the reduction of policymaking to questions of yeah or nay. For many people democracy means voting. But majority rules implies that a ready-made agenda exists, when in fact there is none. And the secrecy of the vote, while protecting individuals from intimidation and thus enhancing freedom of choice, eliminates the need to justify our vote to others or ourselves and thus think publicly (Barber, 1984).

Alienation of citizenry from the institutions and practices of governance
The second major challenge of contemporary democratic society is the extraordinary alienation of citizenry from the institutions and practice of governance. Three main sources of alienation are closely tied to the disintegration of community and civic life. These sources are:

1   the mistrust of the political process and the public realm;
2   domination by the bureaucratic welfare state; and,
3   inadequate vehicles for authentic and effective public participation.

Mistrust: why citizens hate politics   We did not need the 1994 American congressional elections to recognize what the electoral process confirmed: a deep hatred for politics. As the humorist Ian Shoales observes, 'If there's not a twelve-step program for believers in the political system, there surely ought to be. Or at the very least, free brain scans'.[3]

Two sympathetic studies explain why this is so. They suggest that the appearance of political apathy has nothing to do with a disinterest in public life. Dionne (1991) argues that there is good reason why the quality of involvement in democratic institutions has declined over the past three decades: there is little encouragement from existing political institutions that public engagement is worthwhile. A society which no longer supports community or common purpose has resulted in a flight from public life. People have fewer common activities and feel fewer obligations towards others as divides, such as those between blacks and whites, grow wider.

Dionne traces these failings to the dominant ideologies of conservatism and liberalism, and the cultural civil war between the two which is the legacy of the 1960s. Both conservatism and liberalism, he claims, serve upper-middle-class interests. Reformers of both left and right argue morality, communism, imperialism and abstract personal rights, ignoring the economics which matter most to people and the needs of basic governmental institutions such as schools, transportation, and criminal justice. In effect, politics has little to do with what really matters.

Why is this so? Instead of a politics of deliberative processes, public arguments, and persuasion, there is an insider industry of fundraising, polling, media relations, advertising. Instead of problems, there are issues – instruments to divide the populace and advance insider interests. Instead of honor of public service, there is notoriety. Even success often leaves not a sense of accomplishment but a determination never to get involved again. Involvement in public interest can be very costly, both literally and personally, for those fighting its battles. As Kemmis (1990) observes, the political system leads people to pursue their visions in ways which alienate people from public life entirely.

The Kettering Foundation ('Citizens and Politics', 1991) released a study which reports the results of a series of focus groups of ordinary citizens held throughout the United States. According to this report, citizens feel disconnected from the political process in three areas: how the political agenda is set, how policy issues are framed, and how they are debated. The study reports that the political system is perceived as being run by an oligarchy of professional politicians, special interest groups, political action committees, media, and lobbyists. Politics is viewed as a kind of disease people don't want to get near to. The major forces that dominate politics, such as special interests, negative campaigning, and political action committees, reward the pursuit of self-interest and ignore or even punish those working for the common good.

This report debunks the conventional wisdom of an apathetic public; indeed, it characterizes that conventional wisdom, and how it writes off a sizeable portion of citizenry, as part of the problem with politics. The public is decidedly not apathetic; rather, citizens feel impotent concerning politics. They simply do not feel that they make a difference.

Domination by the bureaucratic state   In examining the socio-political dimensions of the public domain which gave birth to public conflict resolution, it was made clear that the institutions of governance – legislative, administrative, and judicial – were unable to deal with the changing demands placed upon them. This failure is a key element within the ideology of management. But the reasons offered by the management ideology for the inadequacies of the institutions of governance have more to do with inefficiencies of decision-making than with their impacts upon human lives.

As the size and influence of government has increased, the role of citizen has given way to that of dependent client of the state (Luke and White, 1985). In this form, the bureaucratic nation state stands as a dominating agent of moral impoverishment (Wolfe, 1989). The development of contemporary political and economic arrangements has damaged the civil society of autonomous families, voluntary associations, religious communities, and neighborhoods. Strong moral ties are abandoned in favor of weaker ones; lives are dominated by routines untied to any sense of moral conviction; no longer are there truly autonomous individuals.

New rights and social insurance, while providing for the immediate satisfaction of basic needs, endanger freedom by making clients dependent upon the bureaucracies constituted to administer them. This dependency, what Habermas (1987) refers to as 'internal colonization by the legal-bureaucratic systems' (in Handler, 1988: 1045), removes from these individuals their own capacity to interpret their lives and needs (Fraser, 1989).

Barber's (1984) discourse about the relationship between citizenship and governance explains the paradox of a citizenry so dependent upon the state while at the same time independent of civic obligations:

> When the citizenry is a watchdog that waits with millennial patience for its government to make a false move but that submits passively to all other legitimate governmental activity, citizenship very quickly deteriorates into a latent function. Civic virtue remains, but it is a civic virtue that is defined by reciprocal control or *accountability*. Government is responsible to and for the body of citizens but is in no way comprised of that body (p. 220).

Inadequate authentic public participation   One of the conundrums of any representative democracy is the structural antipathy between representation and participation. Representation can serve both efficiency and accountability, but it does so at an enormous cost to citizenship (Barber, 1984). Representation can be disempowering of individual initiative. It takes from individuals responsibility for their behavior (Barber, 1984). Tocqueville himself warned that a citizenry which relies on representation tends to judge public affairs by how they meet their private economic interests (Schroyer, 1985).

Thus a representative democracy cannot rely on representation alone. But the institutions of governance – executive, legislative, and even judicial – have little skill, and generally less interest, in enhancing citizen participation. Consider some of the common ways public officials respond to controversy. One immediate response is to keep information confidential, with the hope that they can limit the impact of the controversy. But when information is limited or slow to be revealed, the assumption of the public is not that officials know best, but that they are hiding something that will make them look bad. Constraints on information create confusion, contribute to uncertainty, and exacerbate any previous suspicion and antagonism individuals or groups might have about an organization. An organization which becomes known for not responding to requests for information and for discouraging public access to its records and meetings will have no legitimacy when it makes mistakes or deals with truly confidential issues.

Too often organizations wishing to avoid controversy delay opportunities for involvement until those affected by proposed plans have no recourse other than protest (Potapchuk, 1991b). Certainly, decisions often need to be made in timely fashion, not only to meet legislative, administrative, funding, or other deadlines, but to address problems promptly and to deal with issues when people and organizations are most willing to be engaged. But early deadlines and time limits can heighten uncertainty and increase suspicion about the motivations of parties responsible for those time constraints. Such suspicion is heightened when an issue is controversial and/or the organization has a reputation for imposing unreasonable time pressures.

All too often the first time citizens hear of an action which will affect them is when such action is already initiated or even confirmed. Officials often will propose a plan of action or a limited number of options in order to get discussion started. But a public presented with a single solution or a limited range of options often assumes that their input is not wanted or valued. Exclusion of individuals or groups from decision-making processes not only gives an impression of secrecy and fosters a sense of victimization, it wastes the potential ideas and support that those who are excluded from the process might bring.

When public institutions receive criticism, a standard response is to characterize it as misunderstanding or obstructionist. All too often, the next step is to label and demonize the opposition. It is rare to find an official who can acknowledge the meaning and importance of an issue to individuals or groups voicing concern. Such behaviors may be made with good intention. But public officials and organizations which practice consistently these arts of secrecy, defensiveness, rationalization, and animosity will destroy their personal and institutional legitimacy.

Arnstein's (1969) classic 'ladder of citizen participation' presents a typology based on citizens' power in determining government plans and/or programs. She suggests three categories of participation. 'Nonparticipation' ranges from manipulation to therapy; 'degrees of tokenism' includes informing, consultation, and placation; 'degrees of citizen power' range from partnership, to delegated power, to citizen control. Participation is only a 'new Mickey Mouse game' for have-nots if control is offered without sufficient resources to accomplish what is needed (p. 224). Without real distribution of power, participation is an empty exercise in frustration.

Even the public hearing, a bulwark of democratic participation, is not free from problems. Public inquiries may be biased and inegalitarian, and actually distort communication and legitimize actions and interests of already dominant groups (Kemp, 1985). The Kettering study *Citizens and Politics* (1991) notes that citizens believe that current vehicles for participation, such as hearings or public surveys, are designed to tell them what is going to happen, not to ask them what should happen.

Inability to solve public problems and resolve public conflicts

Strong community and civic ties and legitimate participatory practices of governance are necessary, but insufficient, preconditions for sustaining democratic society. For conflict is a natural part of the human existence, even (and sometimes especially) in the closest communities. And the unmitigated effects of severe conflict can break even the strongest social fabric.

The ability to resolve conflict productively requires understanding of the nature, sources, and dynamics of disputes. And it requires an understanding of why the predominant vehicles used today for settling disputes – power and rights – are unsuitable, and how even the alternative to power and rights proffered by the conflict resolution field – the mutual satisfaction of interests – is itself inadequate to the task of resolving public conflict.

The theory of conflicts in question   The previous chapter described the 'management' conception of disputes and disputing, a conception heavily influenced by the methodologies of game theory. This conception was challenged as long ago as 1976 by the social psychologists Apfelbaum and Lubek. They were among the first to describe how the field of conflict research, by accepting certain basic assumptions about conflict, marginalizes other, more important, issues. The thrust of their argument, an argument still relevant today, is that the theory of conflict which dominated the research of the late 1950s persisted beyond the point where the theory was viable. The preoccupations of the time, during which concerns over the Cold War overshadowed all such research and conflict theorizing, superimposed upon the research a time-locked paradigm which did not keep abreast of actual conflicts.

Apfelbaum and Lubek suggest that two factors were responsible for the contemporary conception of conflict. The first of these was the socio-historical-political climate of the 1950s, a climate dominated by the spectre of two superpowers, equally armed, equally distrustful, and each desirous to win. The second factor was the development of a new social science research tool. Game theory, then gaining a foothold in a number of areas of social science, appealed to social psychologists seeking a formalization suitable for the experimental laboratory.

The focus of research and theorizing then was upon *conflicts of interests*. The task of the research was to find ways to achieve a satisfactory division of resources between protagonists with similar interests. This concentration on conflicts of interests misleadingly reduces the many complexities of human behavior to one single component of that behavior: the drive to maximize individual gains.

There are two adverse consequences to this over-simplification of behavior. The first is that a false parity is assumed to exist between conflicting parties. Conflicts among parties with significant differences in resources either are obscured or it is presumed that there are no differences in values and goals of the opponents.

A second consequence is that by focusing on the 'final confrontation', conflicts are narrowly defined as time-locked rather than being seen as dynamic processes of evolving goals, strategies, and confrontations. The effects of choices of goals and means used to reach those goals, as well as the relationship itself, are ignored. The strong implication of this theorizing is that conflicts can be ended if the right strategic solution is found. Solutions based upon this narrow conception of conflict deny the sources of the conflict and the effects of those sources on its development. And, while important elements generic to all conflicts are rightly identified, equally important differences are discounted. The questions of conflict as vehicle of social change, of its functions, and of its place within society, are ignored.

Unsustainable vehicles for settling conflict: Power, rights, and interests The concept of 'sustainability' of ecological, economic, and social systems garnered much support among environmentalists and others during the 1980s and early 1990s (Stein, 1991). For example, Daly and Cobb (1989) propose a quality-of-life substitute for the Gross National Product, the 'Index of sustainable welfare', one component of their work towards a 'sustainable future'. The Worldwatch Institute and World Resources Institute works towards 'sustainable development' (Anderson, 1990). The Public Disputes Network publication *Consensus* even describes the use of conflict resolution procedures in Canada, 'Provincial Roundtables', to assist in strategizing for sustainable development ('Canadians take up the challenge', 1990).

There is possible a new application of the term, an application which, as conflict theory advances in its understanding of the requirements for resolution, makes both practical and moral sense. This new conception may be termed *sustainability of human relations*: the capacity to resolve conflicts in ways that allow individuals and communities to maintain relationships and to find not only common ground but new and higher ground. The framework for this application for the concept of sustainability uses as a starting point one of the most influential works for practitioners in the conflict resolution field, *Getting Disputes Resolved* (Ury et al., 1988). The authors suggest that there are basically three ways of dealing with disputes: by application of power; by determining who is right; and by reconciling underlying interests. I argue that, while the triad of power, rights, and interests provides a useful conceptual framework, they are ultimately unsustainable ways for settling disputes.

Power The power-based methods of settling disputes are familiar. These range from the fairly trivial – a bully taking the lunch money away from a less combative schoolmate – to the global – a nation state imposing its will upon a neighbor. In many circumstances this is to be expected and, indeed, the world would not work very well without legitimate exercise of power. A traffic policeman ought not to ask motorists their preferences about who should precede whom in an intersection.

But there is enough truth in Lord Acton's maxim, 'power corrupts, and absolute power corrupts absolutely' to recognize how easily power lends itself to abuse. Indeed, at least one theorist presents a credible argument that power over others is the most significant cause of crime and violence. Pepinsky (1991) declares that theories of control, opportunity and deterrence together suggest that individuals who victimize the most are those with command of the greatest resources and with the capacity to avoid detection and punishment.

It also appears, with support from both empirical evidence and needs theory, that authority maintained by coercion is ultimately untenable. If human needs theorists (Burton, 1990; Sites, 1973) are correct, people have needs which must be satisfied and which cannot be suppressed. These needs include identity, both individual and collective; security, for themselves and their loved ones; and recognition, of themselves and their communities.

The dissolution of post World War II Eastern Europe and post World War I Soviet Union serves to illustrate this principle. The authoritarian governments of that era maintained control of their populations in great part through force and the threat of force. As needs theory would predict, the consequences of those decades of repression are now being realized, as ethnic and national identities unleashed after years of forced containment are finding their expression through political violence.

Thus the unlegitimized exercise of power may be thought of as an ultimately unsustainable means of maintaining human relations.

Rights How do people protect themselves from the abuses of power which characterize so much of human relations? In contemporary democratic society, power is supposed to be mitigated by an established system of rights. These rights allow for various individual freedoms: of religion, of the press, and of speech. They protect individuals and their private property from theft and from assault. And they give a vehicle, through adjudication or arbitration, for making decisions when people disagree and interests clash.

The political system itself, Ury *et al.* (1988) note, is in many ways a large, rights-based dispute resolution system. It is a system devised to replace 'high-cost contests' (p. 170), including violence, with such lower-cost contests as elections.

Auerbach (1983) observes that the shift from religious or secular authority to legal administration presumably was a step towards rationality and formal justice and away from dominance and social instability. But this vision of an 'inevitable, linear development' (p. 42) of progressive evolution too easily overlooks the adverse consequences of these changes. The more mundane of these problems of the legal rights revolution, such as expense and delay, are obvious. But other problems exist as well. Too often rights merely license abuses of power. An obvious, and powerful, reminder of that abuse is the legal segregation and apartheid which denied protection to blacks in the United States and South Africa, respectively.

As Legal Realism and its step-child the Critical Legal Studies movement have made clear, it is those who make the most use of legal rights who generally have their interests and perspectives reflected by these rights (Gordon, 1988). The categories and images of legal discourse tend to justify the existing social order as 'natural, necessary, and just' (Gordon, 1988: 16). While law does sometimes overlap and even coincide with justice, it is nonetheless essentially a condensed expression of social power, and the justice which does exist is most dependent upon those with that power (Levinson, 1989).

The Critical Legal Studies movement also demonstrates that the autonomy of the ideology of legal rights is incompatible with participation and community (Handler, 1988). Many legal rights in fact decimate relationships by imposing intimidating formality and unwieldy barriers to communication; they 'create zones of privacy and discretion' (Handler, 1988: 1037) which preclude ties of mutual responsibility. This framework of rights, held to by both social liberals and economic conservatives, leads to a 'procedural republic' (Kemmis, 1990) of due process, notice and hearing. Auerbach's (1983) indictment is telling:

> The legal process can be threatening, inaccessible, and exorbitant – usually it is all of these for the least powerful people in society. It is more likely to sustain domination than to equalize power. Litigation expresses a chilling, Hobbesian vision of human nature. It accentuates hostility, not trust. Selfishness supplants generosity. Truth is shaded by dissembling. Once an adversarial framework is in place, it supports competitive aggression to the exclusion of reciprocity and empathy (p. vii).

As he concludes, the shelter which law affords increases the very isolation which makes such shelter necessary. And it is thus apparent that dependency upon rights is also an unsustainable way of maintaining human relations.

Interests Ury et al. (1988) contend that the aim of conflict resolution has been to move away from dependency upon power and rights to their third means of resolving disputes, that of interests. First proposed by Mary Parker Follett (1918; 1930), the role of interests in dispute resolution has been popularized by Fisher and Ury (1981), who illustrated the principle of interests by repeating a story Follett related some fifty years earlier.

A woman was in a stuffy Harvard library reading room one day when she went to open a window to let in some air. Another patron of the library objected, declaring that there would be too much of a draft. The first individual probably did not have enough power to force the window open over someone's objection, and it is likely she had no right to do so, either. If she did have the power, or the right, perhaps she would have used either or both of them. But at what cost? She might have made such a commotion that she and the other patron would have been expelled from the library, or she might have made a new enemy, or she might not have liked the draft, either.

What she did, after some discussion with the objecting party, was go into a neighboring room, open a window, and keep a door between the two rooms open, so as to allow cooler air to enter her room without causing a draft. Thus, what these two people did was move beyond their positions – 'I want the window open' versus 'I want it shut' – to their interests – the need for fresh air, on the one hand, and the desire to avoid a draft on the other. And once they reached the level of interests, they were able to discover a solution that satisfied both of them.

Ury *et al.* (1988) are not suggesting that a turn to interests will eliminate the influence of power and rights. They acknowledge that interests are always constituted within the context of power and rights, and resolution of differences will always rely upon the balance of power and rights for some component of the resolution framework. But the goal of any system for resolving disputes, according to their argument, is to minimize the power and rights-based means for resolving disputes and maximize those based on interests.

The emphasis on interests as the basis for dispute resolution has been enormously influential within the public conflict resolution arena, as it has been within the larger conflict resolution field. The idea that parties in conflict with one another may find ways in which their own interests may be satisfied without denying those of others has been a powerful and useful inspiration to many. But a transformative practice of public conflict resolution demands more than the interest-based conception of dispute resolution can offer.

Disputes are not solely clashes of interests. They also involve struggles for recognition, identity, status, and other resources less tangible than are immediately apparent. Disputes are not fixed. They are instead socially constituted, dynamic organisms, whose actors, issues, and consequences are invariably shaped and transformed by the means available and used to contest them. If the crisis of governance is an inadequate representation of contemporary problems; if the individualistic conception of human nature is incorrect, and human beings are something greater than possessive individuals who come together to maximize self-interest; if governance is something besides the province of an elite, whose authority needs shoring in order to provide for that self-interest; then there is a need for more than another vehicle for satisfying self-interest.

Thus, like power and rights, reliance upon the mutual satisfaction of interests is ultimately also an unsustainable way of maintaining human relations. If disputes are more than diferences of interests, if their resolution requires more than a balance of power, rights, and interests, then other remedies must be developed.

Notes

1   As Kennedy (1990) points out, women are largely absent from this discussion.
2   This form of social control adopts the language of the helping professions to express state power in 'socio-legal concepts and understandings', rather than 'brute force or official punishment' (Harrington and Merry, 1988: 713).
3   In 'Funny Times', date unknown.

10

Philosophical foundations of a transformative practice

The legacy of modernity

The challenge to the vision of humanity, society, and governance offered by the ideology of management begins with a rethinking of modernity. As Friedmann (1989) notes, the philosophical antecedents of our age are found in the revolutionary changes of Western Europe of the late seventeenth and eighteenth centuries. Ushered in by philosophers such as Locke, Descartes, Rousseau, and Adam Smith, the Enlightenment offered the promise of a world which might be studied, understood and changed through the use of reason. That the world might be changeable and brought into accord with a universal Reason was an exhilarating promise: 'Old myths yielded to scientific understanding. Everyone had a capacity for reasoning. All institutions might be challenged as being "contrary to reason". Secular goals could be put forward and persistently pursued ... Progress was an imminent possibility' (p. 220).

The practical and material consequences of this promise were immense. The feudal order gave way to the institutions of modernity: empirical science, liberal democracy and industrial capitalism.[1] These institutions were to be the vehicles for the realization of the goals of individual happiness, fulfillment of material needs, and liberty.

In some ways, this project and promise have been realized. Empirical science, liberal democracy, and capitalism have brought much to be grateful for. For those to whom they are available, the miracles in areas such as medicine, transportation, energy production, agriculture, and information technology, allow a degree of health, mobility, productivity, and material wealth unimaginable only a few generations ago.

Yet it is clear to all but the most pollyanna-ish apologists of the status quo that, at the least, modernity has not yet fulfilled its promise. Indeed, while modernity is still lauded by some for its scientific prowess and economic prosperity, it is also argued that problems such as environmental destruction, totalitarianism, and general dehumanization are also intrinsic to the project (Kellner, 1989).

What has gone wrong with this promise? Three key institutional legacies of the project of modernity – empirical science, industrial capitalism, and liberal democracy – and their unanticipated progeny – the rites and doctrines of instrumental reason, market rationality, and possessive individualism – help answer this question. While these products have brought many valuable products to contemporary society, they also have contributed to the decline of public thinking and the impoverishment of civil and social life.

Empirical science and instrumental reason

Technology affords achievements ranging from the microchip to the space ship, advancements which extend human capabilities in ways not even dreamed of only generations ago. But accompanying these achievements has been the growth of a kind of instrumental reason, whereby the world is viewed as an object and knowledge as a tool. Three centuries of domination by the philosophy of empiricism has elevated instrumental reason and transformed Western civilization in ways never envisioned by its progenitors.

The institutionalization of scientific rationality offers a number of major 'pathological' consequences (Friedmann, 1989). Because of the single-minded pursuit of objectivized knowledge, schools and their curricula have been emptied of ethical content (Skolimowski, 1985). A value-vacuum has been created whose space is filled by the doctrines of 'objectivity' and 'efficiency', which have become the dominant values of contemporary Western society. Most problematic is how social repression is encouraged by the isolation of morality and ethics from abstracted knowledge. Instrumental reason provides for scientific rationales to justify existing social arrangements. The human being is either ignored or treated as another component of a functioning society (Murphy, 1989).

White and McSwain (1990) argue that within the context of abstracted knowledge, a context they term the 'technicist consciousness', human beings cannot discover the language of mutual values and shared knowledge which is necessary for discussing humankind's fate and destiny. Their highly relevant explanation is worth quoting:

> Such questions are not open within technicist consciousness because, in effect, it imposes on us a kind of artificial language, one that does not carry true meaning because it does not carry human sentiment. Language, as the primary organizing agent of sentiment, acquires this quality when it arises spontaneously from indigenous patterns of living together. As we increasingly substitute calculated technical routines for folkways, we begin to speak technically, communicate technically, and the direction of our lives comes to be set by technical necessity and opportunity, that is, by the requirements of the system rather than the people within it (White and McSwain, 1990: 36).

Market rationality

The collapse of communist authoritarian regimes in the Soviet Union and Eastern Europe in the early 1990s was a triumph for advocates of human rights and democratic government. Yet this change hardly validates all of contemporary capitalism, despite euphoric claims to the contrary. Indeed, with the bogeyman of communism no longer perpetually spooking any questioning of capitalism, and the future no longer simply a choice between two polarities of totalitarian communism and industrial capitalism, thoughtful critics of capitalism may finally gain some currency outside of leftist circles.[2]

The free market is a system in which goods and services are produced and distributed according to consumer demand, the profit–production–investment–profit cycle, rather than by a means for achieving various social values (Giddens, 1989). This system has proved to be an enormously productive means of creating wealth and fostering innovation and technical breakthroughs. But it has not been without its costs. Capitalism can be, and often is, criticized along three distinct lines: conditions in the workplace, including issues such as wages, authority, and health and safety; the extraordinary power of multi-national corporations and the consequences of trans-boundary movement of capital; and the privatism engendered by market economics, in which all differences become subsumed beneath the monolith of supply and demand (Friedmann, 1989). While the first two sets of criticisms are not unrelated to the themes of this work, it is the third set of issues which sustains the ideology of management.

Habermas[3] (1973; 1984) has carried this argument into the domain of relationships and communication. Habermas considers two types of action characteristic of human life. 'Purposive-rational action' is interaction with nature to produce the material means of subsistence. It involves manipulating nature and human beings as 'forces of production' to achieve certain goals (Hallin, 1985: 122). 'Communicative action' is the means by which humans interact and produce 'reciprocal expectation' in order to live socially (Hallin, 1985: 122). The difference between purposive-rational action and communicative action is drawn from Aristotle's distinction between techne – 'the skillful production of artifacts and the expert mastery of objectified tasks' – and praxis – 'action directed toward human education and the realization of human potential' (Habermas, 1973: 42).

There are thus two types of knowledge, technical and practical, corresponding to these two types of action. Capitalism, while developing the capacity for purposive-rational action beyond that of any previous social order, overextends that type of action and its corresponding discourse and knowledge into the realm of praxis. All issues then are framed in technical or strategic terms of producing given ends by the most effective means (Hallin, 1985). Within these constraints, society then cannot develop its capacity for communicative action to resolve questions of ends and standards of conduct.

Liberalism and the 'possessive individual'

Empirical science and capitalism found their political counterpart in the liberal democracy which arose as the cornerstone of this triad of modernity's institutions. Liberalism and its focus on individual rights played an important role in the challenge to the authoritarian institutions of feudalism and monarchy (Barber, 1988). Liberalism as 'dissent theory' created the 'ideology of emancipation' necessary for the development of the modern democratic state (Barber, 1988: 18).

Of course, the liberal project was never complete; nor was it ever universal. The liberty, equality, and fraternity promised by liberalism was limited by gender, by class, and by race from the beginning. Lerner (1990) explains that liberty 'was only the freedom of each person to pursue his or her own individual interests – and in a context in which previous inequalities could be passed on to the next generations'; equality was 'equality before the law – and the laws were written in the interests of the industrialists and bankers'; and fraternity was for men, 'allowed to perpetuate a personal feudalism in their own families by reigning over wives and children whose rights were severely curtailed in law and in fact' (p. 75).[4]

The fundamental premise of modern Western democracy has become the importance granted to the individual's right to freedom. Not only is it the most important social value; the prime function of the state has become the preservation of that right. And this is a locus of the problem: the pursuit of freedom to the point of license, and the exclusion of the values of community to the point of detachment. Barber (1984) argues that liberalism, more concerned with liberty and the advancement of interests than with justice and public goods, resists every assault on individual rights of privacy, property, and interests, but fails to provide for community, justice, citizenship, and participation. To the extent that social values such as constraint, commitment, responsibility, and tradition interfere with the individual's right to freedom, they are suspect (Clark, 1989).

The underlying conception of human nature engendered by this focus on individual rights was identified in Chapter Eight as the 'possessive individual'. In this view, people are seen as 'asocial, egoistic individuals whose fundamental motivation in acting is the satisfaction of their own interests' (Gould, 1988: 4). This conception of human nature is incapable of explaining behavior inconsistent with its premises, such as affection, altruism, and cooperation (Gould, 1988). Like contemporary economics, enthralled with man [sic] the maximizer of self-interest, this ideology cannot account adequately for sociality or cooperation. Indeed, this image acts, in effect, to legitimate selfishness and marginalize anything else.[5]

The veneration of individual liberty and subsequent devaluation of economic, social, and personal activities, countenances and justifies extreme economic and social inequalities (Gould, 1988). Because of this emphasis on individual liberty these other activities are viewed as private, not public, matters, and thus excluded from the political sphere. In the battle against a hierarchical and oppressive order, the idea of a solitary individual may have been helpful.

> But it may appear as an obstructive exercise in nostalgia in an era when the extent and quality of citizenship are in question and when the bonds that hold together free communities are growing slack. For centuries, there was a need to stake out a circumscribed private ground in an otherwise statist, mercantilist, all-too-public world. In our own day, the need would seem to be to identify and fence in some small public space in an individualistic, anomic, all-too-privatized world (Barber, 1988: 13, 19).

It is a perspective which does not know it is a perspective, a worldview which admits no other possibilities, a vision which fears enslavement of the individual if not accepted in its totality.

Reconstituting modernity: Acknowledging our heritage

Yet this all-or-nothing choice is neither a historical nor a practical necessity.[6] And despite these criticisms, there are important elements in the traditions of science, in the suitability of the market, and in the protection of individual rights found in liberalism's legal-political order, that are worth maintaining for ourselves and future generations.[7] It is not the destruction of modernity, but its redefinition and redirection, that is necessary (Friedmann, 1989).

This revision faces numerous obstacles, not the least of which is resistance to ideas which challenge long-established beliefs. Many on the right are suspicious of any new thinking which hints of criticism of the icons of democracy and capitalism, a criticism they associate with a Marxism equivalent to the communism of Mao, Castro, and Stalinists. And many on the left have traditionally seen the institutions of modernity only as instruments for the perpetuation of the status quo (Boyte and Evans, 1986); indeed, the generation of radicals who came of age in the 1960s defined themselves by their opposition to the liberal past (Zaretsky, 1988). For them, the very notion of progress means attacking traditional identities (Boyte and Evans, 1986).

Yet this revision is essential. The vast majority of thought which informs contemporary institutions and practices, whether on the left or the right, has its origins in the world of the eighteenth and nineteenth centuries, a world far removed from contemporary society. As Dahl (1982) observes, the powerful ideologies of this age, including liberalism, conservatism, capital-

144

ism, socialism, Marxism, and democratic ideas, 'all face a world that in its form and thrust confounds the crucial assumptions, requirements, descriptions, predictions, hopes, or prescriptions they express' (p. 3). This thought cannot sustain the world today.

What it means to be human: The individual as social being

The search for a social ontology

At the base of the reconstitution of modernity and the challenge to the ideology of management is a reconsideration of what it is to be human. The bounded parody of what it means to be human which dominates economic, political, and social thought and practice – the possessive individual – is unacceptable not because it is undesirable, but because it is inaccurate. This perspective of what individualism means fails to acknowledge the roles community or relationship play in constituting human nature, in shaping human behavior, and in fulfilling human needs. In broadest terms, any conception of the human being must acknowledge that there is no individual identity absent relationship. As Clark (1989) declares, human beings, *'above all else*, are bonded social beings' (p. 23).

This search for a 'social ontology' (Gould, 1988) is hardly new. There has always been a social dimension to liberalism, including philosophers such as Spinoza, Hume and Rousseau, who argued that humans are essentially social beings (Zaretsky, 1988). But the social dimension of human nature has been obscured by the liberal effort towards removing the bonds of feudalism and liberating the general population from hierarchy and oppression (Barber, 1988). It was assaulted by social Darwinism, which became an apology for late nineteenth century imperialism and the worst excesses of industrial capitalism. And it has finally been eclipsed by the prevailing neo-Madisonian perspective on human nature, politics, and society and its accompanying values of selfishness, materialism, competitiveness, and natural inequality.

A number of social and political theorists have tied this 'new person' to contemporary democratic theory. Four dimensions of this reconceptualized human nature are key.

First, humans are not innately competitive. The argument that humankind has progressed through the competitive evolution of the 'survival of the fittest' is simply not true (Kohn, 1986; Montagu, 1950). We have within us an inherent potential for both cooperation and competition, for good and evil.

Second, we are and have always been inherently social beings. Our human ancestors were never, despite the Western myth, selfish, aggressive, and individualistic (Clark, 1989). Before they became human they were social, cooperative, and closely bonded.

Third, there is a synergistic relationship between individual development and social opportunities. It is through social interaction that the individual reaches full autonomy (Gould, 1988), and it is fully realized human beings who take responsibility for others and who best nurture community.

And fourth, by virtue of their capacities and their communal needs, humans are political beings. The essential qualities of human beings – our 'unique abilities for abstract thought and speech, freedom, technology, morality, self-awareness, and sense of community' (Lea, 1982: 212) – indicate that humans are political, rather than apolitical, beings. And democracy is the form of governance which most honors this nature.

If these four propositions are accurate, then it becomes possible to endorse a return to the liberal Jeffersonian view of human nature, of society, and of governance. This view embraces a populist optimism, including a faith in the human capacity to reason and learn. In this perspective humans are independent, moral, rational, and equal by nature. They are endowed with a reason which is the source of human dignity. There is also a reciprocal moral responsibility upon the part of individuals, who are independent and who have the right to make their own choices, to develop their qualities for the use of the common good.

Constituting human nature

What remains to be understood in this reconception of the human being is how such nature is constructed. Are humans a product solely of biology and genetics – Social Darwinism and its many variations? Are we sculpted by the hand of God – Protestant predestination and its variations? Or are we simply the derivative of circumstances – the structuralist argument that people are not the authors of their thoughts and actions, the so-called 'death of the subject'?

None of these propositions is acceptable. Genetic and biological imperatives do exist, of course. But these imperatives only outline the area of potential behavior, an area which is wide indeed. Thus, there may be posited a human nature which is fluid rather than fixed; which imbues meaning into its surroundings instead of adopting a given reality; and which is capable of being an agent, rather than merely a product, of change. In Berger and Luckmann's classic work, *The Social Construction of Reality* (1966), the human organism is constituted by the dialectic between nature and the socially constructed world: 'Its limits are set by nature, but once constructed, this world acts back upon nature ... In this same dialectic, man [sic] produces reality and thereby produces himself' (p. 183).[8]

The search for the human(e) society

If one accepts the Jeffersonian argument that it is the purpose of society and government to honor the dignity of humanity (Lea, 1982), the question then becomes, what kind of society and government might that be? More specifically, having postulated a human being whose nature is developed within a social milieu, what kind of society is desirable, and what forms of governance might create and support this society?[9]

This search, and challenge, is undoubtedly as old as society itself. There are, however, a number of contemporary answers to this problem which, while perhaps not unique when considered separately, nonetheless represent as a whole an original mode of thought which promises a defensible answer. There are at least three dimensions of this inquiry appropriate for consideration here. These are:

1 the considered search for shared social values;
2 the dual ethics of needs and care; and,
3 the means of valuing successful societies and communities.

The values of a humane society

Lappé (1989) drops the gauntlet:

> The challenge of the twenty-first century will be, then, to create a values-based politics, one in which our values provide the moorings. Continually tested against reality, debated, refined, and deepened, our values must become the beacons casting light on the road ahead, so that no preset economic and political absolutes can constrict our vision (pp. 4–5).

The contemporary search for a healthy society has inspired a number of individuals and organizations to attempt to identify the key values such a society would succor. Finding agreement on such values may be an impossible task, given how fundamental cleavages along socio-economic, ethnic, racial, and cultural lines are sharply reflected in competing worldviews (Bellah *et al.*, 1985; Hunter, 1991). But this search for core values reflects a current which runs deep within society; as Lappé (1989) observes about the United States, 'More than anything, we are proud that *America stands for something*, a set of enduring values that have given us a common identity in the midst of incredible diversity – values that have made us one people' (p. 3).

As the following examples illustrate, there are many ways of framing these values. In some cases, this attempt has actually taken the form of listing such values. For instance, the National Civic League (The National Civic League's Citizen Democracy Project, 1990) sponsors a 'Core civic values of democracy report card'. The values being graded include:

- dignity and importance of the individual;
- equality of right;
- fairness;

- freedom to participate in self-governance and to seek one's own goals;
- responsibility to balance personal and community needs;
- participation;
- access to processes of public decision-making; and,
- respect for diversity.

Skolimowski (1985) offers a more general path:

- *responsibility* for all, including future generations;
- *reverence*, as a mode of interaction with other beings and with other cultures;
- *frugality*, defined as grace without waste, as this mode of behavior vis à vis other cultures which is cooperative, economically viably [sic] and life-enhancing in the long run;
- *equity*, defined as the elementary standard of justice for all (p. 66).

The vision offered by Clark (1989) proceeds along somewhat different lines. She emphasizes decentralization and local self-sufficiency. Cultural diversity would occur within a context in which there is a shared global vision. She contrasts cooperation, diversity, social bondedness, and sacred meaning with their antitheses – competition, uniformity, self-centeredness, and material consumption.

And the final word from this sampler will be offered by Friedmann (1989), who returns to the theme of a reconstituted modernity:

a restructured project [of modernity] would acknowledge the legitimacy of values such as differences in cultural identity, people's increased autonomy over the life spaces they inhabit, ecological preservation, equality of women's rights, and the priority of the claims of needy populations on common resources (p. 230).

This brief survey does not do justice to the complexity of contemporary conflicts over the construction of, belief in, and enactment of differing social values. But certain broad themes may be identified consistent with the vision of humanity offered earlier. A human(e) society would support the following values:

- individual and societal respect for the needs and, indeed, inherent dignity, of each individual;
- a focus on individual responsibilities to all levels of community, from the family to the globe;
- a stress on partnership and cooperation;
- the acceptance of differences (the celebration of 'diversity'), and the attending search for means of productively dealing with those differences.

The ethics of needs and caring

Two broad principles stand out as the underlying foundation of these more specific values. These are the twin ethics of needs and caring.

There is a strong instrumental argument for needs satisfaction as a basis for conflict resolution. As Burton (1989) argues, human beings have certain needs that cannot be denied and which must be satisfied for individual development and for social behavior. But there is also a more profound argument for the ethic of needs. The antecedents to this attention to needs are found in the humanist work of Maslow (1954) and Fromm (1955) in the 1950s, and even Freud (1961) from a generation earlier. Fromm in particular argued that the health of a society ought to be defined in terms of its ability to satisfy individual needs, such as relatedness and identity. The satisfaction of human needs can serve as a kind of benchmark for the evaluation of society (Lerner, 1990).

In contrast to needs theory, with its extensive antecedents, the focus on 'caring' as a founding principle of social ethics is more recent. In fact, its origins can be pinpointed to the publication in 1982 of Carol Gilligan's book, *In a Different Voice*. In brief, Gilligan distinguishes between two modes of thinking about relationships. The one mode is concerned with the logic of rights, the other with caring and responsibility. She finds empirically that the first is generally associated with males, the latter with females. In this view, men resolve disputes according to rights and rules; women try to satisfy the needs of all parties (Handler, 1988: 1041).

The division of rights and caring along gender lines is not above challenge. Tronto (1987) lists a large body of studies finding no such differences. She argues that, while the ethic of care is of obvious concern for feminists, the focus should not be on gender difference but on the adequacy of the ethic as moral theory. Tronto argues the point eloquently on both empirical and strategic grounds:

> The equation of 'care' with 'female' is questionable because the evidence to support the link between gender difference and different moral perspectives is inadequate. It is a strategically dangerous position for feminists because the simple assertion of gender difference in a social context that identifies the male as normal contains an implication of the inferiority of the distinctly female. It is philosophically stultifying because, if feminists think of the ethic of care as categorized by gender difference, they are likely to become trapped trying to defend women's morality rather than looking critically at the philosophical promises and problems of an ethic of care (p. 646).

Gilligan's initiative has inspired a virtual cottage industry of devotees and critics. What they have found in her work that is missing in previous accounts of moral theory is an ethic of care. It is this 'voice', whether female or not, which has been left out of the study of moral development and thought. Within this ethic, moral predicaments are resolved not through some weighting of rights but by relationships of caring. Among the developments spawned by the discourse surrounding the ethic of care has been the social movement of communitarian feminism. Communitarian feminists adopt the constitutive view of human nature wherein individuals develop within relationships. Communitarians are interested less in the enforcement of rights than in the quality of relationships.

Advocacy for the ethic of care advances naturally from a moral theory for individuals into social and political theory (Tronto, 1987). The implications for such social and political theory are profound. As Jones (1989) argues, acceptance of an ethic of care would mean that 'the individualist, rights-based, contractual model of citizenship that views the public realm as one of competition rather than community building' would be replaced by a conception of citizenship which honors 'commitment to relationships, love, and caring for others ... as ideal bonds between citizens' (p. 810).

The ethic of care thus has implications for conflict resolution theory. As Tronto (1987) explains:

> The perspective of care requires that conflict be worked out without damage to the continuing relationships. Moral problems can be expressed in terms of accommodating the needs of the self and of others, of balancing competition and cooperation, and of maintaining the social web of relations in which one finds oneself (p. 658).

The valuation of the desired society

A number of economists and other theorists have been attempting to devise standards for measuring how successful societies are in actualizing these values. Lerner (1990) argues that a politics based on human needs would assess social relationships by how they assist or block the actualization of human capacities. Craib (1984) suggests that this assessment would be based upon how well societies support social relationships, by which ways they encourage cooperative work, by how they enhance our ability to cooperate with one another in our decision-making. Societies which fail in these tasks can be systematically criticized: they are 'oppressive, unfree societies' (p. 168).

The search for a means of determining the quality of life (QOL) is a difficult task; the history of efforts to create such indicators dates at least from Homer's time, through the Bible, to the Enlightenment, and beyond (Marlin, 1987). Actual standards used to make this valuation take a variety of forms. Some are quantitative alternatives to the standard Gross National Product (GNP) or Gross Domestic National Product (GDNP); others are tailored for communities to assess the quality of civic life. What distinguishes today's efforts in particular is the sophistication of some of these newer indices and the focus on values other than economic welfare. For instance, Daly and Cobb (1989) have produced an Index of Sustainable Welfare as a key gauge of a society's progress towards their desired 'sustainable future'. The 'Henry David Thoreau' quality of life index reflects environmental costs not tallied by the GNP (Grossman, 1988). And Waring (1990), has attempted to record the contributions of previously uncounted domestic (i.e. family) labor.

One creative example of how civic effectiveness might be measured by individual communities is to be found in an experiment being conducted by the National Civic League. The National Civic Index offers these ten qualitative indicators by which communities can judge their performance: citizen participation, community leadership, government performance, volunteerism and philanthropy, intergroup relations, civic education, community information sharing, capacity for cooperation and consensus building, strategic/long-range planning, and inter-community cooperation (Gates, 1987).

Governance in a humane society: Rethinking democracy

Democracy triumphant – which democracy?
How might this revised vision of the individual and society be reflected in the political structures and practices of democracy? With what forms of governance may a humane society – a society which rewards caring, satisfies needs, and honors the social individual – be created, nurtured, and sustained?

The struggle for democracy is *the* dynamic of contemporary human history (Quinney, 1991). But it is more particularly the struggle to decide which kind of democracy we shall have: not only the forms and processes of government, but indeed the purposes. Shall we have the liberal democracy that conceives of citizens at their worst and which thereby isolates us from one another, or shall we have one which insists upon equality and unity within diversity, care and respect, and shared resources (Quinney, 1991)?

At the beginning the twenty-first century, well into the third century of its revival, democracy has never been more popular. As a matter of fact, there is a menu of democracies from which to choose: old standards such as pluralist democracy (Dahl, 1982; 1989) and participatory democracy (Cook and Morgan, 1971; Zimmerman, 1986); some former contenders, anticipatory democracy (Dator, 1978) and the little known third universal theory democracy (Gaddafi, 1976); current challengers, strong democracy (Barber, 1984) and discursive democracy (Dryzek, 1990); and even one kind of democracy – unitary – pitted against the other – adversary (Mansbridge, 1984). Frances Moore Lappé and Paul DuBois have their Center for

Living Democracy. Officials from former Soviet bloc republics hound American universities, local planning commissions, state legislatures, and Congress, to find out how democracy works. Indeed, there is even a petulant reaction to this plethora of attention, 'obsessive' democracy (Funk, 1989).[10]

What does not exist is any consensus about what democracy really is. As Dahl (1989) observes, democracy is viewed in many ways: as a set of institutions and practices; as a collection of rights; as a particular social and economic order; and as a process for making lasting decisions. More importantly, there is no consensus about what democracy ought to be.

Perhaps the different conceptions of democracy have never been more prominent than at the prelude to the twenty-first century. On the one hand there are the former Soviet bloc countries now enthralled with the ideals of democracy, individual rights, private property, and the free market. On the other hand, this enchantment is occurring at the same time that many Western theorists are pointing to the adverse consequences of the excesses of liberal democracy. Indeed, despite pride in political heritage, including accomplishments such as extension of suffrage, individual rights, and freedom of speech, many Americans do not even believe that they live in a democracy (Matthews, 1991).

Rethinking democracy: Foundations

Barber (1984) suggests that there are essentially three models of liberal democracies: 'authoritative'; 'juridical'; and, 'pluralist'. These three models correspond to what he terms the 'realist', 'anarchist', and 'minimalist' dispositions within society. Authoritative democracy is embodied in the representative rule of elites. It is unsatisfactory because of its tendency toward hegemony, because it is inegalitarian, and because its view of citizenship is limited to the selection of elites. Juridical democracy, which stresses legal rights and their enforcement, ultimately fails because it subverts the legislative process and it discourages citizen activity, because of its reliance upon representative principles, and because it seeks to introduce abstract grounds such as natural right or higher law, into political life.

Pluralist democracy imagines a governance by which individuals and groups who are free and equal pursue their private interests in a free market governed only by the social contract. Barber is particularly scornful of pluralism, arguing that it fails because it:

> relies on the fictions of the free market and of the putative freedom and equality of bargaining agents; because it cannot generate public thinking or public ends of any kind; because it is innocent about the real world of power; and (as with the first two models) because it uses the representative principle and reintroduces into politics a covert independent ground – namely, the illusions of the free market and of the invisible hand and the simplistic utilitarianism (Man-

152

deville, Smith, and Bentham) by which the pursuit of private interests is miraculously made to yield the public good. (p. 144)

The latter part of the title for this section is borrowed from Gould, whose
1988 publication, *Rethinking Democracy: Freedom and Social Cooperation in
Politics, Economy, and Society* highlights much of that recent rethinking.
Gould articulates the thesis that traditional liberal democratic theory, while
protecting individual rights, has been unable to account for the equivalent
values of social cooperation and social equality. A new democracy which
does so must be based upon a rethinking of its philosophical foundations.

This democracy would have to account for how the values of social equality and cooperation might be achieved without increasing state power and
centralized authority. Contemporary alternatives, socialist and holist, subordinate individual rights to community needs or societal welfare. Gould
asserts that values of individual freedom and liberty are not incompatible
with social cooperation and equality. In fact, the exact opposite is true: they
actually depend upon each other for their realization. And the key for real-
izing this compatibility is democracy, since it is in democracy that individual freedom and self-determination is 'exercised jointly and equally with
others' in common activities (p. 26).

In this conclusion she echoes Barber (1984):

> Without participating in the common life that defines them and in the decision-
> making that shapes their social habitat, women and men cannot become indi-
> viduals. Freedom, justice, equality, and autonomy are all products of common
> thinking and common living; democracy creates them (p. xv).

The alternative to liberal democracy, for Barber, is 'strong democracy'.
Strong democracy he defines as follows:

> politics in the participatory mode where conflict is resolved in the absence of
> an independent ground through a participatory process of ongoing, proximate
> self-legislation and the creation of a political community capable of transform-
> ing dependent, private individuals into free citizens and partial and private
> interests into public goods (Barber, 1984: 132).

Barber has prepared an agenda for the institutions of strong democracy
which may serve as a blueprint for a transformative practice of public conflict resolution. These institutions, if they are to be viable, practical, and in
keeping with democratic theory, should be realistic and workable. They
should complement representative institutions of today; that is, strong
democracy must come as modifier of liberal democracy, not as destructive
revolution. They must provide safeguards for individuals and minorities,
and against majorities governing in the name of community, in order to
counter the tendencies of participatory communities towards irrationalism,
prejudice, uniformity, and intolerance. The institutions of strong democracy

must also deal with such obstacles of modernity as scale, technology, complexity, and parochialism. And they must favor talk and judgment instead of relying on representation, voting, and bureaucrat/technocrat rule.

Democratic societies face many challenges. Past challenges have served as catalysts for changes in democratic practice (Boyte and Evans, 1986). From the struggles for independence, to movements such as anti-slavery, labor, and civil rights, to the neighborhood and citizen movements of the 1970s and 1980s, the citizenry has been called upon to remedy democracy's faults and modify its course. Again and again citizens have endorsed a vision of engagement and civic virtue that revitalizes democracy. There is every reason to continue to renew that vision.

Notes

1   The term 'modernism' actually acquired its current meaning in conjunction with the notion of 'postmodern'. 'Postmodern' was first used to describe the rebellion of architecture against the dogma of form of the modernist movement of over half a century ago (Friedmann, 1989). During the past two decades, the concept 'postmodern' has been embraced by social theorists as a means of expressing the contention that the demands of contemporary society have overwhelmed the foundations of what is considered modernity.

2   See, e.g., Galbraith (1990) and Rohatyn (1990).

3   Habermas has been one of the most influential critics of the contemporary state, the anointed heir of Critical Theory. The analogy with royalty is appropriate – the crown invites its courtiers, rivals, and enemies as well. Habermas, like Rawls (1971) or Gilligan (1982), is one of those social theorists who serve as touchstones for attention by critics who find their ideas too close to essential truths to be ignored and too provocative to go unchallenged.

4   The last condition has engendered a biting feminist critique of liberal democracy. Jones (1989) argues that the essence of citizenship 'is derived from a set of values, experiences, modes of discourse, rituals, and practices that both explicitly and implicitly privileges men and the "masculine" and excludes women and the "female"' (p. 781). In this argument, even if women were to eventually achieve juridical/legal equality by gaining admission to the institutions of governance and acquiring the economic and personal resources to take advantage of their rights, their membership would be diminished by its dependency on men's terms.

5   A number of observers condemn this focus on individualism and self-interest to the exclusion of other human characteristics. While invoking the need to protect ourselves from our own Hobbesian natures, this perspective of competitiveness, isolation, and natural inequality 'pervades the political system and the socialization experience and rationalizes the stratified sociopolitical and economic structure' (Lea, 1982: 212). It serves as a prop to the modern, technological society as it 'encourages a mechanistic approach to life: to rational thinking, efficiency, utilitarianism, scientific detachment, and the belief that

the human place in nature is one of ownership and supremacy' (Glendinning, 1990: 50-1). Indeed, Clark (1989: 317) argues that 'This presumed image of man is the underlying basis of most of what is wrong with Western society – both in terms of our behaviour toward our environment and toward one another.

6 It may surprise many readers to realize that during the classical and early Christian periods of Western thought and practice terms such as 'individual' and 'privacy' had a decidedly negative connotation (Barber, 1984). It took eighteenth-century capitalism to transform the vocabulary of virtue so as to 'put selfishness and avarice to work in the name of public goods' (Barber, 1984: 195).

7 Bookchin (1990), one of the severest critics of modernity and its devastating effects on ecology and community, offers a testament to this paradox.

Our present civilization is nothing if it is not Janus-faced and riddled with ambiguity. We cannot simply denounce it as male-oriented, exploitative, and domineering without recognizing that it also freed us, at least in part, from the parochial bonds of tribalism and an abject obedience to superstition, which ultimately made us vulnerable to domination. By the same token, we cannot simply praise it for its growing universality, the extent to which it fostered individual autonomy, and the rational secularism it brought to human affairs without recognizing that these achievements were generally purchased at the cost of human enslavement, mass degradation, class rule, and the establishment of the State (p. 170).

8 See also Giddens (1982; 1987; 1989), Murphy (1989), and Weedon (1987).

9 Or, as Lea (1982) proclaims, the challenge is 'to go beyond a set of cultural values, a political socialization process, and a socioeconomic structure which largely reinforce the negative and undeveloped dimensions of man as he is, to a society which encourages and facilitates the realization of what he might become' (p. 213).

10 Funk (1989) suggests that the Left has an 'obsession' with democracy, which she associates with 'the fading of the New Left in the 1970s, the subsequent hardening of an orthodox Marxism-Leninism and eventually a rejection of Marxist theory in general' (p. 171).

11

The practical foundations of a transformative practice

In Chapter Nine three fundamental expressions of the problems of the contemporary public domain were identified. These were (1) the disintegration of community and the relationships and meaning found in community life, (2) the deep alienation of citizens from the institutions and practices of governance, and (3) the inability to solve public problems and resolve public conflicts. The previous chapter developed the philosophical foundations of a public conflict resolution practice which would respond to these challenges. In this chapter, these three problems will be addressed along the lines of the following themes of a transformative practice of public conflict resolution:

- inspiring, nurturing, and sustaining a vital communal life: an engaged community;
- invigorating the institutions and practices of governance: a responsive governance; and
- enhancing society's ability to solve problems and resolve conflicts: a capacity for problem solving and conflict resolution.

An engaged community

Community

Within the ideology of management, concern for the crisis of governance focuses primarily upon the deficiencies of political institutions and their functions. But the search for institutional reform is insufficient for the present condition.

It is easy to belittle such 'soft' concepts as affiliation and community, particularly in relation to life-threatening issues such as shelter, food, health, and safety. But citizens, even those for whom these needs are at risk, both desire and need more than good institutions of governance. They need and long for a sense of meaning, a sense of purpose, and a sense of shared community. Indeed, West (1993) argues that it is especially degraded and oppressed people who hunger for such intangibles as identity, meaning, and self-worth. It is participation in community life which plays an essential role in transforming the private interests of individuals into the public concerns of citizens, a transformation which is essential to deal with these persistent problems. It is as important for individuals to be with their communities, and with one another, as it is to reform political processes and institutions.

The decentralization of governance, of work, and of social life called for by advocates of community and place[1] would make community easier to achieve. But the structures of a global society make such radical reordering unlikely, at least to any substantial degree. Yet it is possible to find community despite the giant scale of so much of the public realm. The commonality of citizenry comes not only from geographical proximity; it also arises from the consciousness produced by common activity, a bonding which develops out of common procedures and work (Barber, 1984).[2]

Boyte and Evans (1986) suggest that community is found in what they call the 'free spaces' of public life. These free spaces, rooted in the common, voluntary activities of daily life, nurture values of citizenship and the common good. Free spaces are inhabited by those community-based, mediating institutions which have traditionally served as buffers between the indifference of faceless bureaucracies and community life.

Both the left and the right misjudge the meaning of these free spaces. The left assesses these voluntary associations as instruments of the status quo, and is convinced that these communal identities must be replaced by modern and rational forms of association. The right argues that they may provide a counterweight to the potential of a totalitarian state. Both miss the important point: that these mediating institutions are the source of constructive social change. It is in these places – churches and synagogues, PTAs, Boy Scouts and Camp Fire Girls – where democracy acquires its true meaning for most people. It is there that people learn the values and skills of democracy and democratic practice. And it is in these spaces where people express their 'democratic aspirations' during the most difficult times.

A significant leader of this pursuit of community renewal has been Etzioni (1991; 1993), a leader in the developing communitarian movement. Etzioni argues that public life in contemporary democratic society inculcates citizens with a strong sense of rights and entitlement without the necessary accompaniment of a sense of obligation. True freedom requires a community which affirms the 'language of social virtues, interests, and, above all, social responsibilities' (Etzioni, 1993: 2). In order to minimize the role of the state, one must enhance the role of the community.

Yet the connections found in community do not come without risks, both Etzioni and Boyte and Evans admit. Too often traditional communities have been restraining and authoritiative. Free spaces may and often do contain biases based upon class, gender, racial or other divisions. The search for community must be accompanied by continued efforts to care for the individuals such community is supposed to nourish. A community which does not care for its individual members offers little towards a vital public life (Theobald, 1978).

Thus, an integral component of the pursuit for communal life is to find the means by which caring may be inculcated in community members. Communitarian feminism suggests that the development of an ethic of care depends upon the experience of care both by and for others (Tronto, 1987). Conversely, the absence of caretaking experiences leads to a kind of moral deprivation, a misleading morality based on cognitive terms alone. Community life must at the same time offer individuals the affiliation they seek and the responsibility to offer the same for others – an opportunity found in inclusive, consensus-based public conflict resolution processes.

Public discourse

The role of dialogue A key component of the effort to nurture such caring is through developing a capacity for honest, responsible, and effective public talk. As Barber (1984) observes, talk has the power to make the 'I of private self-interest' into a 'we that makes possible civility and common political action' (p. 189). Talk nourishes empathy, and empathy develops bonds and promotes public thinking.

In the introduction to the study, *Citizens and Politics* (1991), Kettering Foundation president David Matthews argues that citizens long to restore the integrity and vitality of public discussion. That restoration begins with how the public discusses major issues. Citizens realize that they must gain an informed understanding of public issues in order to participate in the governance of society. Citizens want forums which encourage free and open discussion. They truly want elected officials, the media, and others to listen to their concerns; they yearn for open discussions both among themselves and with public officials.

Matthews' assessment of the role public dialogue must play in halting the erosion of political legitimacy is enlightening:

> Why is the public dialogue so pivotal? The public dialogue is the natural home for democratic politics. That is the 'home' people feel forced out of and want back. People depend on the dialogue to provide opportunities for the public to hold counsel with itself and give public definition to the public's interest. ... The only way to get at the base of the problem is through greater public definition of its own interests. That means the public has to be invested in deliberations over the difficult choices that are involved in delineating the public's interests. That definition is necessary to give direction to government. And public direction makes for public legitimacy (*Citizens and Politics*, 1991: vi).

The two theorists of democracy most concerned with the transformative role of dialogue are Samuel Barber and Jürgen Habermas. Barber (1984) embraces language – or rather, the harvest that the proficient use of language may reap – as the salvation of democracy. He declares that transformations in ideology and political power always coincide with major shifts in language. In the clash of established power and tradition versus change, language is the battlefield. When language lives, growth is possible. He identifies no fewer than nine functions of talk (pp. 178–9):

1 the articulation of interests; bargaining and exchange;
2 persuasion;
3 agenda-setting;
4 exploring mutuality;
5 affiliation and affection;
6 maintaining autonomy;
7 witness and self-expression;
8 reformulation and reconceptualization;
9 community-building as the creation of public interests, common goods, and active citizens.

In Barber's strong democracy an 'entire citizenry' is engaged in such talk:

> Democratize language, give each citizen some control over what the community will mean by the crucial terms it uses to define all the citizens' selves and lives in public and private, and other forms of equality will follow. We may redistribute goods and make power accountable, but if we reserve talk and its evolution to specialists – to journalists or managers or clerics or packagers or bureaucrats or statesmen or advertisers or philosophers or social scientists – then no amount of equality will yield democracy (p. 193).

And all the various functions of talk serve a single essential purpose: 'the development of a citizenry capable of genuinely public thinking and political judgment and thus able to envision a common future in terms of genuinely common goods' (p. 197).

Barber claims that Habermas has understood that the meaning of democracy, above all else, is 'equal access to language' (1984: 197). Habermas (1984; 1987) has constructed a theory of communicative action which is aimed at prescribing a kind of ideal speech situation of undistorted communication. His objective is to define the conditions under which communicative action is not distorted by power disparities, in which results are not tainted by coercion, and during which the dialogue of equals would arrive at a 'rational consensus' (Gould, 1988: 17). He posits the conditions for an 'ideal speech situation', including the truth of a statement, its legitimacy, and its reflection of the intentions of the speaker.

There has been considerable criticism of Habermas for promoting a 'fiction' of ideal speech and for disregarding the distorting effects of entrenched power relations on political dialogue (Mészáros, 1989). Gould (1988) argues that the level of abstraction with which he describes the ideal speech situation leaves unclear how such a situation might be actually created. She complains that his emphasis on consensus as the goal of communication overemphasizes agreement to the exclusion of appreciation of differences. Such an emphasis on consensus may pressure for conformity while denigrating dissent.

But critics who find ideal speech unrealistic mistake Habermas's project for something it does not pretend to be (Hanson, 1985). Habermas is not offering ideal speech situations as blue-prints for the Good Society. Without a principle like ideal speech and the reminder of how discourse may be distorted, there is nothing to distinguish genuine, legitimate consensus from mere agreement.

A responsive governance

Elevating politics

Before various material crises and problems can be solved the powerlessness and alienation which disengage people from politics must be addressed (Lerner, 1990). Thus, a first task of a vital democracy is to remove the term 'politics' from the linguistic and moral junkyard and relocate it into the midst of everyday lives. One task of a transformative practice, then, is to assist in recentering political power in civil society (Friedmann, 1987).

People do care, and care deeply, about public life. Kettering Foundation interviews of citizens revealed that there does indeed exist a strong foundation for building productive democratic practices which encourage public participation in politics. Citizens want to play a central role in the effort to reinvigorate the public domain. And citizens do become engaged in the areas of public life in which they believe that they make a difference. They are most likely to become involved under certain conditions, at the center of which is possibility of being heard, of contributing to their community, and of creating change (*Citizens and Politics*, 1991).

The Kettering Foundation has developed an agenda for change which offers a broad program for providing these conditions and reinvigorating democratic public life. This agenda emphasizes the need for informed and meaningful involvement by citizens:

- *AGENDA ITEM #1:* find ways to refocus the political debate on policy issues and how those issues affect people's everyday lives.
- *AGENDA ITEM #2:* find ways for citizens to form a public voice on policy issues – as an alternative to the clamor of special interests – and for public officials to hear that public voice.
- *AGENDA ITEM #3:* find public places where citizens – and citizens and public officials – can consider and discuss policy issues.

- *AGENDA ITEM #4:* find ways to encourage the media to focus more on the public dimension of policy issues.
- *AGENDA ITEM #5:* find ways for citizens and public officials to interact more constructively in the political process.
- *AGENDA ITEM #6:* find ways to tap Americans' [and others] sense of civic duty in order to improve our political health. (*Citizens and Politics*, 1991: 8-9)

Authentic participation

A return to a politics of deliberative processes, public arguments and persuasion, can give participatory forums real meaning (Dionne, 1991). And, conversely, effective participation in governance is tied to constructive community; one cannot exist without the other (Barber, 1984).

Despite current rhetoric, the abandonment of government by the middle class is not a demand for less government; rather, it is a cry for better government (Dionne, 1991). But asking for better government does not mean that citizens expect to reform existing institutions only to remain passive bystanders. Rather, they are asking for the means to actively participate themselves (*Citizens and Politics*, 1991).

Needs theory indicates that active participation in self-governance is more than morally desirable. Social stability is not possible without people's involvement in the decisions that affect their lives (Clark, 1989). Furthermore, in a healthy society, citizen participation is what Alinsky (1972) calls the 'animating spirit and force' (p. xxv). And participation brings a moral power to communities that cannot be otherwise developed (Barber, 1984).

Liberal democracy too often fosters a polity of interest-maximizing individuals. Participation then can become at best only a vehicle for expression of the multitude of private interests. As Barber (1984) observes, democracy requires not 'efficient private interests', but 'effective public judgments' (p. 173). And public participation must allow for the transformation of self-interested individuals into citizens who can rethink their interests in terms of communal norms and public goods (p. 173).

Philosophers such as Rousseau and Mill, and, more recently, Pateman, recognized the role participation plays in educating for citizenry (Gould, 1988). It is through the act of participation in decision-making itself that people learn self-governance and self-management. Bookchin (1990) presents the argument most forcefully. He declares that:

> no substantive democracy is possible and no concept of self-administration is meaningful unless the people convene in open, face-to-face assemblies to formulate politices for society. No policy, in effect, is democratically legitimate unless it has been proposed, discussed, and decided upon by the people directly – not through representatives or surrogates of any kind (pp. 174–5).

Reconceiving the administrative task

Participation ought not to be taken as a means in and of itself (Walker, 1988). While participation can renew a sense of involvement in community, it is also possible for it to manifest a selfish struggle for private gain. Participation can be also be distorted by the manipulation of those controlling the keys to public access. Thus, public officials have a special, and challenging, responsibility to offer avenues for public involvement that are fair, effective, and democratic. And public conflict resolution practitioners, who are often called upon to guide such involvement, have a unique opportunity to advocate for that responsibility.

This need for involvement suggests to many observers a significant reconsideration of the role of public agencies and officials away from their traditional role as authoritative decision-makers or as arbiters of public judgment. Instead, they are to become advocates for as well as designers and facilitators of public consideration. For instance, Barber (1984) calls for institutions which would facilitate civic participation in all areas – agenda-setting, deliberation, legislation, and implementation. Friedmann (1989), intending to reverse the Enlightenment model of central planning, supports a transactive mode which joins expert knowledge to people's practical experience. Habermas (1984; 1987) envisions public agencies which deliberately promote consensus-based decision-making.

Public administration and planning, and their respective accompanying roles of public administrator and planner, are the twin foundations of professional public service. White and McSwain (1990), for public administration, and Webber (1978), for planning, demonstrate how these roles may be enacted. White and McSwain deny the prevailing conception of the public agency as program implementer. Public administrators must view their agencies less as institutions than as 'enclave[s]' against 'technicism' and the 'social incoherence' that it produces (p. 30). The agency must become the arena 'where reason can be spoken' (p. 31).

The changes in the role of public agencies mean a corresponding shift in the role of the public administrator. Rather than merely implementing programs, the public administrator would act as a 'mediator of meaning' (p. 30), whose basic task would become creating a '*lingua franca* by which value issues can be discussed' (p. 31). The role transformation is significant:

> The public administrator must play the role of both mediator and negotiator, sometimes of meaning, sometimes of policy and action alternatives, as when contractor relations are involved. We see this mediator-negotiator role as even more important, and indeed dramatic and exciting, than the program implementation role idea of the past (p. 33).

Webber (1978) calls for a paradigm shift in planning. In place of a planning which offers right answers, the new planning would contribute effective and acceptable decision-making procedures. The central function of this planning would be to 'improve the processes of public debate and public decisions' (p. 156). The task of planning would be to ensure that all voices are heard, that all options are considered, and that all consequences and their effects on the public are identified and assessed.

The orientation of this planning is towards strengthening the democratic means of governance. And the methodology is that of an active mediator. Its aim is to 'foster free exchange of dissimilar ideas and the open confrontation of divergent opinion, thus to encourage the generation of new ideas and innovation of all sorts'. It is aware of the potential 'tyranny' of majority rule, and 'hypersensitive' to minority concerns and interests. It therefore is 'constantly seeking to assure that their interests are ably represented and that they attain equal access to opportunities' (pp. 158–9).

Yet the planner, unhampered by the strictures of 'neutrality' which may plague the mediator, is more than a facilitator of dialogue.

> The permissive planner is literally a troublemaker. Finding persons or groups unconcerned about latent problems that will later affect them, he seeks to agitate those latent interests until they rise to the surface, then to find ways of involving those persons in pursuit of their self-interests. Finding dialogue lagging, he seeks to ignite conflict so that latent issues will become manifest. (Webber, 1978: 160)

The transformative conception of the administrative task is clear. Instead of the efficiency of top-down decision-making by an elite, a transformative practice strives for participatory processes, for consensus-building from the bottom-up (Clark, 1989), and for dialogue among parties conceived as equals (Handler, 1988). The administrative practice must be responsive to the public, rather than directive of that public. The role of government is redefined from that of a provider of solutions to that of the public's servant (Boyte and Evans, 1986).

Because of the structural impediments, the necessary desire and capability cannot be expected to be achieved simply as a matter of individual will. Handler (1988) argues that there must be administrative and legal changes along reflexive lines in order for there to be the needed 'participatory relationships' between the public and the agencies which serve them. The bureaucracy must be staffed such that professionals reconceive their professional tasks along 'dialogic or client-empowerment lines' (p. 1108). Dialogism must be incorporated within professional norms. This process might be aided by creating 'reciprocal concrete incentives' (p. 1012) for administrative personnel. That is, by structuring the definitions of administrative success such that active participation of clients becomes integral to the professional task, there might be nurtured the 'respect, dignity, caring, and listening' (p. 1091) essential to create the understanding and cooperation these relationships need.

Conflict resolution and problem solving

The value of conflict

A healthy democracy would embrace conflict as central to the political process (Barber, 1984). Public conflict is not only as an inevitable feature of political life, it is entirely appropriate and necessary (Dahl, 1982). And unlike traditional liberalism, which suggests that conflict is intractable and best managed through adjudication or avoidance, a strong democracy uses conflict as a vehicle for participation, informed deliberation, civic education, and, ultimately, cooperation (Barber, 1984).

Achieving this disposition towards conflict is not an easy task. Deeply rooted in the traditions of organized religion and reinforced by what Alinsky (1972) calls 'Madison Avenue public relations, middle-class moral hygiene' (p. 62), there is a strong current within society which favors harmony, conformity, and quiet, and the regularity, order, and predictability these bring.[3]

The experience of the last three decades has caused some reconsideration of this attitude. Conflict does make some people uncomfortable; however, the benefits of avoiding differences are illusory (Bingham and Laue, 1988). Observers of conflict recognize that the ability to challenge useless precedents and outmoded practices is lost in the quest for conformity (Blake and Mouton, 1970). Experience of organizations involved in efforts to resolve conflict suggests that avoiding or suppressing conflict may actually exacerbate it, making it only more destructive (Adler *et al.*, 1988).

As public conflict resolution practitioners know, conflict and its expression can have many positive consequences. By increasing public awareness of issues it can mobilize constituencies and foster leadership (Bellman *et al.*, 1982). Without conflict there is no acceptance of any need to seek multilateral solutions (Cormick, 1987). Creative solutions to problems come only through the acknowledgment of differences and through learning to work through those differences (Bingham and Laue, 1988). Adler *et al.*, (1988) see a deeper function: the empowerment of education and unification as members of a community accepts its problems as their own. Its presence can even be an indication of the health of a community.

Ultimately, in a democratic society conflict is the basis for social change (Bellman *et al.*, 1982). If there is to be a just relationship, if change is to occur, latent conflicts must be made clearly visible to all parties (Stoltzfus, in Price, 1989b). It is through confrontation and advocacy that needs gain currency and legitimacy; in many situations it is this confrontation alone that forces the recognition of interdependence that makes negotiation possible (Lederach, 1989). Indeed, it may not be too extreme to argue along with Alinsky (1972) that 'Conflict is the essential core of a free and open society' (p. 62).

The environmental arena is an example of the dual potential of conflict. On the one hand, what Gladwin (1987) terms the 'golden age of environmental conflict' (p. 14) of the 1970s and early 1980s had numerous deleterious consequences, including reduced economic growth, exacerbated energy shortages, an overburdened court system, increased civil disobedience, and time and resources diverted from more productive activity. But that conflict also increased protection for human health, left natural resources for future generations, stimulated environmentally-sensitive planning, enhanced the overall quality of life, and served to bring about a rethinking of how development can proceed within the natural limits of the Earth.

While the transformative practice parts with consensus theorists in its appreciation of conflict, it similarly differs with many activists of the left and right in the use it makes of this conflict. As Blake and Mouton (1970) recognized over two decades ago, 'Just stimulating people to challenge and contest status quo conformities, however, is likely to do little more than provoke disagreement and controversy, increase polarization, and ultimately end in win–lose, impasse, compromise, or chaos' (p. 421). Making conflict productive is the challenge.

Understanding conflict

The conflict resolution field has a long way to go before it can claim an understanding of social conflict adequate to the needs of disputants, practitioners, and others seeking to resolve conflict in ways that provide for individual and social justice and that promote relationship and community. To be sure, there are some substantial contributions to the conflict resolution literature which reflect a good understanding of micro- and mid-level conflict theory, e.g. the dynamics of interpersonal and group relationships and of multi-party negotiations. Practitioner-theorists such as Moore (1987), Susskind and Cruikshank (1987), Carpenter and Kennedy (1988), Cormick (1989), and Potapchuk (1991a) provide thoughtful, practical, and effective counsel about the strategies and tactics of intervention.

One need look no further than two early influential theorists of the public conflict resolution field, Laue and Cormick (1973), to find a convincing mid-range generic theory of conflict. They contend that conflict occurs when allocations of resources are seen as inadequate and divisions of power are perceived as illegitimate. Central cleavages may occur around divisions of race, age, sex, life-style, employment, provider/consumer or constituent/representative. No matter the arena, they observe, the goal is to change the existing system of power and resources distribution.

But most public disputes also reflect deep societal divisions. It is true that some public disputes are the product of circumstances unique to a particular situation, such as a history of local partisanship or personal animosity. All disputes contain these particularist elements. However, it is in these disputes that these larger social conflicts are articulated and enacted, where positions are drawn, parties coalesce, misrepresentations established, and so forth. An understanding of the basis for these divisions must precede any efforts of intervention.

However, there is no established and coherent body of conflict theory which offers a clear path towards such understanding. There is instead a rather messy mosaic of theory, of practical advice which passes for theory, and of wishful thinking, at intra- and inter-personal, small group, multi-party, societal, and trans-national levels. To sort through this mosaic in any comprehensive manner would require far more space than is available here. An overview of other perspectives, however, will suggest the limitations of the understandings of conflict offered by the management ideology. Two components of conflicts not addressed by the management program stand out in particular: the importance of power and inequalities of power, and the new arenas of social conflict which have emerged since the 1960s.

Early challengers to mainstream conflict theorizing were heavily influenced by Marxist notions of class conflict. Except for psychological explanations which focused upon misperception, miscommunication, and psychological disturbance, there was little available which acknowledged the significance of inequalities of power and resources.

Yet it became apparent to many conflict theorists that a singular emphasis on class difference alone was inadequate to explain the many kinds of conflicts which began appearing in the 1960s. The economic order of capitalism, while having a profound influence, is only one of several structuring dimensions of modernity (Giddens, 1989). Dahl (1982) offers a persuasive argument about why Western industrial democracies do not conform to the analyses of Marxism. Dominance theories correctly emphasize universal tendencies toward suppression. But Marxist focus on class ignores the endurance of 'primordial' affiliations which center on religious, regional, ethnic, and racial identity. Furthermore, there are many other forms of identity reflecting other social and economic differences that transcend a single cleavage line. And elites, rather than reflecting a single interest, are subject to an 'ideological diversity' which reinforces these crosscutting patterns. It is this 'crosscutting' or 'segmentation' of numerous cleavages which weakened the effects of class polarization.

The emergence of feminist theory brought the role of gender, and the character of power and dominance along lines of gender, out of the shadows. More than that, it eventually enriched conflict theory through the extension of its principles beyond gender. Feminists such as Fraser (1989) demonstrate how the differentiation of class, gender, race, ethnicity, and age translated into inequalities of status, power, and resources.

Hunter (1991; 1994), however, has observed that there is a wide range of ideological conflict which cannot be explained by these familiar divisions. He argues that the 'culture wars' over issues such as family, law, politics, abortion, and education stem from deep and incompatible differences over the sources of moral authority. The progressivist visions, generally associated along so-called liberal political lines, are counterposed against an orthodoxy represented by so-called conservatism. This line of division transcends long-standing religious, gender, and racial differences.

Habermas (1987) has carried this assessment of sources of conflict beyond divisions over power and resources. Industrialized capitalism has institutionalized class conflict, taming the labor movement through a normalization of occupational roles and elevation of consumerism. The role of citizen participant has been supplanted by that of dependent client of the welfare state (Habermas, 1984). Thus, since the 1960s, the dominant conflicts in Western societies no longer fit the 'welfare-state pattern of institutionalized conflict over distribution' (Habermas, 1987: 392).

These newer problems involve issues of quality of life, of equal rights, of participation, and of human rights. Social movements which have coalesced around these issues include antinuclear and environmental, peace, single-issue and local, minorities (elderly, gays, handicapped), religious fundamentalism, tax-protest, school protest, women's, and movements for autonomy for regional, linguistic, cultural, and religious independence (p. 393). And, despite their differences, these 'heterogeneous' groups are united in a single bond: except for the women's movement, which Habermas sees as a movement seeking new qualities of rights, these new social movements are defensive protests. They seek to protect the environment, communities, and accustomed values from the 'colonization of the life-world' by which all the demands of contemporary society, including capital, technology, and the state dominate private and public lives (Luke and White 1985: 219).

It is Burton (1987; 1989; 1990) who has most forcefully linked a generic theory of conflict to the means for its resolution. Burton posits a conception of deep-rooted conflict which sees such conflict as embedded in the frustration and denial of basic human needs. The drive for these needs such as identity, recognition, and security is ontological and universal; they must be met before there can be individual development and socialization. The drive to fulfill these needs does not cease until they are met. They cannot be suppressed, and they will be pursued despite obstacles.

The norms and rules of social institutions (including culture, community, and government) channel the means for meeting these needs. If these norms and rules do not allow the fulfillment of these needs, then the individual will go outside of these boundaries to fulfill them. Deep-rooted conflicts are encouraged by problems such as denial of political participation, as well as job, educational and housing discrimination. Such means of identity and achievement as the drug market and terrorism are caused by a minimal level of development, combined with access to tools of violence and communications. And no level of coercion and containment, no response which does not directly deal with the sources of frustration, can resolve these problems. Burton sees needs fulfillment as a practical necessity:

> It is the politically realistic observation that unless there is development and fulfillment of needs of individuals and groups, unless problems are solved and the need for coercion avoided, a social and political order may not be stable and harmonious, no matter what the level of coercion. Protest movements, violence at all social levels, terrorism, communal conflicts, dissident behaviour, strikes, revolts, revolutions, wars may be only observable symptoms that are a misleading clue to unobservable motivations (Burton, undated: 7).

What is one to make of this jumble of identity, gender, cultural, ideological, and class conflict? It is clear that no single theory of conflict is adequate to the task of understanding public conflict. The search for the single answer, the oracle which once found will condense the complexities of human behavior and organization to a few simple laws, is not defensible.

It is equally clear that an understanding of the dynamics of disputes and strategic considerations in negotiations alone is insufficient to the task of designing, convening and mediating these disputes. To focus only on these dynamics, however sophisticated such understanding may be even in encompassing gender and cultural differences, is to ignore the deeper meaning of these divisons and the potential for oppression and injustice.

Yet how can the many truths of these different theoretical perspectives be integrated without wandering aimlessly from one to another, or oversimplifying? None of these schools are a single mode of thought and practice; rather, they are a cauldron of evolving debate, with internal competition for primacy in some areas waged as fierce or fiercer than the battles against their external opponents. Thus it is all too easy to get caught in the morass of arguments and counter arguments internal to each tradition.

The answer, as unsatisfactory as it may be, is simply to warn of the pitfalls of this eclectic approach, and to proceed forewarned with these few propositions:

- There is much work in social theory and political practice during recent decades which has examined the nature of the circumstances circumscribing public conflict resolution.
- This work is not in any one field, with many of its currents outside of academia.
- Its influences on related areas of practice, such as planning, law, and public administration, is substantial but spotty.

- For those practitioners, public officials, foundations, and others concerned with the societal consequences of these divisions, it is worth the effort, and risk, to bring this wide-ranging inquiry to bear on the questions being studied.

Accepting the challenge: Building sustainable relationships

In Chapter Nine I offered a new use of the term 'sustainability', an application intended to have both practical and moral appeal. This new conception I termed *sustainability of human relations*. The starting point for this new application for the concept of sustainability is the book *Getting Disputes Resolved* (Ury *et al.*, 1988), and the triad of ways of dealing with disputes it describes: power, rights, and interests. I argued that these three vehicles of conflict resolution were ultimately unsustainable means of resolving conflict. A transformative practice of public conflict resolution must add a fourth choice to those three.

Relatedness

In order to move beyond power, rights, and interests, there must be vehicles for transforming, to paraphrase Barber (1984), the *I* of self-interest to the *we* of common welfare. I have asserted earlier the need to seek not only common ground, but higher ground. The metaphor of higher ground represents both new ground, or the creation of what has yet to be imagined, and an appeal to morality, to principle, indeed to virtue. Community life, institutions of governance, and the new forums being created to solve our public problems and resolve public conflict, must both insist upon as well as offer the opportunity for seeking that higher ground. The vehicle offered for this opportunity is that of 'relatedness'.

Relatedness is an imperfect term; it certainly has no currency yet within the conflict resolution field, and it carries rather vague connotations of good feelings. But relatedness as I am using it here embraces a host of qualities. While it need not exclude such dispositions as friendship, love, or altruism, it is much more than those dispositions alone. For relatedness does not depend upon the good feelings one might have for others.

Relatedness is also found in such qualities as a sense of responsibility for one's actions; a sense of obligation to those who are dependent; and loyalty to those who have extended themselves for others. It is found in a respect for the traditions of one's own and others' cultures; recognition of one's shared humanity; and understanding of, and even empathy for, the meaning others impart to their beliefs, values, and needs. It is, in short, a way of honoring the individual integrity which so often is hidden or assailed in adversarial situations and institutions.

These qualities of responsibility, or respect, of recognition, are of course enacted in relationship to other individuals and groups. But there is another important dimension to relatedness for public conflicts: an affiliation to place. Place, by virtue of its physical characteristics (e.g. landscape, climate, natural resources, visual beauty) and its historical antecedents (e.g. the built environment, culture) conditions the ways people live on the land. Each place thus has both physical and cultural qualities which exert a claim on its inhabitants, a claim which again and again is demonstrably honored. Indeed, Kemmis (1991) makes a strong argument that public life can only be sustained by linking it to real and identifiable places.[4]

Berry (1987) uses the example of a public hearing about a nuclear power plant to speak of a rapidly deepening division between people defending 'the health, the integrity, even the existence of places whose values they sum up in the words "home" and "community", and people for whom those words signify no value at all' (p. 84). People 'with local allegiances and local points of view' have an interest 'different in both quality and kind from the present *professional* interest' (p. 84). The transience of the population may weaken the visceral linkages to place, but the appeal is still very strong. Witness the enthusiastic connection felt by much of the population to sports teams, whether professional, collegiate, or even in many towns and counties at the secondary school level. At the professional and collegiate level these teams often lack a single native player; yet the teams are seen as embodying what is best about a particular community, win or lose, e.g. hard work, teamwork, persistence, the ability to recover from loss.

The challenge

The formidable challenge for the field of public conflict resolution is to develop the kinds of forums which acknowledge as well as cultivate the meaning and appeal of relatedness. It is a tall order, to manifest and foster relatedness amongst people with very different goals, and in situations with a history of antagonism and mistrust. It is tremendously hard and time consuming work, often undertaken with no guarantees of success. And yet, in contemporary society, where the legacy to posterity and the interdependence of individual, community, and society are so much at risk, there is little choice.

It is one thing to do this for interpersonal relations – albeit still a very difficult task – and another to do so for public issues involving multiple parties, each representing different personal and institutional interests. But much can be learned from practitioners working at the level of relatedness in a variety of forums.

While I disagree with Bush and Folger (1994) that the fundamental goal of mediation ought to be changing people through individual moral growth, I think they demonstrate truly extraordinary insight into processes of empowerment and recognition at the interpersonal level. Similar insights have been practised and articulated for years by Davis (1989, in Merry, 1994). The experiences and understanding demonstrated by Burton (1987; 1990) and Kelman (1990) through their work with identity groups at the intra- and inter-national levels are applicable at other levels as well. Saunders and Slim (1994), thoughtful and articulate, have begun to apply lessons learned at the international level to the domestic public arena. The powerful distinction between claiming goods and creating solutions offered by Kritek (1994) is but one small part of the useful and inspirational guidance she offers for conflict in general.

Among those leading the search for forums of relatedness and conflict transformation are many faith-based practitioners, including most prominently Chupp (1991), Lederach (1989; 1995), and Kraybill (1980; 1988). Potapchuk (1991a) and Potapchuk and Polk (1994) are doing pathbreaking work in the arena of civic and community development. Bremner and Visser (1994) have used their experience in community development in South Africa to articulate a transformative vision for meeting human needs. Brown and Mazza (1991) have developed a model of prejudice reduction which has been expanded for inter-group identity disputes and dialogue over other contentious issues. Chasin and her colleagues (Becker *at al.*, 1992) are devising creative ways of engaging dialogue on controversial issues. And these innovators are joined by many other practitioners, educators, and trainers whose wisdom and experience awaits description in print.

Notes

1   See, e.g., Berry (1987), Clark (1989), Bookchin (1990), and Kemmis (1990).
2   Barber (1984) also contends that local public activity, whose affective links are vital to democratic governance, can be supplemented by communication technologies which counter the problems of scale.
3   For acknowledgment of the problems with this 'harmony' orientation see Bellman *et al.*, (1982), Blake and Mouton (1970), and Nader (undated).
4   Kemmis explains that 'A politics of citizens working out the problems and the possibilities of their place directly among themselves implies a revival of the old republican notion of citizenship based upon civic virtue; it rejects the federalist use of procedures to "supply the defect of better motives"' (p. 123).

12

Agenda for a
transformative practice

This chapter presents recommendations to the public conflict resolution field for a transformative practice which would be consistent with the visions of humanity, of society, and of governance outlined in the previous three chapters. This practice would challenge the problems of the contemporary public domain through its acceptance of three projects:

1 inspiring, nurturing, and sustaining a vital communal life: *an engaged community*;
2 invigorating the institutions and practices of governance: *a responsive governance*; and
3 enhancing society's ability to solve problems and resolve conflicts: *a capacity for problem solving and conflict resolution.*

The bulk of the chapter is given to suggestions for actions which practitioners, researchers, funders, and supporters of public conflict resolution might take in order to develop a field which would support such a practice.

The components of a transformative practice

The engaged community
A transformative practice seeks to nurture a strong democracy by helping constitute and support communities of dialogic relations at local, state, regional, and national levels. It seeks to establish and sustain a standard of public discourse that empowers people to articulate their needs freely and to explore their differences fairly. It moderates powerlessness and alienation by insisting on inclusion and participation. It opposes the polarization and demonizing which too often accompany conflict by offering recognition of shared humanity and purpose.

A transformative practice educates for a civic consciousness. It recognizes that individuals, through their participation in the public realm, are capable of transcending pressures of self-interest in search of common goals.

And it encourages productive, realistic relationships both within and among communities of all kinds that recognize and affirm their interdependence – their relatedness – within this shared public domain.

A responsive governance

While not ignoring the need for improved capabilities of public management, the transformative practice conceives of these desired capabilities as responsive to, rather than directive of, the public. A transformative practice acknowledges the importance of well-functioning administrative, legislative, and legal institutions. It recognizes their expanding role in a society whose problems are rapidly increasing in complexity and in scope. It views these institutions as potential channels of participation by an engaged citizenry. It wishes to enhance their capabilities by sensitizing them to public needs and by facilitating appropriate responses to public demands. And it strives to strengthen these public institutions by encouraging active, lasting and meaningful public participation in decisions made on that public's behalf.

A capacity for solving problems and resolving conflicts

A transformative practice addresses a wide range of problems, including pivotal issues of race, ethnicity, class, and gender. It recognizes that underlying many disputes are struggles over power, status, and human needs such as identity, recognition, and security. It also recognizes that ordinary disputes are often the manifestation of these deeper societal divisions. It acknowledges the disparities of power that favor relations of dominance along these divisions, and embraces the opportunities for revealing injustice and mobilizing concern presented by the inevitable conflicts that accompany and uncover these relations. It assists in efforts to equalize and even transcend power, by acknowledging these disparities in public forums open to previously unseen faces and unheard voices. It recognizes that movements for justice are also capable of harm. It intervenes in the demonizing and polarization which pervade these disputes by advocating for openness, inclusion, fairness, and understanding.

A transformative practice also recognizes that site-specific disputes are the manifestation of larger social conflicts. The struggles over these many disputes define the ground of these larger conflicts. Thus, in some fashion, the battles over such issues as the siting of waste facilities, commercial development in historical districts, AIDS policy for a school district, and thousands of similar disputes also have at stake matters such as the bounds of privatism and public life; the responsibility of a generation to its inheritors; an ethic of care competing with an ethic of rights; domination counterposed against partnership; corporatism (including nationality) opposed by appropriateness of scale; and continued economic growth relative to sustainability and quality of life. It is in the resolution of these individual disputes that these larger conflicts will be transformed.

The transformative agenda

What would a field which supports this transformative practice look like? Several substantive components of the transformative practice might serve as a benchmark. They are centered around these six themes:

1 the conception of disputes and dispute resolution;
2 the third party role;
3 the types of problems and conflicts addressed in practice;
4 evaluation of success and failure;
5 the research agenda; and,
6 development of the field.

These will be addressed in turn.

Disputes and the resolution of conflict

The effects of public conflict resolution cannot be measured by the intervention of mediation and facilitation alone. Indirect activities, such as training and development of mediators, research, funding, public speaking, and writing, are not at all peripheral in terms of their impact upon public conflict. The impact of the field of public conflict resolution must be measured by the cumulative effects not only of intervention but of these other endeavors as well.

But the practices of dispute resolution – mediation and facilitation – are certainly a most important component of the field. In a transformative practice, the conception of disputes as static clashes of interests, and negotiation as a process solely of bargaining and exchange, a conception reinforced by game theory and the collective bargaining experience, would be rejected as incomplete. Disputes would be seen as socially constituted, dynamic organisms, whose actors, issues, and consequences are invariably shaped and transformed by the means available, offered, and used to contest them. These clashes of interests would be recognized as involving as well struggles for recognition, identity, status, and other resources less tangible than are immediately apparent.

The many values and functions of conflict would be acknowledged. Conversely, while embracing conflict, a transformative practice would also offer less public gloss and more acknowledgment of the real world of conflict, including the important roles played by organizational imperatives and constraints, competition for power both between and within parties, and the personal factors of fears, hurts, insults, anger, and ego. It is a gross misconception to believe that conflict resolution avoids this aspect of conflict.

Indeed, negotiating the resolution of public disputes requires parties both to transcend and at the same time be faithful to their differences, at least insofar as they reflect their underlying goals.[1]

The dispute resolution process would then become more than a vehicle for reaching agreements and for exchanging interests. It would offer, as presented in Chapter Eleven, a higher ground – the opportunity to add to human relations maintained by power, rights, and interests the opportunity to discover and to claim the relatedness a vital public domain demands. The focus would be upon the creation of *sustainable* relations between and among individuals and communities.

The responsible and independent third party

There are three arguments for rejecting the conception of neutrality established in labor-management dispute resolution for intervention in public disputes. First, it is demonstrably untrue that perceived neutrality or impartiality is essential for successful intervention in public disputes. Public conflict resolution procedures are being used by city managers, planners, and others who might be considered to have a stake in the issues under contention, such as authorities invested with decision-making power.[2]

Second, it is also demonstrably untrue that practitioners act neutrally or impartially in actual practice. Researchers in the fields of labor-management, community dispute resolution, and public conflict resolution have found that the actual behavior of practitioners defies the rhetoric of neutrality.[3] To pretend to a practice which does not exist is both dishonest and impractical.

Third, and most importantly, the assumption of a so-called 'neutral' stance in public disputes is morally and ethically untenable. Too often a stance of neutrality merely serves to legitimize the disparities which provoked the dispute. As Forester and Stitzel (1989) affirm, neutrality in the face of inequalities of power promises acquiescence to the perpetuation of the status quo.[4] Indeed, neutrality within a setting of power differentiation and injustice is another form of partisanry (Chesler, 1989).

Thus, in a transformative practice a neutrality which actually reinforces an undesirable status quo would be replaced by a conception of third-party *independence* and *responsibility* which recognizes and embraces the values implicit in the conflict resolution process. Independence means being responsible for, aligned with, or obliged to no one individual, group, or interest. Responsibility means that this independence is not merely an exercise in unrestrained self-indulgence, and that the power inherent in the third-party role is used with full awareness of its potential consequences to disputants and affected publics.

Abandoning the conception of neutrality does not mean becoming an advocate for one party relative to another. Laue (1990) offers the distinction between advocacy for party, advocacy for outcome, and advocacy for process. Individuals may assume any one or more of these roles in any given situation. But a responsible and independent third party cannot be an advocate for any one party, nor for any particular outcome. Rather, an independent third party explicitly advocates for processes seeking certain qualities of outcome, including fairness, inclusiveness, openness, and endurance. This role may also be thought of as non-partisan (Susskind, in Forester, 1994), impartiality, or even 'co-partiality' or 'co-advocacy'.

This more active conception of the third party role also admits the interests of stakeholders not at the table, including the general public, groups or individuals without the power to force their inclusion into public conflict resolution forums, and also of future generations (Susskind, 1981; Stephens *et al.*, 1995). In effect, practitioners would accept responsibility for the implications of their practice.

In some ways the attention granted to neutrality and its alternatives is misdirected. Neutrality is not a goal or a value in and of itself. Rather, it is a means to another end: it is, in fact, trust, acceptance, and, ultimately, entry, which are the desired products of neutrality and integral to the dispute resolution process.

The willingness with which so many disputants accept the intervention of a third party (albeit conditionally) ought perhaps to be seen less as a positive sign of the field's success than as an indictment of contemporary society's fragmentation of communities and traditions. In effect, this third party 'neutral' is fulfilling a role which in traditional cultures is filled by intermediaries such as a village elder or tribal council (Gulliver, 1979).

Individuals and organizations involved in disputes often have invested significant portions of their lives, at great emotional and financial cost, in the struggles over issues having the deepest meaning to them. How unique to contemporary Western culture must be this willingness to extend trust to strangers in these circumstances! Indeed, acceptance of these third parties occurs in good part for three reasons: because they have little or nothing at stake in the substance of the outcome, because their involvement will be transitory, and because they have only professional relationships with those involved.

It seems likely that the idea of the 'neutral' public conflict resolution practitioner will eventually be seen as a brief, if necessary, interlude in the history of the advancement of conflict resolution. Even if one does not accept that neutrality is not possible, or desirable, the growing acceptance of mediation of public disputes will force changes in the third party role, as more and more parties return to the table more and more often. The University of Virginia's Institute for Environmental Negotiation, for instance, in existence since 1981, already finds many repeat players, some of whom have participated in five or six negotiations mediated by the Institute. These parties represent all of the various interests (i.e. industry, environment, government, citizenry) involved in local, regional, and state-wide public issues. Indeed, some of these players are former students, who are gradually finding their way into senior level positions. It is impossible to avoid the kinds of relationships with these parties which neutrality claims to deny. Yet these relationships are far from being the obstacle advocates for neutrality might predict. Quite the contrary; these participants become advocates for the dispute resolution process as well as for particular individuals and/or organizations.

This new conception of the third party role will undoubtedly bring its own problems. As the weaknesses of the classic conception of neutrality are acknowledged, other means will need to be found for developing the requisite trust and acceptance. While confidence in those providing negotiation assistance will always be an important part of the dispute resolution practice, such confidence can be developed in other ways. It may also be developed when disputants know that third party assistance is offered by those with more than a professional investment in achieving a workable, fair, and self-sustaining resolution; by those whose involvement with the issues is more than transitory, and whose investment in the community will outlast any one particular case; and even, in some cases, by those who may share some stake in the consequences of the outcome, by virtue of their interest in the larger commuity.[5]

One constructive way of developing such confidence is by developing institutions rooted in the communities (geographic or political) which will use them. For example, a number of community dispute resolution centers founded to deal with interpersonal disputes have also created a public dispute resolution capacity (Sachs, 1988; 1989). These centers, rooted in the communities that use them, can serve as a model for this kind of institution building.

The types of problems addressed in cases

In a transformative practice, sensitivity to the problems of women (e.g. the feminization of poverty), the poor, minorities,[6] and others found most often at the low end of the power scale would be actualized through a caseload that deals with issues of concern to those too often left out of the political process. It is perhaps less popular, and therefore even more important, to recognize that this category includes groups across the political spectrum. A field which addresses issues such as environmental racism and AIDS discrimination ought to acknowledge as well the likes of rural property rights advocates, elderly tobacco farmers, and champions for home schooling among those who have been marginalized and excluded from decisions which affect their lives.

The market will continue to play a dominant role in the types of issues addressed by public conflict resolution practitioners. In order to ensure attention to these issues, which do not necessarily respond to market-driven forces, the field needs to lobby diligently for continued foundation support. And sensitivity to these needs must retain a prominent position on the field's agenda. One concrete suggestion aimed at accomplishing this goal would be for interested practitioners to create a pooled, revolving fund which would allow attention to those disputes and issues which do not attract conventional funding.

Evaluating success and failure

In a transformative practice, the methods of evaluating success or failure would broaden well beyond such existing standards as efficiency of time, cost savings, and numbers of agreements reached and implemented. One must answer many questions in order to adequately evaluate the results of specific cases, to assess the worth of different processes, or to judge the impact of the field. Is the process accessible and affordable? Does it protect participants' rights? Are unrepresented interests acknowledged and safeguarded?

If an agreement is reached, does it provide a sense of finality? Does it reflect up-to-date knowledge? Does it have an impact on policy? How is it implemented? How well does it last?

These are not easy questions to answer. Even more difficult to assess are the kinds of long-term changes in individuals that many practitioners seek. Do participants gain greater understanding of themselves, of their interests, and of each other? Do they gain the ability to continue on their own, without the assistance of a third party? Do they find the process useful for dealing with other disputes or problems?

A final question concerns the degree of institutional change resulting from the intervention. Although this concern is not commonly included in assessment, in some circumstances it may be the most important criterion for success (Chesler, 1989).

Shifting considerations of success and failure beyond agreement and efficiency may require considerable education of users of dispute resolution services, particularly those funding these applications. For decision-making forums, agreement will always be an important goal; however, as practice becomes more proactive, other benefits may become more apparent. Research which demonstrates the utility of processes that may not reach formal agreement is an essential component of that education.[7]

The research agenda

While more research of public conflict resolution is necessary, it is well to remember – and to remind the researchers – that it is not so much research that is needed as it is understanding embedded in fact. A transformative practice would encourage honest efforts at understanding the meaning of this work as well as sharing this understanding with those who have the most at stake. Crowfoot (1988) suggests seven items within the field of public conflict resolution needing theory-building and empirical research, including the sources of conflict and their relationship to social change, experiences of interest groups with negotiations and mediation, concerns with social justice, and the cross-cultural dimension. While his focus is the environment, his ideas may be extended to other issues (e.g. health care, housing, group violence) as well, since these issues transcend any single field.

Thanks to the journal *Consensus* public officials and practitioners now can keep up with the basics of the public conflict resolution field – the issues, processes, and experiences of practitioners. But the 1983 Report of the National Institute for Dispute Resolution-sponsored Ad Hoc Panel on Dispute Resolution and Public Policy is still current in its sensitivity to the needs of the field. The report, 'Paths to Justice', argues:

> Very little of the experience with these programs has been documented. The information that does exist is fragmented and housed in many separate places. The result is that, while jurisdictions have problems in common, there is no mechanism for finding out what has been tried elsewhere and with what success. Moreover, dispute resolution methodologies are developing in various substantive areas with little cross-fertilization. As a result, knowledge, experience, and resources are wasted (p. 25).

While there has been some documentation of the experience with dispute resolution programs, it is still quite fragmented. Program evaluation is sorely lacking (Susskind, 1986). Publication of research is scattered across many journals, some of them quite obscure.

The dissemination of this information to affected audiences, including some of whom may not realize that dispute resolution concerns them, is equally as important as garnering the information. Such information must be tailored to the specific audience, whether researchers, policymakers, the legal profession, or the general public. The research agenda ought to balance innovation, evaluation, and education. The Panel recommendations – pilot programs and research, a clearinghouse for information, and outreach to expand awareness and dialogue – remain appropriate guidelines for the field.

Development of the public conflict resolution field

The future of the field cannot be taken for granted (Susskind, 1986). Laue (1988) observed that experienced practitioners inevitably ask whether third parties can do more than react to cases. As they do so, their attention turns from case intervention towards social change. Judging from interviews and presentations and discussions at conferences, many public conflict resolution practitioners are eager to effect such change.

Their ability to do so will depend in good part upon whether and how the field defines its role. The following recommendations are offered to stimulate the kind of self-assessment required by those involved in the field who care about its future.

The meaning of practice   Practitioners would engage in continual reflection and discussion about their own values and practices, and how those practices do and do not reflect those values. Practitioners would also seek an understanding of public conflict resolution embedded in historical, political and social perspectives. This understanding can be actualized through conference sessions devoted to this subject, continuing education, and granting considered reflection the same priority as other demands of organizational development.

Linkage with the conflict resolution community   There would be more linkage with others with similar aims in the conflict resolution community, including practitioners in other fields, in order to garner the benefits of mutual education as well as develop and use political power to advocate for the purposes of the field. Practioners would, following Susskind's (1986) advice, oversee the development of the conflict resolution field as a whole.

This linkage would be accompanied by the recognition that conflict resolution is itself a social movement, with citizen advocates (especially within the community mediation arena), foundation support, and other elements characteristic of other such movements. Social movements perform many functions; they can make people aware of problems, change ways of thinking about those problems, empower people to act, and change institutions.

Education   The field would recognize its potential as a vehicle for education. Such education starts with the demystification of practice (Susskind, 1986), and is very broad. It includes education in the skills of negotiation and conflict resolution, about the sources and structures of violence, and about creative participation in social change (Clark, 1989).

It would be well to remember that this is a learning movement as well. Many of the participants in these conflict resolution forums have their own skills and inclination for problem solving, consensus building, and conflict resolution to share.

Linkage with allied social movements   The relationships which already exist with 'established' interests, including training and consultation, would continue to be developed. The benefits brought to these interests by collaborative solutions can be powerful inducements to advocate for the virtues of democratic and participatory decision-making.

But there would also be efforts to link conflict resolution with social movements that have related aims and values, including those of citizen action, feminism, populism, peace action, and ecoactivism. This linkage might occur in a variety of ways: through participation in the community of dialogue, writing, conferencing, and general networking common to these other groups; by sharing expertise (e.g. by offering trainings in principled negotiation and conflict resolution); or by assisting in organizational development.

Conflict theorists realize that escalated conflict is often the only viable means for gaining attention and resources for groups denied justice (Chesler, 1989). In situations involving these groups, practitioners might also offer training and assistance along the lines of conflict assessment, negotiation advice, and skills in working in multicultural settings.[8]

Cultural sensitivity   The field of public conflict resolution, with only a few exceptions, is dominated by white middle-class individuals. To judge by participation at seminars and conference discussions of cross-cultural issues, many practitioners do recognize the increasing significance of issues of ethnicity and race (with less attention paid to class). And practitioners cannot simply be labelled as products of contemporary Western privilege and culture; indeed, many entered the field because of their dissatisfaction with the less attractive themes of Western culture.

But sensitivity to and awareness of the realities of life for minorities cannot fully alleviate the 'demographic biases' of the field, which place the concerns of social justice for these minorities somewhere at the back of the agenda (Chesler, 1989). A field which advocates fairness and inclusion ought to demonstrate a visible commitment to the same internal standards. A two-track approach to this concern, combining education about racism and class discrimination for practitioners and recruitment of minorities, is an important component of a transformative agenda.[9]

Resistance to problems of professionalism   Within the community of practitioners there would be awareness of the bureaucratic and organizational pitfalls which other human service movements have discovered make every profession, to varying degrees, a 'conspiracy against the laity'. As Davis (1989) wryly admits, ideas started with the best intentions get pulled into establishments: 'Most reforms eventually go sour' (p. 3). Susskind (1986) offers a plea to 'not allow the competitive impulses of some practitioners to set up barriers to entry into the profession', and to 'resist all efforts at guildism (p. 52). Forewarned is forearmed; while public conflict resolution is not immune to such pressures, acknowledgment of their influence is a first step towards continued resistance to them. It is well to heed this reminder of

Lederach (1989): 'The best mediators have the passion and vision of activists' (p. 14).

Conclusion

The two conceptions of public conflict resolution presented in this book – the ideology of management and the transformative practice – are broadly drawn. They certainly overlap at several points, and few practitioners, if any, would find themselves exclusively in one camp or the other. Nonetheless, the cumulative effects of the current body of practice, writing, publicity, and, particularly, sponsorship, indicate a growing acceptance of the terms of management to the exclusion of the transformative potential.

I do not claim by any means that all the problems addressed by the management practice are illusory. Rather, I fear that acceptance of the terms of management means that the field might become far less than what it could be and what it needs to be. At worst, the field risks becoming a self-deceiving caricature of its own promises, devoured like so many other social reform movements by the conditions of its own success. At best, it can play an important role as one vehicle of the movement for social justice and transformation. While the future may not force a choice of all of one or all of the other, it will most certainly offer a choice of which will dominate.

Few expect that public conflict resolution can significantly alter the destiny of society. Most practitioners would agree with the assessment of its acceptance by one mediator, who termed it 'a mile wide and an inch deep'.[10] The resolution of difficult disputes; the creation of dialogic, consensual, problem-solving forums; the education of citizens and officials in principles of conflict resolution; any or all of these, in and of themselves, will be inadequate to the task of creating and sustaining the kind of world that is as yet only imagined.

But can anyone believe that such a world can ever be constituted or maintained without a capacity for engaging different viewpoints, confronting difficult issues, and resolving difficult problems? Public conflict resolution offers a unique challenge, and opportunity, to help build this capacity.

Notes

1 Cormick (1987) in particular advocates this view: 'Unless parties remain mindful of their conflicting interests, they are unlikely to strike a bargain that is viable when faced with the difficult realities of implementation; both the parties and their agreements will be repudiated by their constituents. Established, confident adversaries aware of their own interests make the best negotiators and work out the best agreements' (p. 33).

2 See, e.g., Forester and Stitzel (1989).
3 See, e.g., Kolb (1983a), Cobb and Rifkin (1990), Forester and Stitzel (1989).
4 See also Laue and Cormick (1978), Chesler (1989), and Edmonds (1990).
5 Dan Kemmis (1990), the mayor of Missoula, Montana, provides a model for such a role.
6 As Edmonds (1990) contends, 'how the conflict resolution field defines itself and its models, in preparing to respond to the realities of a multicultural society, is the most critical developmental task our field will encounter' (p. 15).
7 See, e.g., Buckle and Thomas-Buckle (1986), Dotson (1993).
8 See Chesler (1989) and Chesler *et al.*, (1978).
9 See the 1994 SPIDR Proceedings for report of a series of workshops concerning these issues.
10 Howard Bellman, personal conversation, 1990.

Appendix: Terminology

Problems of terminology

The field of conflict resolution, whose study so clearly reveals the costs of distorted communication, does not itself have a shared language. This irony is not lost on observers (Burton and Dukes, 1990), but as yet there has been no solution to the problem.

What is the difference between a dispute and a conflict? Between mediation and conciliation? Between dispute resolution, dispute settlement, conflict management, and conflict resolution? Individual authors often attach different meanings to these various terms, and the answers to these questions vary from one publication to another. While some of the differences are merely matters of terminology, others can reflect substantial contradictions in the understanding of disputes and conflicts, the appropriateness or inappropriateness of various processes, and goals of intervention efforts.

The term 'ADR' (alternative dispute resolution) may serve as a notable example of the significance of terminology. The use of the term ADR has significant implications for the ways people conceptualize the field, their work, and the meaning attached to this work. There are two meanings to the term. The first is the limited domain of alternatives to formal adjudication, including arbitation, mini-trials, summary jury trials, and so forth (Burton and Dukes, 1990). The second, and more common, meaning is the entire galaxy of non-litigative means of dealing with disputes, including not only those aforementioned procedures but others such as mediation, ombudsmanry, and negotiation.

As a descriptive term ADR has several problems. It is misleading, in that it ignores both the many facets of adjudication – there is no single standard judicial procedure – and the fact that much of so-called ADR deals with issues the courts have never touched. And the assumption of a single descriptor means that the significant differences in values and goals among practitioners and institutional interests become swept under the same rug.

'Alternatives' do not exist on their own terms. As Auerbach (1983) notes, the alternatives do not have a name of their own; instead, they become defined by that which they are not. Because the term alludes to the legal system, its meaning is embedded within the framework of legal practice. The acceptance of the term ensures that discourse is bounded within a litigation paradigm.

Finally, the term 'alternative' itself has a self-limiting, indeed self-marginalizing aspect. For the past few decades the term has often been associated in a pejorative manner with radical and misguided practices by an alienated minority of society: witness the 'alternative press', an 'alternative lifestyle', and now 'alternative dispute resolution'. As long as the field is identified by what it is an alternative to, rather than what it stands for, it is bound to have a role prescribed by its referents.

A call for clarity

While the choice of particular words is open to interpretation and argument, it surely is useful to be able to distinguish among the many different concepts evoked by these terms. But repeated ambiguity of terminology causes issues to be framed in such a way that sometimes very real differences are obscured, while the substantial becomes confused with the superficial. And to the extent that the use of labels such as 'resolution' or 'settlement' substitute for clearly presented and shared understandings of the concepts they represent, debate will inevitably fail to uncover the true sources of any disagreement over those concepts.

The absence of a shared language presents problems not only to practitioners and academics trying to communicate with one another, but to a general public bewildered by the sudden proliferation of choice offered them. How many people forced into mandatory mediation or arbitration may have been permanently alienated from any other 'alternative'?

No one individual or institution has a mandate to impose standards of meaning upon others. One set of definitions will not change the meaning of its terms to others; the need for precision and clarity within the field must be balanced with consideration of actual current usage. What can be suggested is that there be awareness of the consequences of the use of language, and the potential for misunderstanding; that care is taken to make explicit what is intended by the choice of terms; and that analysts of conflict work towards a clear, unambiguous communication within the field and between the field and the public.

Selected definitions

Adjudication (public)

The process of settling a dispute, during which the judge, an official representative of the state, renders a binding decision (subject to appeal) based upon application of a formal system of laws and precedent.

There are many variations on the familiar jury trial format. These variations include a *pre-trial conference*, in which the parties present their cases informally to the judge, who may then recommend a settlement. A *moderated settlement conference* involves a panel of experts, often attorneys, who hear presentations by each side and give advice to the parties for their negotiations. A *summary jury trial* is a brief mock trial, with a real jury (who may not be informed beforehand that their verdict is not binding), which allows each side to realistically assess their chances were they to proceed to a full trial.

Neutral experts, also called *fact-finders*, give advice, opinion, and testimony during a trial; they may be appointed in some situations without the approval of the disputants. A *special master*, appointed by a court, has a good deal of leeway with which to work, and may act as a mediator as well as recommend a specific settlement to the parties and the court.

Adjudication (private)

A class of non-official processes similar to public adjudication in which disputants themselves approve the choice of process and judge.

In some states these proceedings have the force of law. The two most common procedures are called *private judging*, or *rent-a-judge*, and the *mini-trial*. Private judging allows disputants to avoid the long delays common to litigation by hiring their own adjudicator, often a retired judge. The mini-trial involves a neutral advisor and, sometimes, a mock jury, both of whom can make a decision and give their opinions of the merits of the case. This independent appraisal enables the sides to negotiate their own agreement with a realistic understanding of how others perceive their case.

Most of these private alternatives to public adjudication proceedings have been developed to deal with corporate disputes.

Alternative dispute resolution (ADR)

This term is used narrowly to refer to a select set of courtroom alternatives and in a very broad sense to include a wide range of conflict processes. Some critics of the term prefer the designation *appropriate dispute resolution*, suggesting that it is in fact adjudication which is the alternative, since most disputes are handled through non-adjudicatory procedures.

Arbitration

A private, relatively informal process in which a third party hears arguments and renders a decision based either upon the disputants' own criteria or applicable statutory provisions. Arbitration is commonly used for labor-management disputes, automobile warranty complaints, insurance problems, and international business disagreements. The arbitrator may be an individual or a panel.

There are many variations of arbitration. It can be *binding* or *non-binding*. *High-low* arbitration limits the minimum and maximum amount of potential awards. In *final-offer* arbitration the arbitrator must select one of the final positions of the two sides. *Med-arb* is a recent innovation combining mediation with mandatory arbitration should mediation efforts fail. Some judicial systems use *court-annexed* arbitration to divert minor cases from crowded dockets.

Conciliation

Steps taken by a third party to reduce hostility, lower tension, correct misperceptions, improve communication, and create a favorable climate for negotiation. Often a figure of some stature recognized by the disputants uses *good offices* to begin the conciliation process. Conciliation is particularly associated with religious groups such as the Quakers and Mennonites.

Conflict

Conflict is the opposition of two or more parties, one or more of whom have or perceive incompatibility of values, interests, or goals, and one or more of whom attempt to persuade, neutralize, injure, or gain advantage over the other party or parties.

Conflict is a natural, inevitable, and recurring part of all human interaction occurring at all levels of society, from interpersonal to international. It is not deviant or pathological, *per se*, nor does it necessarily result in serious harm; its manifestation may be a revealing expression of injustices or strains in the social system which demand attention. Left alone, however, conflict behavior can become destructive, and destructive behavior can be self-reinforcing and self-escalating.

Conflict is not the opposite of 'order' or the same as 'chaos', for behavior of parties in conflict often follows identifiable and even predictable patterns. Conflict is rooted, not only in scarcity of resources, aggressive behavior, and personality, but in universal human needs for individual and cultural identity, security, and recognition, as well as in the policies and structures of political and economic systems. Struggles over identity, values, power, and limited resources are at the heart of all social conflicts.

There is also a special meaning of conflict where it refers to fundamental, deep, and widespread societal and inter-societal divisions over issues such as distribution of resources, values, and behavior. In the latter meaning, a distinction is made between *conflicts* and *disputes* (see *Dispute* and *Public conflict resolution*).

Conflict assessment

Determination of the parties, issues, history, and feasibility of any proposed intervention for a particular conflict or dispute. A conflict assessment is the first step undertaken by a third party entering into a dispute.

Consensus

Consensus-based processes are used increasingly for decision-making for public policy issues, from informal meetings within organizations to lengthy, formal, multi-party negotiations. Despite the prominence these processes have achieved, there is still wide misunderstanding about the uses and purposes of consensual decision-making.

Typically, consensus may be defined by the following characteristics:

- Decisions are made either by unanimity or by a substantial majority (e.g. all but one member) depending upon the preferences of the group.
- Everyone can live with the final agreements without compromising issues of fundamental importance.
- Individual portions of the agreement may be less than ideal for some members, but the overall package is worthy of support.
- Individuals will work to support the full agreement and not just the parts they like the best.

Consensus building

Developing agreement on issues where parties bring different perspectives and interests to the table but before the issues have crystallized into a dispute. Inclusive participation, full exploration of issues, and agreements based upon substantial majorities or even unanimity are characteristics of consensus building efforts.

Convening

Commonly used in conjunction with *negotiated rulemaking*, a convenor identifies the scope of issues and parties to a dispute and determines whether negotiations would be feasible.

Dispute

The individual grounds upon which larger social conflicts are fought. For instance, a series of disputes across the nation between white supremacists and localities is one manifestation of deeper societal racial and class conflicts (see *Conflict* and *Public conflict resolution*).

Facilitation

For the purposes of this work, facilitation refers to those activities which are exploratory, educational, or otherwise directed at gathering information and developing understanding short of agreement. These serve a variety of functions: educating various interested parties and/or the general public, increasing public involvement, demonstrating an unfamiliar process, engaging different viewpoints, or raising consciousness about an issue. They may precede or accompany efforts more directly tied to reaching and implementing agreements.

The term is also used to describe the process direction given by a third party structuring and running a meeting or other gathering. Facilitators encourage full analysis of issues, open expression of opinion, exploration of options, and consensual choice of action. Facilitation is often a part of other processes, but is sometimes distinguished from mediation by virtue of the facilitator adding little or no substantive input into the process.

Fact-finding

The process by which the facts relevant to particular issues under contention are determined. A *neutral fact-finder* may be appointed to develop the necessary information, or the parties may engage in *joint fact-finding*.

Mediation

The term 'mediation' has been used to identify a wide range of practices. Because of this, much of the discourse surrounding 'mediation' is unproductive; arguments about its viability or promise or problems are inherently meaningless without specifying exactly which procedure, in which circumstances, producing which results, is meant. Indeed, the term often 'obscures more than it reveals' (Adler *et al.*, 1988: 333).

The terms 'mediated negotiation' (Susskind and Ozawa, 1985; Dotson *et al.*, 1989) and 'assisted negotiation' (Mernitz, 1980) are perhaps more appropriate descriptions of what is termed 'mediation'. However, while focusing appropriate attention on what is central to the process – the negotiations among the disputants – rather than the activities of an intervenor, these terms have gained little currency among observers.

Claim to possession of the rights to the term 'mediation' is often debated among those advocating different approaches to the dispute resolution process. A sampling of the very different definitions available includes the following:

Mediation involves the intervention of a third party who first investigates and defines the problem and then usually approaches each group separately with recommendations designed to provide a mutually acceptable solution (Blake and Mouton, 1984: 15).

[Mediation is] the process by which participants, together with the assistance of a neutral person or persons, systematically isolate disputed issues in order to develop options, consider alternatives, and reach a consensual settlement that will accomodate their needs (Folberg and Taylor, 1984: 7).

Mediation is the assistance of a neutral 'third party' to a negotiation (Bingham, 1986: 5).

Mediation refers to a site-specific dispute resolution process which results in a written settlement statement (Lake, 1980: 60).

Mediation is a process in which the disputing parties select a neutral third party to assist them in reaching a settlement of the dispute. The process is private, voluntary, informal and non-binding (Millhauser, 1989: 3).

Unfortunately, each of these attempts to define mediation uses 'loaded' terms, terms which argue (perhaps unintentionally) through definition for particular practices. A brief scan of these definitions reveals a number of these hidden arguments. For instance, a good portion of the community mediation literature argues for integrative solutions rather than mutual concessions (e.g. Moore, 1987; Folberg and Taylor, 1984); many argue that 'neutrality' is unachievable or misconceived (e.g. Cobb, 1991; Cobb and Rifkin, 1990; Forester and Stitzel, 1989; Laue and Cormick, 1978); and there are 'mediations' which are public (e.g. regulatory negotiations), involuntary (some court-annexed programs require participation of parties), formal (as is often the case in international forums), and even binding (as in the hybrid process of 'med-arb', a combination of mediation and arbitration).

A broader definition resolves many of these difficulties. The definition proposed by Szanton Associates (1989) is appropriate. They suggest that mediation involves a third party in the following activities:

> any form of active participation in attempts to resolve differences between or among parties in actual or prospective conflict. The participation may be labeled mediation, facilitation, consultation, participatory research, consensus building, conflict management or whatever, so long as it: (a) involves actual intervention (training others to mediate future disputes does not qualify), and (b) is not initially intended to impose a third-party decision, i.e. is not arbitration (p. 2).

The term covers a very broad set of procedures. These range from the *muscle mediation* activities of a Kissinger or a labor mediator, who often bring strong pressure to bear upon the disputants, to *community mediation*, where parties are offered primarily a process of structured communication.

Mediation is used at all social levels. At the community level, many divorce and child custody disputes, consumer-merchant problems, and landlord-tenant disputes are mediated. The Community Relations Service, of the US Department of Justice, intervenes in ethnic and racial disputes.

Many schools now have *conflict manager* programs in which students are trained to mediate student disputes. *Victim–offender* mediation brings together a convicted offender with the victim(s) of the crime to work out restitution. Equal employment opportunity disputes or fair hiring practice cases may be mediated.

An expanding field, *public policy mediation*, is being developed to deal with many public issues, including land use, resource management, energy policy, access to health care, and government regulations. The subset of this field dealing with environmental issues is titled *environmental mediation* (see *Public conflict resolution*).

Negotiated rulemaking

The process by which multiple interests who anticipate being substantially affected by a potential agency rule negotiate the terms of the rule. The agency participates in the negotiations with varying degrees of activity, and retains authority over the promulgation of the rule, but generally anticipates that any consensual agreement would provide the basis for the proposed rulemaking. It is also known as *regulatory negotiations* or *reg-neg*.

Negotiation

The process by which disputing parties directly and indirectly exchange ideas, promises, threats, or other information related to one or more issues. One common distinction currently made is between *positional* negotiation, which involves little or no analysis of the wants and needs underlying a party's stated positions, and *interest-based* negotiation, which attends to those underlying wants and needs. *Bargaining* is sometimes identified as the subset of negotiation involving only trade-offs, compromise, and other fixed-sum activities.

Ombudsmanship

The process by which a third party, on behalf of some authority, investigates complaints and recommends or implements solutions. The ombudsman's duties are often organizational, although in some countries they have a wide range of authority. In Sweden, for instance, ombudsmen oversee the courts and criminal justice system, the armed forces, the tax system, and the social welfare and educational systems.

Policy dialogue

Exploratory discussions of complex public policy issues involving multiple parties. Unlike *negotiated rulemaking*, policy dialogues do not have the direct tie-in to a particular policy apparatus, but the inclusiveness of participation is generally of such a quality that any agreements derived from the dialogues are expected to have a significant effect on policy. Participation may include members of citizen or environmental organizations, regulatory agencies, corporations, legislative and executive branch staff, academic institutions, labor unions, and lobbying organizations.

Process design

Consultation with the parties to a dispute or with an organization about the needs for handling a particular issue or project. The consultant does not actually serve as mediator or facilitator, but may offer training in negotiation or organizational development.

Public conflict resolution

As a descriptor of the entire field, the term, 'public conflict resolution' is favored here over possibilities such as 'environmental mediation' (Amy, 1987, among others); 'policy mediation' (Laue, 1988); 'public policy mediation' (Szanton Associates, 1989); 'public dispute management' (Carpenter and Kennedy, 1988); 'public sector dispute resolution' (Forester, 1989); or 'public dispute resolution' (Susskind and Cruikshank, 1987).

'Environmental mediation' is inadequate for two reasons. Environmental problems comprise only a portion of the host of public issues, including race, health care, and economic development, now being addressed by conflict resolution practitioners. And 'mediation' is simply too limited a term to adequately convey the wide range of activities now common to the field, including process design, training, and other forms of assisted negotiation.

The addition of the qualifier 'policy' is also unnecessarily constraining. Laue (1988) defines policy mediation as 'a proactive form of intervention that involves the use of a mediator, facilitator, or other third party to promote cooperative problem solving in complex multiparty conflicts with major policy implications' (p. 1). But many disputes of a public nature do not necessarily involve questions of policy.

Szanton Associates (1990), while recognizing this broader application, still subsume it under the rubric of 'public policy', by which they mean any dispute involving a 'government or public interest organization or civic or neighborhood group as a substantial party (for example, a dispute betweeen a municipal agency and residents over the location of an airport), or bearing on the interests of some community as a whole' (p. 2). Because 'policy' does connote the active involvement of some governmental authority as one of the principals of the dispute, at whatever level, and because some public disputes (e.g. turf wars between gangs in a particular neighborhood) do not have that element, policy mediation, like environmental mediation, ought to be seen as only one component of a larger field.

The term 'public' refers to any issue with implications beyond any single private entity such as a family, business, or other organization. It is generally restricted to domestic (i.e. non-international) issues. There are also a number of efforts to develop public conflict resolution capabilities for transnational problems (von Moltke and DeLong, 1990; McDaniel, 1990; Trolldalen, 1991; 'Long term capacity building for global environmental negotiations', 1991).

There is no established or definitive distinction between the terms 'resolution', 'management', and 'settlement'. 'Management', like 'ADR', can be used in a general sense to describe a wide range of ways of dealing with conflict: 'all efforts to do something deliberately about conflict' (Sandole and Sandole-Staroste, 1987). Yet it also has a more limited meaning, that of 'managers' keeping conflict in check so as to maintain control of a situation, or 'efforts to maintain the costs of conflict below a maximum level' (Galtung, 1975: 436).

'Resolution' and 'settlement' share several meanings. Both are used to refer to the *means* or *processes* by which disputes and conflicts are brought to an end, as well as the specific *outcomes* of these processes. That is, one may 'resolve' and 'settle' disputes and conflicts by reaching a 'resolution' or 'settlement'.

Like 'management', both 'resolution' and 'settlement' are sometimes used to refer to the entire range of efforts to do something deliberately about conflict. On the other hand, the two terms are at times counterposed against one another. 'Resolution' in this latter context means achieving an agreement which is lasting, engaging the root sources of the dispute or conflict, derived with consensual support, self-enforced, and not contradictory to the interests of the larger society or institution bounding the disputants and the dispute or conflict. 'Settlement', in contrast, refers to any determination made of the immediate issues precipitating a dispute, by agreement of the parties themselves, or by imposition by one or more of the parties or an outside authority (see Cormick, 1982; Laue, 1990; Crowfoot and Wondolleck, 1990; Burton and Dukes, 1990).

Crowfoot and Wondolleck (1990) distinguish 'dispute settlement' from 'conflict resolution'. For them, environmental *conflicts* are 'rooted in different values of natural resources and environmental quality' (p. 6). Conflict (in this specific instance, environmental conflict), they elaborate, involves the:

> fundamental and ongoing differences, opposition, and sometimes coercion among major groups in society over their values and behaviors toward the natural environment. Such conflict is very wide in scope and in part arises from

the rapid change in human population, technology, social structures, and social norms. Within this conflict, there are many smaller and quite specific episodes referred to here as 'disputes' (pp. 17–18).

While this distinction between 'conflict' and 'dispute' is a useful one, so is the distinction offered by Burton (1987). Burton suggests that there is a gradation by *intensity* of conflict, ranging from ordinary 'disputes' involving interests which can be bargained, traded, and compromised, to intractable 'conflicts' involving fundamental human needs which will not and cannot be compromised. But Burton's terminology has little currency. Thus it seems more appropriate to understand 'conflict' as the larger problem or class of problems represented by episodes of 'disputes'. This use is also supported by the availability of the term 'disputants'; there is no comparable term for conflicts ('conflictants'?).

While Crowfoot and Wondolleck use this distinction to argue that the field is one of 'dispute settlement' rather than 'conflict resolution', the opposite conclusion may also be drawn from their reasoning. The use of the term 'dispute' in 'public dispute resolution' implies a limited applicability to specific cases, whereas 'conflict' articulates the relationship between these disputes and the fundamental societal cleavages they represent. Thus, while there are individual incidents of 'dispute settlement' and 'dispute resolution', this broadened conception of the field implied by the term 'public conflict resolution' reflects its impact upon these conflicts, rather than its application to individual cases.

System design

As much a conceptual aid for the analysis of disputes as it is a dispute settlement process, a systems approach recognizes the connections among a series of disputes within a particular institution or relationship. System design suggests that many of the costs associated with conflict can be avoided by removing systemic elements which encourage dysfunctional disputing, and instituting in their place more productive mechanisms to address differences.

Third party

The umbrella term for any of a number of roles of someone assisting disputants in settling a dispute, including arbitrator, facilitator, and mediator.

Visioning

A process whereby community members imagine their desired future and set goals for achieving that future. Visioning emphasizes active citizen participation, long-term planning, imagination, a sense of possibility, and common ground.

References

Abel, R. L. (ed.) (1982a), *The American Experience*: Vol. 1, *The Politics of Informal Justice*, New York, Academic Press.

Abel, R. L. (ed.) (1982b), *Comparative Studies*: Vol. 2, *The Politics of Informal Justice*, New York, Academic Press.

Adler, P., Lovaas, K. and Milner, N. (1988), 'The ideologies of mediation: the movement's own story', *Law and Policy*, 10(4), 317–39.

Alinsky, S. D. (1972), *Rules for Radicals: A Pragmatic Primer for Realistic Radicals*, New York, Vintage Books.

American Bar Association Standing Committee on Dispute Resolution (1990), *Legislation on Dispute Resolution*, Washington, DC, American Bar Association Standing Committee on Dispute Resolution.

Amy, D. J. (1987), *The Politics of Environmental Mediation*, New York, Columbia University Press.

Anderson, W. T. (1990), 'Green politics now comes in four distinct shades', *Utne Reader*, 40, 53–4.

Apfelbaum, E. and Lubek, I. (1976), 'Resolution versus revolution? The theory of conflicts in question', in L. H. Strickland, F. E. Aboud and K. J. Gergen (eds), *Social Psychology in Transition*, New York, Plenum Press.

Arnstein, S. (1969), 'A ladder of citizen participation', *Journal of the American Institute of Planners*, 35, 221.

Auerbach, J. S. (1983), *Justice Without Law?* New York, Oxford University Press.

Bacow, L. S. and Wheeler, M. (1984), *Environmental Dispute Resolution*, New York, Plenum Press.

Barber, B. (1984), *Strong Democracy: Participatory Politics for a New Age*, Berkeley, CA, University of California Press.

Barber, B. (1988), *The Conquest of Politics: Liberal Philosophy in Democratic Times*, Princeton, New Jersey, Princeton University Press.

Becker, C., Chasin, L., Chasin, R., Herzig, M. and Roth, S. (1992), 'Fostering dialogue on abortion: a report from the Public Conversations Project',

Conscience, *13*(3), 2.

Bellah, R. N., Madsen, R., Sullivan, W. M., Swidler, A. and Tipton, S. M. (1985), *Habits of the Heart*, Berkely, University of California Press.

Bellah, R. N., Madsen, R., Sullivan, W. M., Swidler, A. and Tipton, S. M. (1991), *The Good Society*, New York, Alfred A. Knopf.

Bellman, H. S., Sampson, C. S. and Cormick, G. W. (1982), *Using Mediation when Siting Hazardous Waste Management Facilities: a Handbook*, Washington, DC, US Environmental Protection Agency.

Bellman, H., Orenstein, S. and Wondolleck, J. (Speakers) (1990), 'Environmental dispute resolution, Part one' SPIDR Conference Presentation, 26 October.

Bendix, J. (1991), 'The power elite and the state', *Society*, *28*(4), 91.

Berger, P. L. and Luckmann, T. (1966), *The Social Construction of Reality*, New York, Doubleday.

Berger, P. L. and Neuhaus, R. J. (1977), *To Empower People*, Washington, DC, American Enterprise Institute.

Berry, W. (1987), *Home Economics*, Berkeley, North Point Press.

Bingham, G. (1986), *Resolving Environmental Disputes: A Decade of Experience*, Washington, DC, Conservation Foundation.

Bingham, G. and Laue, J. (1988), 'Disagreeing about the rules: negotiation and mediation', *EPA Journal*, *14*(2), 17.

Birnbaum, N. (1986), 'Social theory in the United States: the legacy of the decade 1960–1970', in G. H. Lenz and K. L. Shell (eds), *The Crisis of Modernity: Recent Critical Theories of Culture and Society in the United States and West Germany*, Boulder, CO, Westview Press.

Blake, R. R. and Mouton, J. S. (1970), 'The fifth achievement', *Journal of Applied Behavioral Science*, *6*(4), 413–26.

Blake, R. R. and Mouton, J. S. (1984), *Solving Costly Organizational Conflicts*, San Francisco, Jossey-Bass.

Bookchin, M. (1990), *Remaking Society: Pathways to a Green Future*, Boston, MA, South End Press.

Bosso, C. J. (1988), 'Transforming adversaries into collaborators: interest groups and the regulation of chemical pesticides', *Policy Sciences*, *21*, 3–12.

Boyte, H. C. and Evans, S. M. (1986), 'The sources of democratic change', *Tikkun*, *1*(1), 49–5.

Bradley, R. (undated), *Managing Major Metropolitan Areas: The Application of Collaborative Planning and Negotiation Techniques*.

Bradley, R. (1991), 'Visioning the future', *Synergy: A Newsletter of the Program for Community Problem Solving*, Winter, p. 1.

Bremner, D. and Visser, P. (1994), *Negotiation, Conflict Resolution and Human Needs: Social Transformation for a Sustainable Future in South Africa*, Wilgespruit Fellowship Center, South Africa.

Brookes, W. T. (1991), 'Too many lawyers or laws?' (Editorial), *Richmond*

Times Dispatch, October.

Brown, C. R. and Mazza, G. J. (1991), 'Peer training strategies for welcoming diversity' (unpublished paper).

Brunet, E. (1987), 'Questioning the quality of alternative dispute resolution', *Tulane Law Review*, *62*, 1–6.

Buckle, L. G. and Thomas-Buckle, S. R. (1986), 'Placing environmental mediation in context: lessons from "failed" mediations', *Environmental Impact Assessment Review*, 6(1), 55–60.

Building Consensus for a Sustainable Future: Guiding Principles, (1993), (initiative undertaken by Canadian Round Tables).

Buntz, C. G. (1989), 'Alternative dispute resolution and public policy', paper presented at the 1989 SPIDR conference, 20 October.

Burton, J. (ed.), (1990), *Conflict: Human Needs Theory*, The Conflict Series, no. 2, New York, St Martin's Press.

Burton, J. W., 'The philosophy of public policy', unpublished essay.

Burton, J. W. (1987), *Resolving Deep-Rooted Conflict: A Handbook*, Lanham, MD, University Press of America.

Burton, J. W. (1989), 'On the need for conflict prevention', Vernon M. and Minnie I. Lynch Lecture, 26 April.

Burton, J. and Dukes, F. (1990), *Conflict: Practices in Management, Settlement and Resolution*, The Conflict Series, no. 4, New York, St Martin's Press.

Bush, R. A. B. (1984), 'Dispute resolution alternatives and the goals of civil justice: jurisdictional principles for process choice', *Wisconsin Law Review*, p. 893.

Bush, R. A. B. (1989), 'Efficiency and protection, or empowerment and recognition? The mediator's role and ethical standards in mediation', *University of Florida Law Review*, *41*, 253–86.

Bush, R. B. (1988), 'Defining quality in dispute resolution: taxonomies and anti-taxonomies of quality arguments', Vol. 8, Working Papers, Disputes Processing Research Program, Institute for Legal Studies, University of Wisconsin-Madison Law School.

Bush, R. A. B. and Folger, J. P. (1994), *The Promise of Mediation*, San Francisco, Jossey-Bass.

Carlson, C. (1985), 'Negotiated investment strategy: mediating intergovernmental conflict', in N. A. Huelsberg and W. F. Lincoln (eds), *Successful Negotiating in Local Government* (pp. 57–60), Washington, DC, International City Management Association.

Carpenter, S. (1989), *Community Problem Solving by Consensus*, Program on Community Problem Solving, Washington, DC.

Carpenter, S. and Kennedy, W. J. D. (1988), *Managing Public Disputes*, San Francisco, Jossey-Bass.

Caspary, W. R. (1991), 'Democratic theory and conflict-resolution: a human needs approach, from a contextualist orientation', paper presented at the National Conference on Peacemaking and Conflict Resolution, Charlotte, North Carolina, 5 June.

Chalmers, W. E. and Cormick, G. W. (eds) (1971), *Racial Conflict and Negotiations: Perspectives and First Case Studies*, Ann Arbor, University of Michigan and Wayne State University and the American Arbitration Association.

Chesapeake Bay Land Use Roundtable (1987), *Land Use Initiatives for Tidewater Virginia: The Next Step in Protecting the Bay*, findings and recommendations, Institute for Environmental Negotiation.

Chesler, M. (1989), 'Conflict resolution and social change', revised version of talk given at 1989 National Conference on Peacemaking and Conflict Resolution, 4 March.

Chesler, M. A. (1992), 'Alternative dispute resolution and social justice', intended for Lewis and Douvan (eds.), *Injustice, Social Conflict and Social Change*.

Chesler, M. A., Crowfoot, J. E. and Bryant, B. I. (1978), 'Power training: an alternative path to conflict management', *California Management Review*, 21(2), 84.

Chupp, M. (1991), 'When mediation is not enough', *Conciliation Quarterly*, 10(3), 2.

Citizens and politics: a view from Main Street America (1991), report prepared by The Harwood Group for the Kettering Foundation, Dayton, OH, Kettering Foundation.

Clark, M. E. (1989), *Ariadne's Thread: The Search for New Modes of Thinking*, New York, St Martin's Press.

'Cleaner air, by consensus', (1991), unsigned editorial, *New York Times*, 27 August.

Cloud, S. W. (1989), 'The can't do government', *Time*, 23 October pp. 28–32.

Cobb, S. (1991), 'Einsteinian practice and Newtonian discourse: an ethical crisis in mediation', *Negotiation Journal*, 7(1), 87.

Cobb, S. and Rifkin, J. (1990), 'The social construction of neutrality in mediation', executive summary submitted to the Fund for Research on Dispute Resolution.

Collins, R. C. and Dotson, A. B. (1990), 'Sharing the pain in Virginia: new laws to protect instream flow', *Consensus*, 7, 5.

Collins, S. (1994), 'Mediating chaos', *Track Two: Constructive Approaches to Community and Political Conflict*, 3(2/3), 14–16.

Community Relations Service (undated), *The Community Relations Service* (brochure).

Cook, T. E. and Morgan, P. M. (1971), *An introduction to participatory democracy*, in T. E. Cook and P. M. Morgan (eds), *Participatory democracy*, San Francisco, Canfield Press.

COPRED (1989), 'State support for peace education and conflict resolution', *COPRED Peace Chronicle*, 14(4), 3.

Cormick, G. (1987), 'Environmental mediation: the myth, the reality and the future', in D. J. Brower and D. S. Carol (eds), *Managing Land-use Conflicts*, Case Studies in Special Area Management, Duke Press Policy Studies, Durham, North Carolina, Duke University Press.

Cormick, G. W. (1982), 'Intervention and self-determination in environmental disputes: a mediator's perspective', *Resolve*, Winter.

Cormick, G. W. (1985), 'Resolving conflicts on the uses of range through mediated negotiations: answers to the ten most asked questions', *National Range Conference Proceedings*, p. 84.

Cormick, G. W. (1989), 'Strategic issues in structuring multi-party public policy negotiations', *Negotiation Journal*, 5(2), 125–32.

Cormick, G. W. and Patton, L. K. (1980), 'Environmental mediation: defining the process through experience', in L. M. Lake (ed.), *Environmental Mediation: the Search for Consensus*, Social Impact Assessment Series, Boulder, CO, Westview Press.

Corson, R. (1991), 'Study Circles: building knowledge, participation and power', *Focus on Study Circles*, Winter p. 5.

Craib, I. (1984), *Modern Social Theory: from Parsons to Habermas*, New York, St Martin's Press.

Creighton, J. L. (1992), *Involving Citizens in Community Decision Making: A Guidebook*, Program for Community Problem Solving, Washington, DC.

Critchlow, D. T. (1988), 'Social-policy history: past and present', introduction to D. T. Critchlow and E. W. Hawley (eds), *Federal Social Policy: The Historical Dimension*, University Park, PA, The Pennsylvania State University Press.

Crowfoot, J. E. (1988), 'The emerging literature on environmental negotiations', *Negotiation Journal*, 4(1), 77–89.

Crowfoot, J. E. and Wondolleck, J. M. (1990), *Environmental Disputes: Community Involvement in Conflict Resolution*, Washington, DC, Island Press.

Crozier, M., Huntington, S. P. and Watanuki, J. (1975), *The Crisis of Democracy* (report on the governability of democracies to the Trilateral Commission), New York University Press.

Dahl, R. A. (1982), *Dilemmas of Pluralist Democracy: Autonomy vs. Control*, New Haven, Yale University Press.

Dahl, R. A. (1989), *Democracy and its Critics*, New Haven, CT, Yale University Press.

Dahrendorf, R. (1959), *Class and Class Conflict in Industrial Society*, Stanford, CA, Stanford University Press.

Daly, H. E. and Cobb, J. B., Jr. (1989), *For the Common Good: Redirecting the Economy Toward Community, the Environment and a Sustainable Future*, Boston, Beacon Press.

201

Danzig, R. (1973), 'Towards the creation of a complementary, decentralized system of criminal justice', *Stanford Law Review*, 26(1), 1–54.

Dator, J. A. (1978), 'The future of anticipatory democracy', in C. Bezold (ed.), *Anticipatory Democracy*, New York, Random House.

Davis, A. (1986), 'Dispute resolution at an early age', *Negotiation Journal*, 2(3), 287–97.

Davis, A. M. (1989), 'The logic behind the magic of mediation', *Negotiation Journal*, 5(1), 17–24.

Dawkins, K. (1991), 'New statewide offices plan most far-reaching programs in nation', *Consensus*, 9, 1.

DelliPriscolli, J. (1989), 'New arenas in dispute resolution', presentation at SPIDR Conference, Washington, DC, 20 October.

DeLong, P. J. (ed.) (1991), 'Virginia nontidal wetlands roundtable recommends enhanced use of state authority to protect wetlands', *Resolve*, 23, 12.

DeLong, P. J. and Orenstein, S. G. (eds) (1990), 'Roundtable develops instream flow policy in Virginia', *Resolve*, 22, 15.

Dembart, L. and Kwartler, R. (1980), 'The Snoqualmie River conflict: bringing mediation into environmental disputes', in R. B. Goldmann (ed.), *Roundtable Justice: Case Studies in Conflict Resolution* (report to the Ford Foundation), Boulder, CO, Westview Press.

DeSario, J. and Langton, S. (1987), *Citizen Participation in Public Decision Making*, Westport, CT, Greenwood Press.

Dionne, E. J. (1991), *Why Americans Hate Politics*, New York, Simon & Schuster.

Doob, L. (ed.), (1970), *Resolving Conflict in Africa*, New Haven, CT, Yale University Press.

Doob, L. and Foltz, W. J. (1973), 'The Belfast workshop', *Journal of Conflict Resolution*, 17(3), 489–512.

Doob, L. and Foltz, W. J. (1974), 'The impact of a workshop upon grassroots leaders in Belfast', *Journal of Conflict Resolution*, 18(2), 237–56.

Dotson, A. B. (1993), '"No go" negotiations: reflections on practice', paper presented at Association of Collegiate Schools of Planning, Philadelphia, 29 October.

Dotson, A. B., Godschalk, D. and Kaufman, J. (1989), *The Planner as Dispute Resolver: Concepts and Teaching Materials*, Teaching Material Series, Washington, DC, National Institute for Dispute Resolution.

Dozier, D., Rennie, S., Robinson, R. and Snyder, F. (1989), 'Dispute resolution opportunities in Superfund', presentation at SPIDR Conference, Washington, DC, 21 October.

Drake, W. R. (1989), 'Statewide offices of mediation', *Negotiation Journal*, 5(4), 359–64.

Dryzek, J. S. (1990), *Discursive Democracy: Politics, Policy and Political Sci-*

ence, Cambridge, UK, Cambridge University Press.

Dugan, M. A. (1988), 'State support for peace education: the case of Ohio', *COPRED Peace Chronicle*, *13*(1), 3.

Dukes, F. (1987), 'Faith Mission Home and the Beachy Amish–Mennonites vs. the State of Virginia: a case study', unpublished paper.

Dukes, F. (1990), 'Understanding community dispute resolution', *Mediation Quarterly*, *8*(1).

Dukes, E. F. (1992), 'The development of public conflict resolution: a transformative approach', dissertation.

Edelman, M. W. (1992), *The Measure of Our Success*, Boston, Beacon Press.

Edmonds, D. S. (1990), 'Director's circle', *Conciliation Quarterly*, *9*(2).

Ehrmann, J. R. and Lesnick, M. T. (1988), 'The policy dialogue: applying mediation to the policy-making process', *Mediation Quarterly*, *20*, 93–9.

'Electronic democracy', (1991) (special section), *Whole Earth Review*, *71*.

Ellison, C. (1991), 'Dispute resolution and democratic theory', in S. S. Nagel and M. K. Mills (eds.), *Systematic Analysis in Dispute Resolution*, New York, Quorum Books.

Emigh, P. (1991), 'Kindred souls or kissing cousins?' *Focus on Study Circles*, p. 1.

England, P. (1992), 'Disunity in a nuclear community', *Mediation*, *8*(4), 10.

Esser, J. P. (1988), 'Evaluations of dispute processing: we don't know what we think and we don't think what we know', Working Papers Series 8–10, University of Wisconsin-Madison Law School, Institute for Legal Studies.

Etzioni, A. (1991), 'Too many rights, too few responsibilities', *Society*, January/February.

Etzioni, A. (1993), *The Spirit of Community: Rights, Responsibilities and the Communitarian Agenda*, New York, Crown.

Field, P. (1993), 'A Canadian "road map" for integrating economy, ecology', *Consensus*, *20*, 8.

Fiorina, M. P. (1980), 'The decline of collective responsibility in American politics', *Daedalus*, *109*(3), 25–45.

Fisher, R. and Kling, J. (1989), 'Community mobilization: prospects for the future', *Urban Affairs Quarterly*, *25*(2), 200–11.

Fisher, R. and Ury, W. (1981), *Getting to Yes: Negotiating Agreement without Giving In*, Boston, Houghton Mifflin.

Fiss, O. (1984), 'Against settlement', Yale Law Journal, *93*, 1073.

Folberg, J. and Taylor, A. (1984), *Mediation: A Comprehensive Guide to Resolving Conflicts Without Litigation*, San Francisco, Jossey-Bass.

Folger, J. and Bush, R. A. B. (1994), 'Ideology, orientations to conflict, and mediation discourse', in J. P. Folger and T. J. Jones (eds), *New Directions in Mediation: Communication Research and Perspective*, Thousand Oaks, CA, Sage.

Follett, M. P. (1930), *Creative Experience*, New York, Longmans, Green and Co.

Follett, M. P. (1918), *The New State: Group Organization the Solution of Popular Government*, New York, Longmans, Green and Co.

Fonte, A. (1991), *Working paper: 3/12/91* (draft working paper), Tucson, AZ, Maverick Institute.

Ford Foundation (1978), *New Approaches to Conflict Resolution* (Ford Foundation report), New York.

Forester, J. (1985), 'Critical theory and planning practice', in J. Forester (ed.), *Critical Theory and Public Life*, Cambridge, MA, The MIT Press.

Forester, J. (1992), 'Envisioning the politics of public-sector dispute resolution', in *Studies in Law, Politics and Society*, Vol. 12, pp. 247–86.

Forester, J. (1994), 'Lawrence Susskind: activist mediation and public disputes', in D. A. Kolb (ed.), *When Talk Works: Profiles of Mediators*, San Francisco, Jossey-Bass.

Forester, J. and Stitzel, D. (1989), 'Beyond neutrality: the possibilities of activist mediation in public sector conflicts', *Negotiation*, 5(3), 251–64.

Foster, C. H. W. (1969), 'A case for environmental conciliation', paper presented at the annual meeting of the American Institute of Biological Sciences, University of Vermont, Burlington, VT, 19 August.

Foucault, M. (1986), 'Disciplinary power and subjection', in S. Lukes (ed.), *Power*, Oxford, Basil Blackwell.

Fraser, N. (1989), *Unruly Practices: Power, Discourse and Gender in Contemporary Social Theory*, Minneapolis, University of Minnesota Press.

Freud, S. (1961), *Civilization and its Discontents* (J. Strachey, trans.), New York, W. W. Norton.

Friedmann, J. (1987), *Planning in the Public Domain: From Knowledge to Action*, Princeton, Princeton University Press.

Friedmann, J. (1988), 'Reviewing two centuries', *Society*, 26(1), 7–15.

Friedmann, J. (1989), 'The dialectic of reason', *International Journal of Urban and Regional Research*, 13(2), 217–33.

Fromm, E. (1955), *The Sane Society*, New York, Holt, Rinehart & Winston.

Funk, N. (1989), 'Obsessive democracy', *Telos*, 81, 171–9.

Gaddafi, M. (1976), *Democracy 'The Authority of the People': The Political Base of the Third Universal Theory*, London, Martin Brian & O'Keeffe.

Galanter, M. (1983), 'Reading the landscape of disputes: what we know and don't know (and think we know) about our allegedly contentious and litigious society', *UCLA Law Review*, 31, 4.

Gailbraith, J. K. (1990), 'The rush to capitalism', *New York Review*, 37 (16), 51.

Galtung, J. (1975), *Essays in Peace Research*, Copenhagen, Christian Ejlers.

Gates, C. T. (1987), 'The national civic index: a new approach to community problem solving', *National Civic Review*, 76(6), 472–9.

Giddens, A. (1982), *Profiles and Critiques in Social Theory*, Berkeley, CA, University of California Press.

Giddens, A. (1987), *Social Theory and Modern Sociology*, Stanford, CA, Stanford University Press.

Giddens, A. (1989), 'A reply to my critics', in D. Held and J. B. Thompson (eds), *Social Theory of Modern Societies: Anthony Giddens and his Critics*, Cambridge, UK, Cambridge University Press.

Gilligan, C. (1982), *In a Different Voice: Psychological Theory and Women's Development*, Cambridge, MA, Harvard University Press.

Gladwin, T. N. (1987), 'Patterns of environmental conflict over industrial facilities in the United States, 1970–1978', in R. W. Lake (ed.), *Resolving Locational Conflict*, New Brunswick, New Jersey, Rutgers University, Center for Urban Policy Research.

Glendinning, C. (1990), 'Notes toward a Neo-Luddite manifesto', *Utne Reader*, *38*, 50–3.

Goldmann, R. B. (ed.) (1980), *Roundtable Justice: Case Studies in Conflict Resolution*, report to the Ford Foundation, Boulder, CO, Westview Press.

Gordon, R. W. (1988), 'Law and ideology', *Tikkun*, *3*(1), 14.

Gould, C. C. (1988), *Rethinking Democracy: Freedom and Social Cooperation in Politics, Economy and Society*, Cambridge, UK, Cambridge University Press.

Governor's Peace and Conflict Management Commission (1990), *Moving from conflict to cooperation* (report).

Gray, B. (1989), *Collaborating: Finding Common Ground for Multiparty Problems*, San Francisco, Josscy-Bass.

Grossman, R. L. (1988), 'The Henry David Thoreau quality of life index', *Social Policy*, 2.

Gulliver, P. H. (1979), *Disputes and Negotiations: a Cross-Cultural Perspective*, Orlando, FL, Academic Press.

Gurwitt, R. (1990), 'Black politicians for the '90s', *Governing*, *3*(5), 28–33.

Gurwitt, R. (1991), 'Town tries lecture series as a tool for unity', *Governing*, *4*(6), 19.

Habermas, J. (1973), *Theory and Praxis*, Boston, Beacon Press.

Habermas, J. (1984), *The Theory of Communicative Action* Vol. 1, *Reason and the Rationalization of Society*, Boston, Beacon Press.

Habermas, J. (1987), *The Theory of Communicative Action* Vol. 2, *Lifeworld and System: a Critique of Functionalist Reason*, Boston, Beacon Press.

Hallin, D. C. (1985), 'The American news media: a critical theory perspective', in J. Forester (ed.), *Critical Theory and Public Life*, Cambridge, MA, The MIT Press.

Handler, J. F. (1988), 'Dependent people, the state and the modern/postmodern search for the dialogic community', *UCLA Law Review*, *35*, 999–1113.

Hanson, R. L. (1985), *The Democratic Imagination in America: Conversations with our Past*, Princeton, New Jersey, Princeton University Press.

Harbert, L. and Pollack, D. (1990), 'Leading the way in dispute resolution: the Ohio model', *Arbitration Journal*, 45(2), 56.

Harkness, P. A. (1990), 'Publisher's desk', *Governing*, 3(4), 6.

Harrington, C. B. (1985), *Shadow Justice: the Ideology and Institutionalization of Alternatives to Court*, Westport, CT, Greenwood Press.

Harrington, C. B. and Merry, S. E. (1988), 'Ideological production: the making of community mediation', *Law and Society Review*, 22(4), 709–835.

Harter, P. J. (1984), 'Regulatory negotiation: the experience so far', *Resolve*, 16, 1.

Harter, P. J. (1988), 'Practice and perspective: Regulatory negotiation', *ADR Report*, 2, 62.

Hawley, E. W. (1988), 'Social-policy and the liberal state in twentieth-century America', in D. T. Critchlow and E. W. Hawley (eds), *Federal Social Policy: The Historical Dimension*, University Park, PA, The Pennsylvania State University Press.

Haygood, L. V. (1988a), 'Negotiated rule making: challenges for mediators and participants', *Mediation Quarterly*, 20, 77–91.

Haygood, L. V. (1988b), 'Opportunities and challenges in providing state-level support for the mediation of public disputes', *Resolve*, 19.

Haygood, L. V. and Orenstein, S. G. (eds) (1988), 'Structured public participation for low-level radioactive waste policy development facilitated in Virginia', *Resolve*, 19, 18.

Hayter, S. (1994), 'Institutionalising CR: how the IEC coped with conflict', *Track Two: Constructive Approaches to Community and Political Conflict*, 3(2/3), 6.

Hofrichter, R. (1987), *Neighborhood Justice in Capitalist Society: The Expansion of the Informal State*, New York, Greenwood Press.

Hunter, J. D. (1991), *Culture Wars: The Struggle to Define America*, New York, Basic Books.

Hunter, J. D. (1994), *Before the Shooting Begins: Searching for Democracy in America's Culture War*, New York, The Free Press.

Innes, J. E. (1991), 'Implementing state growth management in the U.S.: strategies for coordination', in J. Stein (ed.), *Growth Management and Sustainable Development*, Newbury Park, CA, Sage Publications.

Institute for Environmental Negotiation and RESOLVE (1994), *The Cutting Edge: Environmental Dispute Resolution for the Nineties*, Washington, DC, RESOLVE.

International Environmental Negotiation Network, (1991), 'Long term capacity building for global environmental negotiations' (program statement), May.

Jones, K. B. (1989), 'Citizenship in a woman-friendly polity', *Signs*, 15(4),

781–812.

Jostes, J. (1989), 'New Florida forum seeks the proper balance between development and the environment', *Consensus*, 2, 2.

Kaplan, M. (1988), 'Mediation of public disputes: the wave of the future?', *National Civic Review*, 77(4), 285–97.

Kellner, D. (1989), *Critical Theory, Marxism and Modernity*, Baltimore, The Johns Hopkins University Press.

Kelman, H. C. (1990), 'Interactive problem-solving: a social-psychological approach to conflict resolution', in J. Burton and F. Dukes (eds), *Conflict: Readings in Management and Resolution*, The Conflict Series, New York, St Martin's Press.

Kelman, H. C. and Cohen, S. P. (1976), 'The problem-solving workshop: a social-psychological contribution to the resolution of international conflicts', *Journal of Peace Research*, 13(2), 79–90.

Kemmis, D. (1990), *Community and the Politics of Place*, Norman Oklahoma, University of Oaklahoma Press.

Kemp, R. (1985), 'Planning, public hearings and the politics of discourse', in J. Forester (ed.), *Critical Theory and Public Life*, Cambridge, MA, The MIT Press.

Kennedy, P. (1990), 'Fin-de-Siècle America', *New York Review of Books*, 28 June, 31–40.

Kettering Foundation (1982), *Negotiated Investment Strategy*, Dayton, OH.

Klugman, J., Soriano, E., Orocheria, M., Westbrook, D., Tonji, G. and Taylor, J. (1990), 'Mediation by and for minorities', SPIDR Conference Presentation, 27 October.

Kohn, A. (1986), *No Contest: The Case Against Competition*, Boston, Houghton Mifflin.

Kolb, D. (1983a), 'Strategy and the tactics of mediation', *Human Relations*, 36(3), 247–68.

Kolb, D. M. (1983b), *The Mediators*, Cambridge, MA, The MIT Press.

Kolb, D. and Rubin, J. Z. (1989), 'Mediation through a disciplinary kaleidoscope: a summary of empirical research', *Dispute Resolution Forum*, 3.

Kraybill, R. (1988), 'From head to heart: the cycle of reconciliation', *Conciliation Quarterly*, 7(4), 2.

Kraybill, R. S. (1980), *Repairing the Breach: Ministering in Community Conflict*, Akron, PA, Mennonite Central Committee.

Kressel, K. and Pruitt, D. G. (1989), *Mediation Research: The Process and Effectiveness of Third-party Intervention*, San Francisco, Jossey-Bass.

Kritek, P. B. (1994), *Negotiating at an Uneven Table: Developing Moral Courage in Resolving our Conflicts*, San Francisco, Jossey-Bass.

Kunde, J. E. and Rudd, J. E. (1988), 'The role of citizens groups in policy conflicts', *Mediation Quarterly*, 20, 33–44.

Kuttab, J. (1994), 'The pitfalls of dialogue', *Conflict Resolution Notes*, 11(3),

36–8.

Lake, L. M. (ed.), (1980), *Environmental Mediation: The Search for Consensus*, Boulder, CO, Westview Press.

Langton, S. (1978a), 'Citizen participation in America: current reflections on the state of the art', in S. Langton (ed.), *Citizen Participation in America*, New York, D.C. Heath and Company.

Langton, S. (1978b), 'What is citizen participation?' in S. Langton (ed.), *Citizen Participation in America*, New York, D.C. Heath and Company.

Lappé, F. M. (1989), *Rediscovering America's Values*, New York, Ballantine Books.

Lappé, F. M. and DuBois, P. M. (1994), *The Quickening of America*, San Francisco, Jossey-Bass.

Laue, J. H. (ed.), (1988), 'Using mediation to shape public policy', *Mediation Quarterly, 20*.

Laue, J. H. (1990), 'The emergence and institutionalization of third-party roles in conflict', in J. Burton and F. Dukes (eds), *Conflict: Readings in Management and Resolution*, The Conflict Series, New York, St Martin's Press.

Laue, J. H. and Cormick, G. W. (1973), 'Third party intervention in community conflict: definitions, perspectives and experience', synopsis prepared for the Conference on Third Party Intervention in Community Crisis, 18–19 September.

Laue, J. and Cormick, G. (1978), 'The ethics of intervention in community disputes', in G. Bermant, H. C. Kelman and D. P. Warwick (eds), *The Ethics of Social Intervention*, Washington, DC, Halsted Press.

Laue, J. H., Burde, S., Potapchuk, W. and Salkoff, M. (1988), 'Getting to the table: three paths', *Mediation Quarterly, 20, 7*.

Lea, J. F. (1982), *Political Consciousness and American Democracy*, Oxford, MS, University Press of Mississippi.

Lederach, J. P. (1989), 'In pursuit of dialogue', *Conciliation Quarterly, 8*(3), 12–14.

Lederach, J. P. (1995), *Preparing for Peace: Conflict Transformation across Cultures*, Syracuse, New York, Syracuse University Press.

Lee, K. N. (1982), 'Defining success in environmental dispute resolution', *Resolve, 1*.

Lentz, S. S. (1986), 'The labor model for mediation and its application to the resolution of environmental disputes', *Journal of Applied Behavioral Science, 22*(2), 127–39.

Lenz, G. H. and Shell, K. L. (eds) (1986), *The Crisis of Modernity: Recent Critical Theories of Culture and Society in the United States and West Germany*, Boulder, CO, Westview Press.

Lerner, M. (1990), 'After the cold war: possibilities for human liberation', *Tikkun, 5*(1), 16.

Levi, B. T. and Spears, L. (1994), 'Public policy consensus building: connecting to change for capturing the future', *North Dakota Law Review*, *70*(2), 311–51.

Levinson, S. (1989), 'On critical legal studies', *Dissent*, pp. 360–5.

Luke, T. W. and White, S. K. (1985), 'Critical theory and an ecological path to modernity', in J. Forester (ed.), *Critical Theory and Public Life*, Cambridge, MA, The MIT Press.

McCubbin, P. R. (1989), 'Consensus through mediation: a case study of the Chesapeake Bay Land Use Roundtable and the Chesapeake Bay Preservation Act', *The Journal of Law and Politics*, *5*(4), 827.

McCrory, J. P. (1981), 'Environmental mediation – another piece for the puzzle', *Vermont Law Review*, *6*, 49.

McDaniel, D. L. (1990), 'Dispute resolution flourishes in Canada', *Consensus*, *5*, 1.

Madigan, D., McMahon, G., Susskind, L. and Rolley, S. (1990), *New Approaches to Resolving Local Public Disputes* (special report), Washington, DC, National Institute for Dispute Resolution.

Mansbridge, J. (1983), *Beyond Adversarial Democracy*, Chicago, University of Chicago Press.

Mansbridge, J. (1984), 'Unitary and adversary: the two forms of democracy', *In Context*, Autumn, 10.

Marlin, J. T. (1987), 'Community indicators, yesterday and today', *National Civic Review*, *76*(6), 480–8.

Maslow, A. (1954), *Motivation and Personality*, New York, Harper and Row.

Matthews, F. D. (1994), *Politics for People*, Chicago, University of Illinois Press.

McDaniel, D. L. (ed.) (1990a), 'Alternatives to acrimony, deadlock', *Consensus*, *6*, 1, Public Disputes Network.

McDaniel, D. L. (ed.), (1990b), 'Canadians take up the challenge of "sustainable development"', *Consensus*, *6*, 5, Public Disputes Network.

McDaniel, D. L. (ed.) (1990c), 'Move over Judge Wapner, make way for "Common Ground"', *Consensus*, *5*, 1, Public Disputes Network.

McDaniel, D. L. (ed.) (1990d), 'A new kind of justice for Native Americans', *Consensus*, *8*, 1, Public Disputes Network.

Mealey, T. J. (ed.), 'Interagency policy dialogue and regulatory negotiation completed on Virginia's groundwater management strategy', *Resolve*, *20*, 14.

Mernitz, S. (1980), *Mediation of Environmental Disputes: A Sourcebook*, New York, Praeger.

Merry, S. E. (1994), 'Community mediation as community organizing', in D. M. Kolb (ed.), *When Talk Works: Profiles of Mediators*, San Francisco, Jossey-Bass.

Mészáros, I. (1989), *The Power of Ideology*, New York, New York University Press.

Miller, K. (1989a), 'Minnesota "juries" tackle policy issues', *Consensus*, 4, 8.

Miller, K. (1989b), '"Negotiated investment" pays off for two regions', *Consensus*, 4, 1.

Millhauser, M. (1989), 'Dispute resolution: an overview of basic processes', unpublished paper, Washington, DC, Conflict Consulting.

Mills, S. (1991), 'Salons and beyond: changing the world one evening at a time', *Utne Reader*, 44, 68.

Minnesota State Planning Agency, Office of Dispute Resolution (1989), *Project Update: January 1986–June 1989*, report.

Montagu, M. F. A. (1950), 'The origin and nature of social life and the biological basis of co-operation', in P. A. Sorokin (ed.), *Explorations in Altruistic Love and Behavior*, Boston, Beacon.

Moore, C. (1993), '"Have process, will travel": reflections on democratic decision making and conflict management practice abroad', *NIDR Forum*, 1–2.

Moore, C. M. (1988), 'Negotiated investment strategy', *National Civic Review*, 77(4), 298–314.

Moore, C. W. (1987), *The Mediation Process: Practical Strategies for Resolving Conflict*, San Francisco, Jossey-Bass.

Murphy, J. W. (1989), *Postmodern Social Analysis and Criticism*, Westport, CT, Greenwood Press.

Nader, L. 'The ADR explosion – the implications of rhetoric in legal reform', unpublished paper.

Nader, L. (ed.), (1969), *Law in Culture and Society*, Chicago, Aldine.

Nagel, S. S. and Mills, M. K. (eds), (1991), *Systematic Analysis in Dispute Resolution*, New York, Quorum Books.

National Civic League (1991), 'NCL proposes Democracy and Citizenship Project', *Civic Action*, 4(1), 1.

National Civic League Committee (1989), 'Metropolitan governance statement', *Civic Action: News from the National Civic League*, 2(6), 4.

National Institute for Dispute Resolution (1986), 'Regulatory negotiation issue', *Dispute Resolution Forum*, January.

National Institute for Dispute Resolution (1989), *Public Policy Program Announcement* (brochure).

The National Civic League's Citizen Democracy Project (1990), announcement prepared by National Civic League.

New Jersey Center for Public Dispute Resolution (1989), *New Jersey Center for Public Dispute Resolution* (report).

Ngwenya, J. (1994), 'Threshold of a dream', *Track Two: Constructive Approaches to Community and Political Conflict*, 3(2/3), 11–13.

Nupen, C. (1994), 'The ultimate conflict handling experience', *Track Two: Constructive Approaches to Community and Political Conflict*, 3(2/3), 9–10.

Office of Policy, Planning and Evaluation, *Regulatory Negotiation Project* (pamphlet).

Olson, M. (1982), *The Rise and Decline of Nations: Economic Growth, Stagflation and Social Rigidities*, New Haven, CT, Yale University Press.

Oregon Visions Project, (1993), *A Guide to Community Visioning*, Oregon Chapter, American Planning Association.

'Paths to justice: major public policy issues of dispute resolution' (1983), report of the Ad Hoc Panel on Dispute Resolution and Public Policy, National Institute for Dispute Resolution.

Pepinsky, H. E. (1991), *The Geometry of Violence and Democracy*, Bloomington, Indiana University Press.

Pierce, N. R. (1991), 'Regional governance: why? now? how?', article adapted from a keynote speech given to the Virginia Local Government Management Association in February 1991, *University of Virginia News Letter, Center for Public Service*, 67(8), 1.

Potapchuk, W. (1988), 'Building forums for the cooperative resolution of disputes in communities', *National Civic Review*, 77(4), 342–9.

Potapchuk, W. R. (1991a), 'Designing the process and building the table in public disputes', conference presentation at National Conference on Peacemaking and Conflict Resolution, 4 June.

Potapchuk, W. R. (1991b), 'New approaches to citizen participation: building consent', *National Civic Review*, 80(2), 14–18.

Potapchuk, W. R. and Polk, C. G. (1994), *Building the Collaborative Community*, Washington, DC, National Institute for Dispute Resolution.

Pound, R. (1912), 'Social justice and legal justice', *Missouri Bar Association Proceedings*, 30,

Price, A. M. (1989a), 'Editor's notes', *Conciliation Quarterly*, 8(3), 1.

Price, A. M. (1989b), 'Whither justice? a quartet of voices', *Conciliation Quarterly*, 8(3), 2.

Price, A. M. (ed.), (1990), 'Responding to prejudice' (special issue), *Conciliation Quarterly*, 9(2).

Program for Community Problem Solving, (1988), *Case Summaries*, Washington, DC, 21 November.

Pruitt, D. G. and Kressel, K. (1985), 'The mediation of social conflict: an introduction', *Journal of Social Issues*, 41(2), 1–10.

Public Disputes Network, (1991), 'AIO programs renew tradition of consensus-building', *Consensus*, 9, 8.

Putnam, R. D. (1993a), *In Making Democracy Work: Civic Traditions in Modern Italy*, Princeton, New Jersey, Princeton University Press.

Putnam, R. D. (1993b), 'The prosperous community: social capital and public life', *The American Prospect*, 13, 35–42.

Quinney, R. (1991), 'Foreword', in H. E. Pepinsky, *The Geometry of Violence and Democracy*, Bloomington, Indiana University Press.

Raiffa, H. (1982), *The Art and Science of Negotiation*, Cambridge, MA, Harvard University Press.

Rawls, J. (1971), *A Theory of Justice*, Cambridge, MA, Harvard University Press.

Reich, R. B. (1987), *Tales of a New America*, New York, Vintage Books.

Reilly, W. K. (1984), 'Who should pay?' *Dispute Resolution Forum*, March, 1.

Renaud, P. (1994), 'Environmental officials in Quebec serve as mediators', *Consensus*, 24, 8.

RESOLVE and Institute for Environmental Negotiation (1994, March 13–15), 'The cutting edge: environmental dispute resolution for the nineties', symposium summary prepared by RESOLVE and the Institute for Environmental Negotiation, 13–15 March.

Richman, R. (1983a), 'Mediation in a city–county annexation dispute: the negotiations process', *Environmental Impact Assessment Review*, 4(1), 55–66.

Richman, R. (1983b), 'Structuring interjurisdictional negotiation: Virginia's use of mediation in annexation disputes', *Resolve*, 15, 1.

Richman, R. (1985), 'Formal mediation in intergovernmental disputes: municipal annexation negotiations in Virginia', *Public Administration Review*, July/August, 510–17.

Richman, R., White, O. F., Jr. and Wilkinson, M. H. (1986), *Intergovernmental Mediation: Negotiations in Local Government Disputes*, Boulder, CO, Westview Press.

Rittel, H. W. J. and Webber, M. W. (1973), 'Dilemmas in a general theory of planning', *Policy Sciences*, 4(2), 155–69.

Rodwin, M. (1982), 'Can bargaining and negotiation change the administrative process?' *Environmental Impact Assessment Review*, 3(4), 373–86.

Rohatyn, F. (1990), 'Becoming what they think we are', *New York Review of Books*, 37(6), 6.

Roth, S. (1994), 'Constructive conversation in the abortion debate: use of the dialogue process', Working Paper 94–9, February, Conflict Research Consortium, University of Colorado, Boulder.

Rubenstein, R. E. (1988), 'Group rebellion in America: the fire next time?', working paper no. 2, Center for Conflict Analysis and Resolution, George Mason University.

Rundle, W. L. (1986), 'Teaching negotiation skills: a simulation game for low level radwaste facility siting.' *Environmental Impact Assessment Review*, 6(3), 255–63.

Rural Southern Voice for Peace (1993), 'The listening project: how it works', *Voices*, 71, 8–10.

Ryan, W. (1971), *Blaming the Victim*, New York, Pantheon.

Sachs, A. (1982), 'Nationwide study identifies barriers to environmental negotiation', *Environmental Impact Assessment Review*, 3(1), 95–100.

Sachs, A. (1989), 'Mediation of local public disputes by neighborhood based dispute settlement programs', *Conflict Resolution Notes*, 6(3), 66.

Sachs, A. M. (1988), *Building the Capacity to Mediate Public Disputes* (manual).

Sandole, D. J. D. and Sandole-Staroste, I. (eds) (1987), *Conflict Management and Problem Solving: Interpersonal to International Applications*, New York, New York University Press.

Sarat, A. (1988), 'The "new formalism" in disputing and dispute processing', *Law and Society Review*, 21(5), 695–715.

Sata, L. S. (1975), 'Laboratory training for police officers', *Journal of Social Issues*, 31(1), 107–14.

Saunders, H. H. and Slim, R. (1994), 'Dialogue to change conflictual relationships', *Higher Education Exchange*, 1(1), 43–56.

Schroyer, T. (1985), 'Corruption of freedom in America', in J. Forester (ed.), *Critical Theory and Public Life*, Cambridge, MA, The MIT Press.

Schwerin, E. W. (1995), *Mediation, Citizen Empowerment and Transformational Politics*, Westport, CT, Praeger.

Shonholtz, R. (1987), 'The citizens' role in justice: building a primary justice and prevention system at the neighborhood level', *Annals, 494*, 42–52.

Sites, P. (1973), *Control: The Basis of Social Order*, New York, Dunellen Publishing.

Skolimowski, H. (1985), 'The role of philosophy and values in the right model of peace', *Dialectics and Humanism*, 3–4,

SPIDR Law and Public Policy Committee (1990), 'Mandated participation and settlement coercion: dispute resolution as it relates to the courts' (discussion draft, 20 July).

Staff (1982), 'Agenda for environmental negotiation', *Environmental Impact Assessment Review*, 3(3/4), 387.

'Statewide offices of mediation: experiments in public policy', (1987), *Dispute Resolution Forum*, December.

Staub, H. O. (1980), 'The tyranny of minorities', *Daedalus, 109*(3), 159–68.

Stein, H. (1990), 'Who's number one? who cares?' *Wall Street Journal*, 1 March.

Stein, J. (1991), *Growth Management and Sustainable Development*, Newbury Park, CA, Sage Publications.

Stephens, W. O., Stephens, J. B. and Dukes, F. (1995), 'The ethics of environmental mediation', in J. W. Blackburn and W. M. Bruce (eds), *Mediating Environmental Conflicts: Theory and Practice*, Westport, CT, Quorum Books.

Stephenson, M. O., Jr. and Pops, G. M. (1989), 'Conflict resolution methods and the policy process', *Public Administration Review*, 49(5), 463–73.

Stulberg, J. B. (1981), 'The theory and practice of mediation: a reply to Professor Susskind', *Vermont Law Review*, 6, 85.

Sullivan, T. J. (1984), *Resolving Development Disputes Through Negotiations*, New York, Plenum Press.

Susskind, L. (1981), 'Environmental mediation and the accountability problem', *Vermont Law Review*, 6, 1.

Susskind, L. (1986), 'Regulatory negotiation at the state and local levels', *Dispute Resolution Forum*, January, p. 6.

Susskind, L. (1986), 'A sharper focus: defining the common issues in dispute resolution', *Environmental Impact Assessment Review*, 6(1), 51–3.

Susskind, L. (1987), 'Experiments in statewide offices of mediation', *Dispute Resolution Forum*, December.

Susskind, L. (ed.) (1989), 'Government finds better way to make all those darn rules', *Consensus*, 2, 1.

Susskind, L. and Cruikshank, J. (1987), *Breaking the Impasse: Consensual Approaches to Resolving Public Disputes*, New York, Basic Books.

Susskind, L. and Ozawa, C. (1985), 'Mediating public disputes: obstacles and possibilities', *Journal of Social Issues*, 41(2), 145–59.

Susskind, L., Richardson, J. R. and Hildebrand, K. J. (1978), *Resolving Environmental Disputes: Approaches to Intervention, Negotiation and Conflict Resolution*, Cambridge, MA, MIT.

Susskind, L., Bacow, L. and Wheeler, M. (eds) (1983), *Resolving Environmental Regulatory Disputes*, Cambridge, MA, Schenkman Books.

Susskind, L. E., Babbitt, E. F. and Segal, P. N. (1993), 'When ADR becomes the law: a review of federal practice', *Negotiation Journal*, 9(1), 59–65.

Swanson, P. (1991), personal communication.

Szanton Associates (1989), 'Public policy mediation: status and prospects', report to the William and Flora Hewlett Foundation and the National Institute for Dispute Resolution, January.

Talbot, A. R. (1982), *Settling Things: Six Case Studies in Environmental Mediation*, Washington, DC, The Conservation Foundation.

Theobald, R. (1978), 'The deeper implications of citizen participation', in C. Bezold (ed.), *Anticipatory Democracy*, New York, Random House.

Thomas, R. L., Means, M. C. and Grieve, M. A. (1988), *Taking Charge: How Communities are Planning their Futures*, special report on long range/strategic planning trends and innovations, Washington, DC, International City Management Association.

Tocqueville, A. D. (1969), *Democracy in America*, Doubleday, New York (originally published 1835).

Trolldalen, J. M. (1991), 'International environmental conflict resolution' (brochure).

Tronto, J. C. (1987), 'Beyond gender difference to a theory of care', *Signs: Journal of Women in Culture and Society*, 12(4), 644–63.

Ury, W. L., Brett, J. M. and Goldberg, S. B. (1988), *Getting Disputes Resolved:*

Designing Systems to Cut the Costs of Conflict, San Francisco, Jossey-Bass.

US Army Corps of Engineers (1990), 'ADR Round Table: US Army Corps of Engineers', working paper #1, Alternative Dispute Resolution Series.

Visser, P. (1994), 'Mediating where it matters', *Track Two: Constructive Approaches to Community and Political Conflict*, 3(2/3), 17.

von Moltke, K. and DeLong, P. J. (1990), 'Negotiating in the global arena: Debt-for-nature swaps', *Resolve*, 22, 1.

Waite, J. (1991), 'Standing to appeal administrative decisons in Virginia', memo to Institute for Environmental Negotiation, 28 March.

Walker, J. L. (1988), 'Interests, political parties and policy formation in American democracy', in Critchlow, D. T. and Hawley, E. W. (eds), *Federal Social Policy: The Historical Dimension*, University Park, PA, The Pennsylvania State University Press.

Wall, J. A., Jr. (1981), 'Mediation: An analysis, review and proposed research', *Journal of Conflict Resolution*, 25(1), 157–80.

Walljasper, J. (1994), 'Chattanooga chooses', *Utne Reader*, 62, 15–16.

Waring, M. (1990), 'Measuring the economy: People, pollution and politics', *Building Economic Alternatives*, Fall, p. 8.

Waskow, A. (1990), 'From compassion to jubilee', *Tikkun*, 5(2), 78–81.

Webber, M. M. (1978), 'A difference paradigm for planning', in R. W. Burchell and G. Sternlieb (eds), *Planning Theory in the 1980s: A Search for Future Directions*, Rutgers University, Center for Urban Policy Research.

Weedon, C. (1987), *Feminist Practice and Postructuralist Theory*, Oxford, Basil Blackwell.

West, C. (1993), *Race Matters*, Boston, Beacon Press.

West, M. B. and Gibson, J. M. (1992), 'Facilitating medical ethics case review: What ethics committees can learn from mediation and facilitation techniques', *Cambridge Quarterly of Healthcare Ethics*, 1, 63–4.

Western Behavioral Sciences Institute (1991), 'Abortion and public policy', a report of the work of the Abortion Task Force of the Western Behavioral Sciences Institute, *Conscience*, XII(3), 12–15.

White, O. F., Jr. and McSwain, C. J. (1990), 'The Phoenix project: raising a new image of public administration from the ashes of the past', *Administration and Society*, 22(1), 3–8.

White, O. (1991), '"Mind control" and the decision process', *Governing*, p. 23, June.

Wolfe, A. (1989), *Whose Keeper? Social Science and Moral Obligation*, Los Angeles, CA, University of California Press.

Wondolleck, J. M. (1988), *Public Lands Conflict and Resolution: Managing National Forest Disputes*, New York, Plenum Press.

Zaretsky, E. (1988), 'Theses on liberalism', *Tikkun*, 4(2), 72–5.

Ziegler, W. L. (1985), 'Can we humanize public policy? – a futures-perspective', *Dialectics and Humanism*, 3–4, 79–84.

Zillessen, H. (1991), 'Alternative dispute resolution (ADR) in the USA – a German perspective', unpublished paper.

Zimmerman, J. F. (1986), *Participatory Democracy: Populism Revived*, New York, Praeger.

Index